THE BEST
CHRISTIAN
WRITING
2000

THE BEST
CHRISTIAN
WRITING 2000

SERIES EDITOR

JOHN WILSON

INTRODUCED BY

PHILIP YANCEY

HarperSanFrancisco
A Division of HarperCollinsPublishers

FIRST HARPERCOLLINS PAPERBACK EDITION PUBLISHED IN 2000

Library of Congress Cataloging-in-Publication Data

The best Christian writing 2000 / series editor, John Wilson ; introduced by Philip Yancey.— 1st HarperCollins pbk. ed.
    p. cm.
    Includes bibliographical references.
    ISBN 0-06-069382-7 (pbk.)
    1. Christianity. 2. Chistian literature, American. I. Title: Best Christian writing two thousand. II. Wilson, John, 1948–
BR53 .B43 2000
230—dc21   00-035051

Designed by Lindgren/Fuller Design

00 01 02 03 04 RRD(H) 10 9 8 7 6 5 4 3 2 1

CONTENTS

John Wilson

It's fitting that this new anthology, *Best Christian Writing*, should debut in the year 2000, a turn of the calendar that has occasioned all manner of speculation, since what we mean when we say "the year 2000" is that roughly 2,000 years have passed since the birth of a Jewish boy, Yeshua (or Jesus). According to Acts 11:26, it was in the city of Antioch that Jesus' disciples were first called *Christians*. Many scholars believe that the name originated outside the group and may have been intended derisively, along the lines of Anabaptist, Puritan, Quaker, or Moonie. In any case, the name pointed to Jesus' identity as the *Christ*, a Greek translation of *Messiah*, the anointed one.

Messiah is a familiar term, but perhaps the familiarity is deceptive. What does "anointed one" mean? In the Old Testament, a new king—chosen by God—was anointed; that is, oil was ceremonially poured on his head. The logic of this ceremony is made plain in Richard Broxton Onians's *The Origins of European Thought*. In common with the Hindus and the Zulus, among others, the Hebrews associated the generative seed of the male with oil. ("Oil was in fact the liquid of seed, the seed of the olive tree.") Hence, Onians explains, "the practice of 'anointing,' infusing oil into, kings, i.e., as a begetting, a bestowing of new life, divine life." And this connection, he adds, "is of vital importance for an understanding of the belief that Jesus was not only the king of the Jews but also divine, the son of God." So Acts 10:38 speaks of "how God anointed Jesus of Nazareth with the Holy Spirit and with power; how he went about doing good and healing all who were oppressed by the devil, for God was with him."

Dabbling with oil? To many good moderns, whether inside or outside the churches, that smacks of the ignorant superstition we're supposed to have outgrown. And talk of the devil? That's even worse! But there's no getting around it: Christianity abounds in such unsettling claims—chief among them that, as Romans 10:8 promises, "If you confess with your lips that Jesus is Lord and believe with your heart that God raised him from the dead, you will be saved," meaning that you also will be anointed by the Holy Spirit and receive new life. That's why the Eastern Orthodox Church still practices the ancient Christian rite of *chrismation*, anointing with oil, whereby newly baptized individuals receive the gifts of the Holy Spirit. If it was good enough for the early church, it's good enough for the Orthodox today; they don't worry that they may scandalize the enlightened.

Numbers are propaganda, as the sociologist David Martin has observed, but there are probably around 1.8 billion Christians in the world today. In the United States, *Christian* means many things to many people. Two or three years ago I reviewed a book from Zondervan, one of the leading evangelical publishers, in which the author suggested using the clumsy term "Christ-followers" in an effort to shed unwanted cultural baggage (as in "the Christian Coalition": ugh). Last time I checked, his rather desperate expedient had not been widely adopted.

"Christian writing," as I understand the term, is writing informed by the distinctively Christian understanding of reality. The essays gathered here range from first-person narratives to analytic arguments. Their province is both the interior castle and the public square. The twenty-eight writers included in this anthology represent a range of faith traditions, though by no means the whole spectrum of North American Christianity (let alone world Christianity). Some of them, like the Reformed philosopher Nicholas Wolterstorff, write from the tradition in which they were born and bred. Others entered as adults, as did the philosopher Alasdair MacIntyre (who moved from Marxism to Catholicism via Aristotle and Aquinas) and the writer and commentator Frederica Mathewes-Green (a convert to Orthodoxy who, by her own account, was dragged there by her husband, formerly an Episcopalian priest; she is now winsome witness to all things Orthodox). Most of the writers are practicing Christians of the small-"o" orthodox variety.

The reader may wish to know something of the editor, to gauge his prejudices. I was raised in mostly Baptist churches. For several years, from fourth through eighth grade, I attended a Lutheran (Missouri Synod) school, which gave me my first extended exposure to another Christian tradition: an invaluable experience. In our late twenties, my wife and I found our spiritual home in the Evangelical Covenant Church, which has its roots in Swedish Pietism, and I happily call myself a Pietist (not Pietism as caricatured by its critics, but Pietism at its best, as in Covenant missions and the classic Covenant questions, "Where is it written?" and "Are you alive?"). My wife and I begin and end each day—or try to—with a monthly Catholic prayer book, *Magnificat*.

If you're the editor of a periodical that you believe should be represented in the next volume of this anthology, *Best Christian Writing 2001*, please enter a complimentary subscription directed to John Wilson, Best Christian Writing, 419 Birch Dr., Wheaton IL 60187.

Many people helped in the preparation of this volume. Thanks first to Steve Hanselman, John Loudon, Gideon Weil, Roger Freet, Terri Leonard, Kathy Reigstad, and the rest of the staff at Harper-SanFrancisco: a delight to work with. (Thanks also to Karen Levine and Mark Tauber, who were with HarperSanFrancisco when this project began.) Phil Zaleski, editor of the *Best Spiritual Writing* series, was extraordinarily helpful and generous. I would also like to thank Joe Durepos, Mickey Maudlin, Phyllis Tickle, Elizabeth Wilson, Rick Wilson, and, above all, my wife, Wendy.

INTRODUCTION

Philip Yancey

> . . . [T]he poet's pen
> Turns them to shapes, and gives to airy nothing
> A local habitation and a name.
> —Shakespeare, *A Midsummer Night's Dream*

To an observer, the writing process must resemble pure mathematics or theoretical physics. Alone in a room, a person sits with a notepad or computer keyboard and manipulates abstract symbols, arranging and rearranging them, experimenting with new patterns. As Philip Roth describes the process, "I turn sentences around. That's my life. I write a sentence and I turn it around. Then I look at it and I turn it around again. Then I have lunch. Then I come back in and write another sentence. Then I have tea and turn the new sentence around. Then I read the two sentences over and turn them both around. Then I lie down on my sofa and think. Then I get up and throw them out and start from the beginning."

Roth has described my day precisely. My wife, who has worked as a social worker among the urban poor, and as a chaplain in a hospice, comes home with incredible stories of humanity living at the extreme edges of life and death. After relating those adventures, Janet asks about my day. Panic strikes. What did I do? I sat at home in my basement office, staring at a flickering computer screen in search of the perfect word. "Uh, let me think. Today? Oh, yeah—I found a very good adverb!"

Like wild animals, words are always trying to run away from me, and with my net I chase after them, hoping to catch just the right ones. After thirty years of corralling words, I have learned that these scratchings on paper do some things very well, and some things not so well.

Writers approach the craft with humility and often fear, for words comprise a very frail medium. Painters get to use color, sculptors three dimensions, and in contrast a writer's abstract markings seem thin and weak. Other art forms—movies, painting, dance, music—we encounter directly, sensually; only writing requires an intermediate step, literacy, just for a person to experience it. As C. S. Lewis observed, "One who contended that a poem was nothing but black marks on white paper would be unanswerable if he addressed an audience who couldn't read."

Once literacy is mastered, however, words allow a writer to leap across the gap that separates us all and enter the consciousness of other human beings. In a scene from the movie *Black Robe*, a Jesuit missionary tries to persuade a Huron chief to let him teach the tribe to read and write. The chief sees no benefit to this practice of scratching marks on paper until the Jesuit gives him a demonstration. "Tell me something I do not know," the priest says. The chief thinks for a moment and replies, "My woman's mother died in snow last winter."

The Jesuit writes a sentence and walks a few yards over to his colleague, who glances at it and then says to the chief. "Your mother-in-law died in a snowstorm?" The chief jumps back in alarm. He has just encountered the magical power of writing, which allows knowledge to travel in silence and dart through space.

The transaction that occurs between writer and reader, unlike the scene from *Black Robe*, usually takes place in secret, at a place and time unknown to the one who initiated it. In the old days of hand-rolled cigars, Cuba had a tradition of hiring lectors to read to the workers who rolled cigars. Because they worked in silence, they could listen hour after hour to literature read aloud. It helped the time pass and, the foremen hoped, might do the workers some good. The cigar-rollers enjoyed *The Count of Monte Cristo* so much that they wrote Alexandre Dumas for permission to name a cigar after the novel—the origin of the still-popular "Monte Cristo" cigar. I doubt that Dumas had a Cuban cigar factory in mind when he wrote the novel, but the portability of words allowed him to cross an ocean, enter another language, and visit that closeted place.

On a trip to Lebanon in 1998, I met a woman who said she had read my book *Disappointment with God* during the Lebanese civil war. She kept it in a basement bomb shelter. When the artillery fire intensified around her high-rise apartment building, she would make her way with a flashlight down the darkened stairway, light a candle, and read my book. I cannot describe how humbling it was for me to hear that, at a moment when Christians were dying for their faith, when the most beautiful city in the Middle East was being reduced to rubble, words I had written from my apartment in Chicago somehow brought her comfort.

As I reflect on my own pilgrimage, I realize that I probably became a writer because as a reader I had experienced this same long-distance power. I grew up in a Southern fundamentalist church that taught blatant racism, apocalyptic fear of Communism, and America-first patriotism. Christian doctrine was dished out in a "Believe and don't ask questions!" style, laced with fervid emotionalism.

For me, words opened chinks of light that became a window to another world. I remember the impact of a mild book like *To Kill a Mockingbird*, which called into question the apartheid assumptions of my friends and neighbors. As I went on to read *Black Like Me*, *The Autobiography of Malcolm X*, and Martin Luther King Jr.'s "Letter from Birmingham City Jail," my world shattered. Like the startled Huron chief, I too felt the power that allows one human mind to penetrate another with no intermediary but a piece of flattened wood pulp.

I especially came to value the freedom-enhancing quality of writing. Speakers in the churches I attended could RAISE THEIR VOICES! and play on emotions like musical instruments. But alone in my room, controlling every turn of the page, I met other representatives of the Kingdom—C. S. Lewis, G. K. Chesterton, Saint Augustine—whose calmer voices traversed time to convince me that somewhere Christians lived who knew grace as well as law, love as well as judgment, reason as well as passion.

I became a writer, I now believe, because I saw that spoiled words could be reclaimed. I saw that writing could penetrate into the crevices, bringing spiritual oxygen to people trapped in airtight boxes. I saw that when God conveyed to us the essence of his self-expression, God called it the Word, the Logos. The Word comes in the most freedom-honoring way imaginable.

In *The Humiliation of the Word,* Jacques Ellul suggests that is why God usually speaks, rarely shows himself, and never allows graven images. The image is too overwhelming. Written words, on the other hand, create a space, a respectful distance, allowing the reader to monitor the gate through which they pass.

Today, of course, we live in a world of images. Movies blast us with surround-sound and rush us along at a frantic pace, switching scenes several times a minute. How different is the act of reading, in which the reader governs the tempo, moving eyes across the page, stopping to reflect, mentally transforming symbols into meaning. The reader maintains control, able at any moment to stop the transaction by simply closing the book.

Seamus Heaney, the Irish poet who recently won the Nobel Prize for Literature, made a striking observation about the only scene from the Gospels that portrays Jesus in the act of writing. That scene came at a tense moment when Pharisees brought Jesus a woman caught in the act of adultery and demanded that he pronounce the death penalty. The woman, stripped to the waist as a mark of shame, cringed before Jesus, expecting the stones to start flying at any moment. Saying nothing, Jesus stooped and began sketching words in the sand. In Heaney's reflections on the scene, he finds an allegory for poetry:

> The drawing of those characters [in the sand] is like poetry, a break with the usual life but not an absconding from it. Poetry, like the writing, is arbitrary and marks time in every possible sense of that phrase. It does not say to the accusing crowd or to the helpless accused, "Now a solution will take place," it does not propose to be instrumental or effective. Instead, in the rift between what is going to happen and whatever we would wish to happen, poetry holds attention for a space, functions not as distraction but as pure concentration, a focus where our power to concentrate is concentrated back on ourselves.

In a kind of miracle, these frail symbols that "mark time" (in Heaney's phrase) achieve a power as great as any on earth. In the scene from John 8, Jesus' words in the sand defused the tension, sent the accusers away convicted, and set a terrified woman free.

Nineteen centuries later the words of a preacher's daughter in the novel *Uncle Tom's Cabin* conveyed the abolitionist message to many who had blocked their ears against sermons and jeremiads, and as much as any other force that book goaded a nation toward change. In another hundred years the fierce words of a lone convict from the Soviet Gulag, Aleksandr Solzhenitsyn, exposed lies and bore witness to a different truth, helping change the course of history.

In a moving passage, theologian Jürgen Moltmann tells of seeing a photo of one of six Jesuits murdered in El Salvador. Lying in the blood was the book that had fallen from the priest's hands as he died: Moltmann's own *The Crucified God.* Reading Moltmann's poignant reaction, I remembered meeting the woman in Beirut, Lebanon, who had read my book *Disappointment with God* in a bomb shelter by candlelight as her world crashed in around her. I felt humbled by, and grateful for, the awesome power of words.

The very power of words, however, makes them vulnerable to a kind of deception. Every writer who touches on spirituality can identify with Thomas Merton's concern that his books expressed the spiritual life so confidently and surely when actually he was plagued by insecurities, doubts, and even terrors. (Perhaps, as Kierkegaard hoped, God in his mercy will judge writers by their work more than by their lives.)

I often have the impression that the words I write have more lasting value than my life, and I sense that the higher I reach in my writing, the more I misrepresent that disorderly life. It is far easier, I find, to edit words than to edit life. When I get letters from readers telling me how my words have affected them, I want to protest, "Yes, but you don't know me—talk to my wife!" Words grant to the writer of faith a vicarious power that he doesn't deserve.

What I write may resemble reality, but it neither reproduces nor does justice to it. I sit in a worship service and look around me. The music, poorly written and poorly composed, jars me but seems to have a mesmerizing effect on others. They raise their hands, palms cupped upward; their eyes squint shut; their bodies sway; they appear transported to a celestial plane unattainable to me. I interview these worshipers afterward. "Exactly what happened out there?" I ask. "I need to understand. Can you break it down for me?"

I get blank stares, mumbled phrases, looks of irritation, pity, or condescension. I learn that such journalism is as intrusive as the TV camera that zooms to a close-up on the woman who has just lost her daughter in a house fire.

Edgar Allan Poe wrote a short story about a man who poured his life into painting one masterpiece, a portrait of his mistress.

Just as he put the finishing touches on her eyes and mouth, and stepped back from the canvas to admire its perfection, he glanced at his mistress the model and discovered that she was dead. Art had killed life—a pattern that writers on spirituality know well. Shine a spotlight on spiritual activity, and it tends to disappear.

Can a person write a prayer for publication without wondering how it will sound to potential readers as well as God? Augustine of Hippo wrote a personal journal addressed to God that became a manual for the church ever after. I can't help wondering how often he let future readers influence the editing process.

All art distorts reality, but words most of all, because they reduce a sensory life of sound, smell, sight, and touch to symbols on a page. When I write about my own experience with God, I break it down, reassemble it, then polish the words. What vanishes in the process? After the thirteenth edit, I begin to question what prompted my writing in the first place. Like a chemist who breaks down complex molecules into simple ones, in my reductionism I may destroy the very substance I am hoping to assay.

Once, after writing an article for *Christianity Today* magazine, I got a phone call from an editor. "We like the piece and plan to run it in our next issue," he said. "But we don't like the lead. Can you come up with a new introduction?" I gave it some thought, and my friend Larry came to mind. He seemed a perfect illustration for what I wanted to communicate in the article. I sent in these paragraphs, which ran as the lead:

> Larry has the most colorful background of anyone I know. An avowed bisexual, he has a history of liaisons with people of both genders. A recovering alcoholic, he attends AA sessions almost daily, has recently celebrated his tenth anniversary of sobriety, and has gone on to become a substance abuse counselor for others. He served in Vietnam, but has since become a doctrinaire pacifist.

Along the way, Larry became a Christian. He says he was converted by two hymns, "Just As I Am" and "Amazing Grace." As he heard the words of those hymns, it sank in for the first time that God really did want him *just as he was.* God's grace was that amazing. In his own way, Larry has been following God ever since.

"In his own way," I say—Larry will be the first to admit that he has not experienced "the victorious Christian life." He eats too much, chain-smokes, and neglects the care of his body. Sex continues to be a problem. And since he never manages to get up in time for church on Sunday, he misses out on corporate worship and Christian community. Once, Larry stated his dilemma this way, "I guess I'm stuck somewhere between 'Just as I am' and 'Just as God wants me to be.'"

A few weeks later I got a phone call from Larry. He mentioned the embarrassment of seeing details of his life in print but acknowledged that few of his friends read *Christianity Today* anyway. Then he gave a rebuke that has haunted me ever since: "Philip, I've lived all my life trying to be a real person, an authentic, three-dimensional person. You've reduced me to a three-paragraph illustration." He was right, of course, and I realized that is what we writers do incessantly. We reduce the magnificent complexity of human beings to statistics and illustrations and article leads.

Janet Malcolm suggests that in the interviewing process, a writer functions like a nourishing, supportive mother. We coax out a person's deepest secrets, nodding sympathetically, gently probing for more details. "You can trust me," we imply. "Tell me everything." But when we move into the writing phase, we switch roles and become the authoritarian, objective father. We make judgments and cull our material until we have a thematic whole to present. That process inevitably distorts, and often wounds.

In *The Ghost Writer*, Philip Roth tells of a writer who offended the Jewish community he came from. A distinguished judge wrote to him and asked him to subject his writing to a series of tests. "Ask yourself these questions," he said, and gave him a list that included the following:

If you had been living in Nazi Germany in the thirties, would you have written such a story?

Would you claim that the characters in your story represent a fair sample of the kinds of people that make up a typical contemporary community of Jews?

Why in a story with a Jewish background must there be (a) adultery; (b) incessant fighting within a family over money; (c) warped human behavior in general?

Can you explain why in your story, in which a rabbi appears, there is nowhere the grandeur of oratory with which Stephen S. Wise and Abba Hillel Silver and Zvi Masliansky have stirred and touched their audiences?

Can you honestly say that there is anything in your short story that would not warm the heart of a Julius Streicher or a Joseph Goebbels?

I have heard eerily similar sentiments from the evangelical community I write about. Essentially, the judge was asking for an artistic immunity against pain. In my writing I have found that few people want truth presented; they want propaganda, or public relations. They want to look good. And the more I strive for accuracy, the greater chance I stand of offending and wounding the people I write about.

Solzhenitsyn's memoir *The Oak and the Calf* tells of the brief period under Communism when the Soviet government acknowledged his genius and thought (fatally, as it turned out) that he might be a writer they could manipulate. Write moral and uplifting literature, they admonished him; be sure to exclude all "pessimism, denigration, surreptitious sniping." I laughed aloud when I first read his account of that scene. The advice Solzhenitsyn got from the Communists bears a striking resemblance to what I sometimes hear from evangelical publishers. Every power, whether Christian or secular, desires moral, uplifting literature—as long as they get to define what constitutes *moral* and *uplifting*.

Several times I have written about my years attending a Christian college, without identifying it by name. I had not realized how much I had upset people there until I revisited the campus and spoke with some of the teachers and administrators. "Why do you hurt us?" said one professor. "Why concentrate only on the negative? We've given you the Alumnus of the Year award, and you turn around and lambaste us every chance you get!"

I tried simply to listen, rather than defend myself. I knew he was reacting against the unfair power of words, *my* words, which had through my books already gone out across the country, presenting one limited and inadequate point of view and causing him embarrassment and shame.

Why do we do it, we writers? "Of making many books there is no end," sighed the Teacher of Ecclesiastes some three millennia ago—and roughly fifty thousand new books will appear this year in the United States alone. Yet we keep at it, cranking out more and more words, with the potential to bring harm as well as comfort. All writing implies arrogance. As I write this sentence, I have the chutzpah to believe it will be worth your time to read it. *Listen to me, please, without the possibility of reciprocation. Subject yourself to my words and thoughts. I, a person you have probably never met, hereby demand your attention.*

I think we do it because we have nothing else to offer—nothing more than a point of view. Everything I write is colored by my family dysfunctions, my upbringing in Southern fundamentalism, my guarded pilgrimage. Indeed, every author represented in this collection sees the world through a unique set of eyes. We can write with passion only about our own experiences, not yours. I find that readers respond, however, not to the specifics of my experiences, but to what those experiences summon up. In the reader, words work a different effect than they worked in me, the writer. I write about Southern fundamentalism: readers respond with stories about a strict Roman Catholic or Seventh Day Adventist upbringing. Somehow my rendering of church, family, and my halting steps toward faith *provokes* something. Walker Percy noted that a novelist reveals what the reader knows but does not know he knows.

Five hundred years ago the Renaissance scholar Pico della Mirandola delivered his famous "Oration on the Dignity of Man," which defined the role of humanity in creation. After God had created the animals, all the essential roles had been filled, but "the Divine Artificer still longed for some creature which might comprehend the meaning of so vast an achievement, which might be moved with love at its beauty and smitten with awe at its grandeur." To contemplate and appreciate all the rest, to reflect on meaning, to share in the power and exuberance of creativity, to revere and to hallow—these were the roles reserved for the species made in God's image.

"What am I?" asked Merton. "I am myself a word spoken by God." Created in God's image, we can only return an interest on that investment. Somehow God perceives his own creation through us, and in the process we reflect back some glimmer of God's own image. Every writer has only a living point of view, which distinguishes him or her from every other person on this planet. We are called to be stewards of that point of view, and stewards of the extraordinary power of words through which we express it.

We do not have to make wine out of water. Indeed, we cannot. We can only provide the water in our leaky clay vessels. If we do so faithfully, God will make the wine.

VINCE BACOTE

COMING TO TERMS WITH MY OTHERNESS

(From *re:generation quarterly*)

My mother and my uncle brought my brothers and me, then three years old, to the tracks near our home to watch the train carrying Robert F. Kennedy's body. I can still remember the train passing by, and my uncle crying, though I had no sense of its significance at the time. They were aware of something I wasn't: the harsh realities of racial prejudice and discrimination. They knew how hard it had been for blacks to gain acceptance as fully human. Now, they watched an iron horse carry what seemed to them their brightest hope away to the grave.

My world, on the other hand, has been vastly different. I always assumed that most of America's race problem had been solved by legislation. Born in 1965, I came of age when busing and other civil rights measures were already in place. My experience was one of racial harmony (or indifference). My world was free from the scars of racism.

I am a true child of integration. It's not that I have never been aware of my race—my early years were full of curiosity about whether our family was black or white, and what that meant. All of this curiosity, however, faded significantly by the middle of elementary school, when my classes were nearly half-black and half-white.

From that time on, while I was aware that there were people of different races, I had also internalized the rhetoric of integration. (Some, I know now, would call it "assimilation" or "cultural self-suppression.") I was on the path toward living a color-blind life. In my world, ethnic and racial differences were incidental. This view made me quite different from some of my African-American friends, who were far more race-conscious. From elementary school through college, I ambled along as though people were people.

Mom and Dad, on the other hand, were both born in the Carolinas in the 1930s, and their experience of living in a segregated world, followed by the victories of civil rights legislation, shaped their view of race. They have been very accepting of my white friends, but they do not have the kind of interracial relationships that I do, nor does it seem likely that they ever will.

I have not been subjected to harassment or discrimination because of my pigmentation. I can count on one hand the number of times I've been called names, and I cannot explicitly remember any experiences of discrimination—socially, vocationally, or otherwise.

Two vivid instances of my neutrality toward race took place on ski trips to Breckenridge, Colorado, with groups from the Navigators, an evangelical (and predominantly white) campus ministry. At some point during the first trip another student came up to me in a souvenir shop and asked me a seemingly random question.

"You're not into that, are you, Vince?" he said.

"Into what?" I asked.

"That" turned out to be a heightened sense of race consciousness that my white friend had encountered in black students back at school (the Citadel, a military college in Charleston, South Carolina). I quickly set his mind at ease: I didn't make race an issue, I said, and I was uncomfortable with black students who would even imply that race was a factor in anything. I truly felt that race was overplayed—the roots of most conflicts lay elsewhere.

Three years later, now a volunteer leader with the Navigators in Memphis, I went on another ski trip. A few other guys and I raced down the mountain, defying common sense and risking injury to beat one another to the bottom of the hill. It was thrilling. I told a black friend about it when I returned. She said, "Well, you know that's how they are."

I had no idea what she meant, until she explained to me how whites (I suppose particularly white males) always have to compete and always have to win. Funny, I didn't know that was only a white trait. Rather than debate, I changed the subject. But I had to wonder. Assumptions about race were clouding either her, or my, perceptions of reality. Whose was it?

In 1990 there were "X" caps everywhere—even in suburban Chicago, where I was starting seminary. I was quite uncomfortable with Malcolm X's resurgent popularity. A fellow black seminarian thought my reaction was too strong. He challenged me to read Alex Haley's *Autobiography of Malcolm X*—something that never would have occurred to me a few years earlier.

Aside from being a great read, the book forced me to open my eyes more fully to the depth of racism in our society. I no longer saw Malcolm and Martin Luther King as polar opposites, one a revolutionary and the other a peacemaker. Instead, I began to see them as different men from different backgrounds and locations who had different, but not completely opposed, approaches to the issue of race. While I hardly became an "X" disciple, Malcolm helped me see more clearly that race did matter, for good and ill, in America.

Now what? What do I do now that I have "color" vision? What do I do now that I realize that humanity's kaleidoscope is not going to melt into one harmonious hue—now that I recognize that my otherness does matter? It is here that the postmodern turn, though fraught with its own dangers, might help.

The postmodern era has called attention to the "other," to difference and diversity. Postmodernism can provide a way to rationalize isolation—even, at its extreme, to justify ignoring those who don't come from our narrow enclave (since communication is impossible anyway). But I see a theological opportunity in this emphasis on otherness.

First, postmodernism has helped us to recapture the startling idea that humanity's kaleidoscopic diversity is made in the *imago Dei*, the divine image. If God is truly three in one, then being in the image of God cannot mean anything less than relationality between differing persons. As a postmodern Christian, I must reckon with the fact that a substantial aspect of my faithfulness in reflecting the *imago Dei* will be my relationships, especially with those who, racially or otherwise, are different from me. The integrationist dream of unity without differences is not only implausible to a postmodern world, it is sub-Christian.

Correspondingly, it may be that rather than trying to obliterate my otherness under the banner of "color-blindness," I should actively bring my own differences into my relationships. This goes against my North American instincts—where friendships are usually constructed on similarity—but it is an inevitable conclusion in a postmodern world filled with inescapable differences. But this extends beyond my own circle of relationships into the church. If the church is indeed a diverse body that requires variety in order to flourish, then the celebration of diversity is actually necessary for ecclesial health. There is simply no way that the church can thrive if everyone is identical. Diversity in a community is as vital as organs in a human body. And since the church is the first fruits of a redeemed humanity, diversity must be equally vital for humanity's own well-being. For those like me who swim easily in the majority culture, it is tempting to smooth over differences, but that shortcut is self-defeating.

It was not easy for my mother and uncle to face a train that seemed to be hauling their hope away. Each of us must face the peculiar challenges of our times; perhaps some today should face the train of hope that was "color-blind" integration, and bid it adieu for a graceful burial. It is not always easy for me to face my otherness, much less embrace it. If I want a life of richness and depth, however, this is one embrace I should never break.

RANDALL BALMER

THE GENERATION OF FAITH

(From *Searching for Your Soul*)

And Jacob was left alone; and a man wrestled with him until the breaking of the day. When the man saw that he did not prevail against Jacob, he touched the hollow of his thigh; and Jacob's thigh was put out of joint as he wrestled with him. Then he said, "Let me go, for the day is breaking." But Jacob said, "I will not let you go, unless you bless me." And he said to him, "What is your name?" And he said, "Jacob." Then he said, "Your name shall no longer be called Jacob, but Israel, for you have striven with God and with men, and have prevailed." Then Jacob asked him, "Tell me, I pray, your name." But he said, "Why is it that you ask my name?" And there he blessed him. So Jacob called the name of the place Peniel, saying, "For I have seen God face to face and yet my life is preserved." The sun rose upon him as he passed Peniel, limping because of his thigh.

—Genesis 32:24–31, RSV

I envied them in a way—their ease and self-confidence, the way they glided smartly across campus, their new American Tourister briefcases in tow. Moving from class to class, they knew—almost instinctively, it seemed—when to laugh at the professor's remarks.

They asked all the right questions; they learned all the right answers. They were clean-cut and well groomed and athletic and earnest and attentive. They smiled most of the time. They socialized effortlessly among themselves, guffawing at inside jokes. More than anything else they exuded an air of confidence and self-assurance.

These were men of God, studying for the ministry at a fundamentalist seminary, and I was supposed to be among them. For as long as I can remember I had been groomed for the ministry, which is to say that my devout parents expected great things of me. My Christmas present following my sixth birthday was a three-foot-high replica of my father's pulpit, and family lore abounds with recollections of me as a six-year-old stem-winding preacher. I sang "Jesus loves me, this I know" in Sunday school, and "The B-I-B-L-E, yes, that's the book for me," and "Jesus wants me for a sunbeam."

I was "saved" at the age of three at the kitchen table in the back of a parsonage overlooking the Minnesota prairie. After breakfast and our family devotions my father asked if I was ready to ask Jesus into my heart. For some reason, I have a vivid mental image of the toaster, its brown fabric-covered cord trailing off the table. Yes, of course I would renounce my sinfulness and ask Jesus into my heart, and from that moment on I was saved. I had been born again.

I grew up in the secure cocoon of fundamentalist faith, society, and dogma. I was a quick study and learned from an early age to detect who was saved and who wasn't. The Lutherans up the road were a bit suspect, what with all their vestments and dead liturgy. Baptists were pretty much okay, though God knows they could get cantankerous at times. Roman Catholics, of course, were beyond the pale. I knew, for example, that I could never pursue the crush I had on Mary Kay Zimmer at school because she was Catholic, and my parents had informed me gently, but in no uncertain terms, that if I married anyone other than a *Christian* girl I would be disowned.

There were, I soon learned, other ways to tell who was saved and who wasn't. Smokers were non-Christians because they defiled their bodies, and our body was a temple of the Lord. Drinking was also a sign of wickedness, and when my dad served Holy Communion at church it was grape juice, not wine, and it came in tiny glass containers barely larger than a thimble. Dancing was also a sign of "worldliness"; the Apostle Paul had admonished us to be separate from the world, to be *in* the world but not *of* the world. As Christians, we were called out of the world; our real citizenship lay in heaven, not on this earth, and this world, after all, was doomed and transitory. Jesus was coming back at any moment, and we had better be ready. Don't let Jesus catch you on the dance floor or in a movie theater.

I learned my lessons well. Rarely did I slip my fundamentalist moorings, and when I did I stayed pretty close to shore, even during the perilous years of adolescence. I shuffled off to Bible camp in the summer, where I swam and hiked and braided lanyards and fell in love and rededicated my life to Jesus at the campfire a couple of dozen times.

What's it like to grow up fundamentalist? I hear that question a lot, along with the corollaries: Is it true your parents didn't let you play cards? Did you really have to bring a note excusing you from square dancing in gym class? Your parents made you go to church more than once a week? What about sex? No sex before marriage, really?

I've always detected an undercurrent of voyeurism in these questions, but, for the record, the answer is yes to all of the above. No cards, no dancing, church three or four days a week and at least twice on Sunday. And no premarital sex. I had to sneak off to my first motion picture at the age of sixteen, feeling dreadfully guilty the whole time. We didn't have a television until I was nearly ten, although I'm not sure if that was because of religious conviction or relative poverty. Probably a bit of both.

Growing up fundamentalist meant living in a tiny world whose every question had an answer. It was a world inebriated with rhetoric about authority and obsessed with chains of command—the authority of the Bible, the authority of the church, the pastor, the husband, the father—and all of it dominated by authoritarian preachers, too many of them sporting egos the size of Montana.

It was a world marked by pious rhetoric, a kind of cloying God-talk. Did you get that promotion? Well, praise the Lord! My heart was really challenged by that message. God has been so good to me; I don't deserve his favors. The Lord has given me a real heart for the unsaved. I just wanna do God's will.

Growing up fundamentalist meant growing up profoundly alienated from my own body, especially my sexuality. I recall my mother remarking to a friend that, even when I was ill, I never complained. The tone in her voice suggested admiration, so I sought to sustain that stoicism, subscribing to the aw-shut-up-and-it'll-get-better school of medicine.

There was comfort in that world, I'll not deny it. There's a certain appeal to being cosseted in a subculture with little room for ambiguity, where my destiny, both heavenly and earthly, had already been determined. Yet here I was watching these seminarians armed with their briefcases and their self-assurance. They had stuck with the program. They had solved the riddle of faith, which for them was really no riddle at all. Ask them a question, any question, and they could supply you with an answer. They could recite the cosmological and the ontological arguments backwards and forward, along with an airtight case for biblical inerrancy, the virgin birth, and the premillennial return of Jesus. Belief for them was effortless and easy, and yes, I envied them.

I was twenty-two at the time, a year out of college, and unemployed. After extensive deliberation I had turned down a career as an underwriter for Allstate Insurance Company, and as I looked for gainful employment I knew I was searching for something else: I was searching for the certainty I saw on the scrubbed faces of the seminarians. I knew I hadn't become the sunbeam Jesus apparently wanted. In the argot of the evangelical subculture, I was "willful" and "wayward"; I had slipped my moorings and was drifting in doubt and uncertainty.

A kind of intellectual restlessness had overtaken me. I was enamored of the world of ideas, so for a time I thought the way to reclaim the faith lay in rational argumentation, intellectual respectability. I was embarrassed by the simple piety of my parents, so I tried to dress up evangelical convictions in Enlightenment finery. Phrases like "reasoned belief" and the "integration of faith and learning" tripped off my tongue and became a kind of mantra. The theological discipline of apologetics seemed like the right course. If only we fundamentalists could come up with a reasonable defense of the faith, then we could hold our heads high in the marketplace of ideas. More important, we could distance ourselves from those loopy charismatics and Pentecostals, who gave us all a bad name with their naïve reliance on religious experience.

Attending church at that juncture of my life was excruciating, so painful that I rarely tried. The sentiments I acknowledged at the time were anger and betrayal, but the subculture still had enough of a hold on me that I felt embarrassed as well, ashamed that the faith had not taken hold of me—or had I not taken hold of the faith?—the way I thought it should. When guilt overtook me and I did show up at church, I heard vapid and self-congratulatory sermons about the goodness of God and the rewards of living a "good Christian life." I heard admonitions about avoiding the perils of worldliness and triumphal assurances that God would eventually vanquish his adversaries, if not in this world then assuredly in the next. This God struck me as austere and demanding; he seemed to be big on rules, to hear the preachers tell it.

After a couple of decades steeped in fundamentalism I found the whole business rather nauseating—the megalomaniac preachers, the cloying God-talk, the overweening moralism—and so I trotted off to graduate school and immersed myself further in the life of the mind. Fundamentalism, with its petty squabbles over doctrinal minutiae and its taboos about beer and hair length and motion pictures, couldn't have been farther from my consciousness. I was busy building a career of my own, and I couldn't care less about the smug seminarians with their self-righteous patter about God's will and sanctification and all their hoary theological schemes.

Despite my satisfaction with the life of the mind, however, the life of the Spirit still beckoned, and I count this as a remarkable working of grace. Shortly after settling into my first academic appointment, I decided, in effect, to revisit my past, although I didn't recognize that I was doing so at the time. I set out on a journey into the evangelical subculture in America with the idea of lending some perspective to the televangelist scandals then titillating the media in the mid-1980s. I visited churches and camp meetings and seminaries and Bible camps. I heard plenty of bad sermons in the course of my travels and more renditions of "Shine, Jesus, Shine" than I care to count, but I also started hearing the gospel. I heard the gospel in the strains of "Amazing Grace, How Sweet the Sound" and in the simple expressions of piety of folks with their arms upraised to Jesus. I heard the gospel in an old friend's lament that fundamentalists had taken the gracious, beckoning words of Jesus and twisted them into demands, threats, and moral imperatives.

I don't think I heard much of the gospel during my visit to a fundamentalist Bible camp in the Adirondack Mountains of upstate New York, but there, as the flames of the campfire licked the darkness, my life began to make sense to me. I saw how desperately my parents wanted to rear me in the faith, how they wanted me to have the same conversion to fundamentalist Christianity that had so profoundly shaped their own lives. At the same time, however, as I listened to teenagers around the campfire talk about their own spiritual lives, I saw how difficult it was for me to appropriate my parents' faith. They had socialized me in the church since infancy—Sunday school, sermons, family devotions, Bible camp—and yet they expected that my moment of conversion would have the same transformative power as theirs. That, I concluded, was unrealistic because my "conversion" at age three was, at best, a ratification of the beliefs and the regimen that had been drilled into me since birth.

I saw myself in the adolescent faces around the campfire that night. I recognized the urge, under the extraordinary pressure of parents and peers, to give my life to Jesus, to conjure the right religious emotions, and then to declare my readiness to live a "good Christian life" and abide by all the fundamentalist strictures. I also recognized myself in those who, choking back tears, were "rededicating" their lives to Jesus, those whose conversions hadn't generated the emotion or the transformation they thought was expected of them, so they were revisiting the moment yet again as the flames danced and the embers glowed.

My experience at the Bible camp prompted me to reconsider my own struggle with faith. With the encouragement of a fellow pilgrim, I discarded my image of the self-confident seminarians and the triumphalist preachers. I even set aside the imposing specter of God the Father, who had been portrayed to me as demanding and authoritarian. I found Jesus a much more sympathetic figure. Jesus, I suspected, wouldn't have felt very comfortable with the briefcase crowd either. As nearly as I could tell, he hung around with ne'er-do-wells, people on the margins of society—fishermen and tax collectors; adulterers and lepers.

In time, it occurred to me that the entire Bible was populated with scoundrels. Paul certainly fits that description, both before and after his conversion. Peter didn't score too well on the loyalty test. David could not have become a member of any fundamentalist church that I'm aware of; he was hardly the poster boy for "traditional family values."

And yet the Bible seems to celebrate these characters. God chooses Paul—irascible old Paul, who had graduated at the top of his class at the persecution academy—to be the conduit for spreading the gospel. Jesus surely must have given Peter his nickname, The Rock, with his tongue at least partially in cheek, to call attention to the fact that, with his spineless dithering, Peter was anything but solid. David, the Scriptures tell us, was a man after God's own heart.

Then there's Jacob. He heads the list of scoundrels. Jacob, you'll recall, is the guy who, disguised beneath a goatskin, cadges his brother's rightful inheritance while Esau is out fetching supper. Jacob gets his comeuppance a bit when, after working seven years for the woman he loves, his devious father-in-law delivers the wrong woman to Jacob's marriage bed. Jacob works another seven years and finally secures Rachel for his second wife. He succeeds pretty well in the ranching business and then one day, camped out in the hill country, word arrives that Esau and his entourage are about to drop by. Jacob, all alone and sweating bullets, finally beds down by the Jabbok River and, in the course of a fitful night, grapples with a phantom—a man or an angel, perhaps, or even God—a wrestling match that leaves him with a bum leg.

Whatever else you care to say about these characters, they strike me as quintessentially human—Jacob and Paul and David and Peter and a hundred others whose images flicker before us in the Bible, however briefly. They are three-dimensional beings with a substance to them that I found lacking in the role models of my fundamentalist past. The religion of my childhood, not to mention the seminarians who so unnerved me, had taken the stories of these wonderfully complex and textured characters and reduced them to morality plays—abject sinners who suddenly are transformed into good, rule-abiding Christians.

Through some unaccountable working of grace, I began to see them not so much as saints but as fellow pilgrims. Like me, they are flawed. They trudge along, step by step, just like most of us mortals. What they share in common, I think, is a sense that the call of God is the call to be human, to embrace our humanity in all of its ambiguity. They see that the call of God is a summons to embark upon a journey of faith whose destiny is not always apparent. The Letter to the Hebrews in the New Testament tells us that when Abraham, another character with a checkered past, answered the call of God, "he went out, not knowing where he was to go."

In David James Duncan's novel *The River Why*, Gus Orviston, the central character, is a maniacal fisherman—like those first followers of Jesus—who unwittingly finds himself on a spiritual quest. After hours of debate and conversation, Gus's spiritual adviser, an aspiring fisherman himself, finally cuts to the chase. "I'm not sane, Gus. I believe in the rivers of living water; I believe our souls swim in that water; I believe Jesus and Buddha and Krishna are the savour in that water; I believe in the Garden World and its Queen. I love the ol' Whopper."

The path of faith is not tidy. For many, belief in itself is an affront to intelligence and even to sanity, especially when you can explain the spiritual quest in psychological or sociological or physiological terms. But, like Gus Orviston's interlocutor, like Paul and David, I believe in the rivers of living water, and those rivers sustain me in my pilgrimage. For me, the path to faith has been rocky and my steps uneven. I am plagued by doubts and fears and anxieties. I feel desolate, at times, and my cries to God meet with silence. I have been locked in a lovers' quarrel with my father, the preacher, for the better part of three decades, a quarrel over faith and belief and theology that has not so much abated as it has taken a different form since his sudden passing a few months ago. Like Abraham, I'm not always certain where I'm going on this pilgrimage, and my progress is slowed, I'm sure, whenever I pause to wrestle with God—or someone—lurking there in the darkness. My trajectory is rarely straight and not always upward. It resembles at times the woven, brown cord of a toaster trailing off the table. . . .

And yet what sustains me is a sense (or at least a hope) of divine presence, a sense that I am not alone on this pilgrimage, but in the company of friends who will pick me up from time to time and point me in the right direction. What sustains me is a suspicion that there is still enchantment in the natural world. What sustains me is the laughter of my sons. What sustains me is the delight of love and companionship and making love. What sustains me is the conviction that the journey brings its own rewards, regardless of the destination, that holiness somehow is embedded in the process itself.

I believe because of the epiphanies, small and large, that have intersected my path—small, discrete moments of grace when I have sensed a kind of superintending presence outside of myself. I believe because these moments—a kind word, an insight, an anthem on Easter morning, a chill in the spine—are too precious to discard, and I choose not to trivialize them by reducing them to rational explanation. I believe because, for me, the alternative to belief is far too daunting. I believe because, in the waning decades of the twentieth century, belief itself is an act of defiance in a society still enthralled by the blandishments of Enlightenment rationalism.

I no longer envy the seminarians I knew twenty years ago, even though I'm sure those spiritual athletes are far ahead of me on the journey. I congratulate them on their self-confidence. They figured out all of their answers before I even knew the questions, and I will never be able to match their strides.

But perhaps you, too, are a pilgrim, and if you look for me, check somewhere toward the back of the pack. Like Jacob, I'm the guy with a limp.

LIONEL BASNEY

IMMANUEL'S GROUND

(From *The American Scholar*)

When I was a boy, there was a camp meeting in my town. Since then it has become a Summer Family Conference and convenes in the facilities of the local college. But in those days it was a genuine holiness meeting, such as used to be common in American country places. The parents of those who came to the conference lived, then, in screened cottages and dormitories on the elm-roofed campground, where their parents had lived in tents with plank or straw floors, and used washstands beneath the trees. It was the middle generation I knew. They were a new population, in town every third week of July; the plates on their large secondhand cars read Ohio and Indiana and Florida. They held three services a day in the tabernacle, preaching and singing and praying. After supper, fanning themselves in the hot westering sun, they listened to missionaries describe the work in Africa, while the supper dishes clinked and someone whistled in the camp kitchen across the gravel drive.

I am writing of events forty years ago, in rural New York State, but these events represented something far older, as old almost as the national frontier once it had crossed the Appalachians. Camp meetings grew out of revivals flaring along southern rivers in 1799 and 1800, among people who, cheated on land and without a cultural fabric, made up a new culture on the spot. Two

generations later, great vacation camp meetings, such as those at
Ocean Grove and on Martha's Vineyard, were built by a Protestant hegemony setting out to reframe American life. Two generations after that, after war, boom, and the Scopes trial, the
hegemony had withered to an embattled minority trying to keep
itself alive in the minds of its children. Ours was a small, obscure
camp meeting. Few came, compared with the crowds on Martha's
Vineyard, though our tabernacle was often full on Sunday nights.
No one would come to argue with us, at least; no one bothered
the cars in the stony parking lot, under the streetlight in its haze
of insects.

The cottages on Martha's Vineyard, with their frilled eaves,
have gone into American cultural history. Our tabernacle was just
a roof of unplaned lumber above a concrete floor—closer, therefore, to its origins, the barn and the preaching-shed. I would distract myself from the sermon by tracking with my eyes the
intricate raftering, the swing beams and purlins, the braces
around the posts that held the roof up. Or tied it down. The
designs worked in the Gothic way, converting mass to suspen-
sion. The more wood that had gone into it, the lighter it had
become. On stuffy evenings the ushers would slide the hangar
doors open on both sides, leaving the roof seemingly without
walls, floating on the uncertain air like a linen of rough pine. "I
tell you . . . !" the preacher would shout, and above his voice, and
above our singing, the tabernacle seemed to brood, impassively,
with shadows under its wings.

The surrounding towns called ours "the holy city." It was officially dry, no hotel or bowling alley, its life dominated by the
alliance of the college and the one big collegiate church. The
town stood on plateaus let into the west wall of the river valley
like balconies—one for the school, another above it for the
campground, smaller ones, like lofts, for houses. To reach the
campground, you wound up from balcony to balcony and finally

bent a steep hairpin curve into the trees. The camp meeting hill was a kind of promontory over the long opening of the river, above the cornfields. Thrust out like a pulpit or castle keep, it was the first thing you saw of the town as you came from the north. You couldn't see the buildings, only the scrubby slope and the high battlement of trees. From among the trees, you couldn't see the valley.

Nor could you see the town, the college, or the lofts of the houses. The campground was closed in. Eleven months of the year it was all but deserted. In summer, before and after the meeting, it was all but wild. Birds filled the trees and flung themselves through the air in front of you. Squirrels scrabbled tail up and tail down on the huge trunks and yelped back at the jays and crows, and at you, the intruder.

On the side of the tabernacle away from the road, weeds grew calf-high right up to the cement sill. The grass was gray with dust that the rain huffed up from the clotted ground. Snakes lived there, sidling off as you walked out into the gravelly worn space, vaguely a drive, that curled around the tabernacle and separated it from the cottages, dormitories, and kitchen. Even in front, the ground was raw and stony, the grass unmown. There were no monuments in the town square of this little temporary settlement. Its monument was itself—that it was just this, just here, that these were the circumstances of the repeated moment when people turned to face the reality they knew could not be negotiated.

When we think about religion, this is what we are looking for—the cultural traces, the formalities, of that encounter, so that by recording and understanding them we might come to understand the encounter itself. It had, for the plain people, the shape, the sounds, the smell of that grove and its wooden shed. You carried the meeting away with you when it was done, in memories of nights that were like the scars of home or of breaking away from home. Corners of the campground, or of the tabernacle itself, would go away in minds to the ends of the earth.

We walk up to the tabernacle in the hot late afternoon, after supper. The July sun has dulled the trees. The college lawns rust in the weeks of heat. Now the white light going orange lies like an abrasion on the tabernacle's matte-white walls. People are arriving from all directions. Their motion, the heated cars pulling up, the exhaust in the ballooning dust are not motion at all, but a property of the frozen heat and light. We live close enough to walk, across the scalded plain of the campus, onto a path as steep and narrow as an escalator trailing up the hill. None of this seems like motion either. Nothing seems to move. Everything is happening in the same moment. In the expectation of God.

The college falls away beneath us as we climb. The path peters out into a rutted, sandy patch of weeds and empties us into the grove. The grass, ropy as kelp, is rank with beaded, unripe ragweed and hoary dandelions. From the cottages and parking lot people assemble, the women with faces lowered into blossoms of shared gossip, the men carrying their jackets over their forearms. Children run and screech among the elms. There is a gush of organ music from the tabernacle. We walk deliberately toward it. I feel caught on a hook, my breath coming fast already.

Now the sun angles in from the deep west, and the white walls shine with light as sharp and flat as acid. Inside the tabernacle it is darker, stuffy. The wide doors are slid back on both sides, the air comes in, the tabernacle roof is airborne above us. The crowd stands with a grumble of chairs and feet; the organ punches the last phrase of a song everyone knows, in the quavery Hammond blat that is like batting in the ears; and we sing.

Around its edges the crowd is still frayed and gathering, people hurrying to places, the ushers walking quickly back up the aisles and signaling to each other to bring people down to empty seats in front. We sit down, the lath folding chairs crackling, and are welcomed. The presiding minister's smile seems to me rank pretense; but perhaps he is not afraid. I watch the line of ministers on the platform. They sing without songbooks, leaning over to speak with one another, nod and smile among themselves; their faces scan the crowd like searchlights. They join the song or leave it for a phrase, beating time on their knees with their Bibles.

They sit in a slight shadow. In the early evening the platform seems dim. All around us the tabernacle is ringed with windows and open doors. As the service begins, it is dark inside and the windows are full of daylight. As evening comes on, the windows grow clear, as if they were display cases in a museum of the real world: you can look out (in) on the summer foliage, western New York, 1955. Then the lights are switched on and the room is ringed with darkness. The tabernacle gathers light into itself, holds it until it is a ship blazing in the dark, the only survivor of the light. Late in the sermon the doors are still open, and the night outside is intense.

There is my family, sitting on folding chairs on the extreme western edge of the crowd, by a door. There I am, I can see myself; I seem composed, grave, but I can feel the terror behind the gravity of the child's round face. He is afraid of the approaching sermon and of what may come next, the call of God, the encounter.

With half his mind, however, he is listening to the crickets outside. He is holding to the world out there, making it real. Sometimes there is a sudden rise in the wind, whipping up dust and blowing through the wide doorway. The wind ruffles sheet music on the piano—the pianist grabs at the pages, smooths them back, rearranges her books—and in a hymnal lying open on an empty chair the pages flap and settle. No one but the boy seems to notice.

Sometimes there is rain. The air suddenly rouses and freshens, turns its cool lining outward, with the clamminess of the storm in its folds. There is a rush of wind, like the swell of an excited crowd, and the trees out of sight above the roof edge hiss and shush. Raindrops wash across the threshold like a scatter of grain and then begin to hammer steadily on the concrete. The roof bellows. In the myth time I am inhabiting, it seems inexplicable that the rain goes on regardless of the sermon. There is a voice in the storm. Which voice should I be listening to? There are two worlds, and I am sitting in both.

But the two worlds are most distinct and intense on perfectly still evenings, when the tabernacle is warmly yellow and the night seems to draw close to hear the preacher shout. The oldest sound outside, a sound so native to that northeastern summer as to be its natural form of silence, is the pulse of crickets. The preaching is an active sound, the crickets' sound contemplative. The preacher drives us toward decision, doing something, standing up, going forward. The sound outside leads you back to the summer evening—isolating, quieting, interiorizing, the song of a world that wants nothing, in which I could want nothing. At the moment, tormented by the preaching, I want that outside world with a desperate pathos. Even the passing of an occasional breeze raising its shallow applause among the trees does not disturb the stillness beyond the light.

Nothing moves. I sit in two worlds. This is myth time: summer, religion. The small enclosed grove, on the hill, is divided between light and dark. The portly women fan themselves, absorbed in the sermon. The evangelist wipes his neck. I can see myself, there, the grave dark face containing its terror and curiosity. The preacher is still calling to me; the evening is still at the door.

We leave the tabernacle and outside it is dark. "It was so dark," my mother writes me of the campgrounds of her childhood.

"There were the little lights on tents here and there among the trees—but it was so dark." In the countryside, the city grid fifty miles away, we are in something like the actual darkness of the planet with the sun out of sight. Camp meeting stranded you in the night and gave you a little light to make it tolerable. It was like being stranded in time and having no more to go on than our small clearings of language. Camp meeting was in a clearing, too, the columnar trees stirring in their invisible tops. I doubt a plane would even have noticed us below—a few porch lights, the one streetlight in its steam of bugs.

The preaching, of course, appealed to brilliantly explosive light, fire falling from heaven (as it was said literally to have done during the Welsh revivals of 1905) and the light on the Damascus road. Our songs were wiser. "Let the lower lights be burning, / Send the news across the waves." Something about a hymn sung in our shopworn voices injected modesty into the project. "God has given me a lifeboat," D. L. Moody liked to say, "and told me, 'Moody, save all you can.'" The *Titanic* of Western culture was, after all, going down. It is a complex image, spiky. There is the triumphalism of watching what Hardy called "this vainglorious-ness" disappear; there is also the tragic modesty of being able to do only a little. And the lifeboat lantern is hard to see past. It is so dark.

I have tried, but I can't recall the tabernacle lights being switched on. It must have happened. We felt the fall of dark. The light seemed not to vanish but to come inside, shrinking and brightening. Things narrowed and focused as the service went on, first to the pulpit, then to the altar rail, the point of energy and desire where people, kneeling, disappeared behind the people who were standing, and then in a minute voices would rise above the singing—"Glory! Hallelujah!" The dark outside served the purpose of the meeting; or, actually, the service had accommo-dated the gigantic event, the arrival of night, adapting itself in a

triumph of cultural invention no less significant for being unconscious, simply accommodating the unavoidable: camp meeting
was an outdoors phenomenon.

Culture is invented when circumstances are welded together
with the widest intuition of their meanings. Religion can be had
anywhere, any day, for a set fee, but faith is time- and place-
specific. This is why the Bible says, *Now is the hour of salvation. Now,
if you will hearken.* But there is also the observation, *You do not know
the day or the hour.* This makes the specificity of faith urgent. We
must be, we were, endlessly accountable for what we did in a particular meeting on a particular night. *Be watchful, therefore.* Back we
go to circumstances: the call is to presence and attention. The
world is about to change around you.

At Cane Run, Kentucky, the Jerusalem of the camp meeting
pentecost, you can enter the cramped log church that was standing on the ridge in August 1801, when the enormous "union meeting" began. The church is clean, restored, and quiet; its keepers
have encased it in a stone basilica to keep the weather away. The
revival itself, by contrast, was loud, out-of-doors, seismic, unpre-
dictable. We can only guess how many people came, but they
overwhelmed the preparations; the meeting expanded like a
storm, or many overlapping tornadoes, and people a mile off
could hear its heavy, abiding murmur, like the sound of a battle.
While the meeting lasted, the rules of normal culture vanished.
The little church has a slave balcony, but outside, slaves and masters marched side by side and women and children preached.
From then on for a century, the signs of the American pentecost
would be night and fire, forest and cleared place, marching, faint-
ing, falling, and crying out, the midnight parade under flaring pine
knots, the sacramental meal in a grove by the river.

Of course when the torches guttered and stank in the damp
mosquito-thick dawn, things went back to normal. But what
does it mean for things to be normal? More changed at Cane

Run than styles of worship. Camp meetings were one source of abolitionist politics and so involved the causes of civil war. They involved its causes in a looser way: they were part of war's imaginative economy. Crossing over Jordan into campground, tenting there, the "hundred circling camps" with their altars and their "righteous sentence" read out in torch light: such images are not chosen or designed—rather, exuded, almost, from intense experience—but they made war plausible and therefore possible.

A new iconography is a new history: a set of conditions in which unprecedented things can be deliberately done. Any intensely religious event is an intensely worldly event. It remakes the world itself by affecting the meanings of the most comprehensive, least avoidable conditions. A religious event that does not change the meaning of light and dark, fire and water, food and drink, field and city, war and peace, birth and death, slavery and freedom has too superficial a connection with us. One that does can create culture.

Not a new mind, but a new world. Conversion changes the actual; things look and sound different. Different conduct, naturally, is required; people change their hopes and common practices. Cranmer's Third Collect for Evening Prayer—"Lighten our darkness we beseech thee"—does not say whether it is physical or spiritual darkness that is to be illumined. This is the prayer's great accuracy: what seems to be praying is the human condition, physical and imaginative at once. Cranmer's writing has the power of Shakespeare's. "The dark and vicious place where he thee got / Cost him his eyes," Edgar says of his father—not that Gloucester's punishment is proportionate, but that, having put himself in the line of darkness, he couldn't calculate or restrain the terrible darkness that might come. If Macbeth murders sleep, he will not sleep. Skeptics who mocked the camp-meeting exhorters for their ecstatic behavior were said to have been struck blind, suddenly groping and stumbling where they had been jumping and howling a moment before.

A circuit rider named Johnson is picking his way through the malarial Indiana woods at night. It is perhaps 1815. He and his horse blunder off the invisible track, slide twice into a ravine, and scramble out. He loses the horse altogether and stumbles on, falling into a river, and then, having recovered his mount, sits drenched and wretched in the utter lostness of the wilderness. The horse is half-asleep; it shifts and stamps. Johnson asks himself where he is. Immediately the answer comes, a hymn line— "We are marching through Immanuel's ground"—and he kicks the horse forward onto Immanuel's ground and is located, a few minutes later, by someone hearing him sing as he rides.

Indiana into Immanuel's ground: the conundrum lies in how it occurs. But then what do we know about religion? We have hardly advanced beyond William James: "If you ask *how* religion thus falls on the thorns and faces death, and in the very act annuls annihilation, I cannot explain the matter, for it is religion's secret, and to understand it, you must yourself have been a religious man of the extremer sort." Setting the condescension aside, James has two important things right: it is the "extremer" case— the genuine believer—who provides the crucial data; and the religious do understand.

But that will not be enough to say, and the condescension cannot be set aside. There are two languages here, two resources of explanation, and James will accept only one of them, that of science. The religious understand, but not in a language James can hear. The gap is as wide as the coming of secular culture, as sharp as the mind-body problem; it is the abyss Kierkegaard insisted on to renew the urgency of faith. Religion can be had anywhere, for a set fee, but it does not correspond to, it only accompanies, the "secret." "For it is in ritual," Clifford Geertz wrote, "—that is, in consecrated behavior—that the conviction that religious concepts are veridical and that religious directives are sound is somehow generated." Somehow: there is always this stop in the argument. It stops at the division of languages, at the tabernacle door, watching the people streaming forward and not knowing what to say.

"There is no criterion," Paul Tillich wrote, "by which faith can be judged from the outside." The question of whether "religious concepts are veridical" will have to be asked by the faithful themselves, who "can say," Tillich went on, ". . . whether the medium through which [they experience] ultimate concern expresses real ultimacy." Then Tillich vacillated: or someone else can say. But how? The truth is that religious believers are always asking themselves this question, though not in Tillich's language, and that if there is a subjective answer in devotion, the objective evidence is the persistence of the community that believes.

For it is finally a matter of how belief is born in the new believer. That it occurs is plain; how it occurs may be told, and the narratives can, within a given community, be formalized, but finally we will have no evidence but the narrative. *I once was lost, but now am found.* Found where? In the place that faith has changed. In that place you meet others whose stories may be radically different from yours; but all of you recognize the place. In the tabernacle most of the young people eventually yielded to the magnetism of the altar and stepped, or were carried, across the threshold. Others went away, up the aisle, hostile and embittered. Their narrative was often political: the service was an exercise of unrationalized authority, an imposition. But they had misread the event; it had shrunk to the size of the preacher's mouth. They had lost track of most of the facts—the singing, the yellow light, the concrete floor so cold through the strip of carpet, the grove outside, where it was so dark. That wasn't where they wanted to be found.

·   ·   ·

In both worlds it is getting late. The sweetness of the grove rides
in the open door on an occasional puff of cool wind. Inside the
tabernacle it is warm, almost hot, in the yellow light, and the air
has its own stuffy sweetness—perfume, hymnal paper, the dusty
plushiness of the old seats. The sermon is almost done. Now it is
done, and the altar call begins. If the altar is not barren, as we
say, many will kneel there, and your private prayer will be
buoyed, or will have to struggle, on the tide of many public ones.

How they swarm up out of my memory, the voices of those
altar calls: "Come home!" the melody rises like a question, "come
home," the question is answered by deeper voices in harmony,
"come home!" the melody sweeps back down and then begins a
stepwise climb, "Ye who are weary, come home!" Then the calmer
prose—"Softly and tenderly, Jesus is calling . . ."

When we get to the high note, the minister is waiting for us.
It has been all the verses and four choruses, and the aisles are full
of people slipping out and going forward in a broken stream, but
the minister knows there are more to be persuaded. He has been
beating time with his Bible in both hands, not singing, but seeming to soak up the music, to become charged with its electricity,
and now as we climb to the song's highest pitch, he calls out,
"Softly and tenderly," and then we sing, back and forth, "Softly
and tenderly," "Jesus is calling," "Jesus is calling," and when we
near the end of the chorus, he says to the song leader, always the
attentive lieutenant at his right shoulder, "Brother Mitchell, could
we sing just one more verse?" And we do.

All around me the song whelms. I am standing on an inside
aisle, sharing a songbook and singing in a choked, subdued voice.
I study the ridges and pits and welts in the concrete floor, just
feet away. My heart is yanking in my chest like a trigger; I am
trembling and cannot move.

Now the minister stops the singing. He tells us how it will be with him in an hour, after the service is done and the last opportunity is gone, when he kneels in his room and the Lord asks him, "Roy, did you give it to them straight?" He is making us responsible for the agony of self-examination he will have to endure. Eventually he comes to the inescapable, mythical story about the young person who resisted the call and that very night, going home from the meeting, was killed by a tractor trailer, trampled into eternity by the screaming tires. The effect of the story is to make you afraid to step out of the tabernacle; but the child had been afraid to come in. There is, he sees, no escaping; now is the day, the hour, the moment.

There is a woman kneeling at the altar not far from the child. She is a regular, the wife of a minister—a small, energetic, kittenish woman who instead of braiding her hair and hiding it, lets it cascade, black and prematurely graying and full of ringlets, down her back. She kneels beside her husband, a strikingly handsome man. We know why they are there. They do not need the grace of the altar themselves, though they would not say so; they are praying for others. But her concern has an edge. She is full of spontaneous resentment—she would probably call it righteous anger—against those who would challenge her place in her understanding of things. She is a small, delicate person, but I cannot remember ever seeing her smile. And now, somehow, she lifts her head and turns from the altar rail to look straight at me. The look—which I remember now, forty years later, with perfect lucidity, as if she were looking straight through time—is as flat and cruel as a lynx's stare.

I do not go to the altar—I cannot move—and eventually the meeting ends. I am still afraid but at the same time intensely relieved, as if after months of testing and suspense I have been told that I have a fatal illness and nothing can be done, and I can set about reconciling myself to it. We are near the door and slip out

into the darkness throbbing with crickets. The two worlds resolve
into one. But it feels flat, one-dimensional. I have lost something.

So the account ends there. The innocent, vacant self is com-
pelled, or required at least, to buckle to the unintelligible, authoritarian demand.

I have told that story to fine, liberal-minded religious people,
and they have been shocked. "How did you survive?" The question shows a misunderstanding, though, and in a modern way, by
assuming that the self is self-ordaining and that any contribution
to its options that is larger than the self is an imposition and
therefore a cruelty. But this is not the meaning of the experience.

The question is, Have you met whatever you take to be non-
negotiable—God, the divine, death, the ultimate ground of
being—and held the encounter until the other declared its name?
"Those who are awakened to the light," Tillich wrote, "ask pas-
sionately the question of ultimate reality. They are different from
those who do not." The awakening and then the question. Whatever interior movement it is that occurs in conversion, that small,
deeply cut turning of a corner, it is a moment when one has no
choice and one's choice is free.

Other nights, other moments. We are singing, many have
gone forward, the altar is not barren. Then one of the seekers
stands and walks back up the aisle toward me. He passes my right
shoulder, and, as he does, he looks me in the face and smiles.

I know him slightly. He is someone caught up and bewildered
by religion, someone who lacks the emotional sturdiness, perhaps, to stand in the beating of that relentless surf. He is odd. He
buttonholes people on Wednesday mornings and demands, "Is
there an angel in that tree? *Right there.* Do you believe that?"
Angels are as palpable to him as bathtubs.

Anyhow, he passes me and smiles. Something happens to me,
more in my face than in my mind. "You were radiant," my girlfriend

says. She also is one of us and knows what it means. It is an evidence, a mark in the flesh.

Another service. The sermon ends, the singing begins. An elderly man, dressed in the flat brown gabardine typical of fifties Sunday best, steps out of his row. But he doesn't go to the altar. Instead, he stands in the aisle, facing the front, and then raises his right hand above his head. He says nothing, doesn't sing, gesticulate, or look around. But the aisles are suddenly thronged.

Of course he may be a plant, a charlatan, one more device. But the more likely possibility is that he has absorbed the power of that gesture, distilled and intensified, from a lifetime of such services. He has raised Moses' hand above the Red Sea. He might even say it that way. It is like the gesture of a great actress who has moved all her life in the literature of her roles, and no longer invents anything, but moves with the authority of her whole community and tradition.

In any case, it is a manifestation. What was hidden has been shouted from the rooftop. That conductivity of looks and gestures, that radiance passed from face to face as a flame is dipped out of one candle by another, is the unofficial sacrament of the whole enterprise.

I remember wandering past the east wall of the tabernacle one evening and finding, to my surprise, that the door was unlocked. I hauled it barely open on its grating track and edged through. It was late summer, the sun was already down, and while under the trees the air was still light, inside it was dim. The hundreds of seats overlapped up the gentle rake of the floor like the ghosts of shells. I sighed harshly, too deeply, I don't know why. Or I do. I had been afraid here—not the needle panic at human violence, but the larger fear that makes the floor shake and your tongue cleave to the roof of your mouth. The tabernacle's air was sweet with the smell of dusty hymnbook paper. There was something in it, though, of Ezekiel's salt-waste valley where the bones stood up. I walked to the center of the altar rail and knelt. But the people had gone for the season, the meeting had left with them, and the tabernacle was silent at my back.

Where does the power of the religious claim come from? *From something having happened.* The event is the source and the subject of ritual. Yet we can idolize events. "What did you come out to see?" Jesus asked the crowd, with his familiar unsettling irony. "A reed shaken by the wind?" They were expecting too little: a newsworthy occurrence, one more in a series, trivial no matter what—not a change of world. What happened to me was a long cumulative event, a location, an opening. I knew the tabernacle for what it was—a tent in the wilderness, a *sukkah*, the proper home for a journey, for a setting-out-one-knows-not-where, for confidence in things summoned by hope.

This is perhaps the place to say that I am a Christian. If you take as a rule James's divergence of languages, you will find it hard to imagine that the camp meeting carried me beyond its terrors, that I learned—I am indebted to the lynx for this—that I was dealing not with one tainted mind but with ultimate concern. The truth is that I never wholly belonged to the camp-meeting people and cannot easily say why. But I had been enclosed, very young, in very old circumstances—the tabernacle and the wilderness. The believer learns to sit in two worlds at once. What a training for a writer!

And fear had its place in this, along with radiance and longing. "Thanks to its tenderness, its joys and fears," Wordsworth wrote of the heart—and the heart must have places to be afraid in, as Wordsworth knew, and to acknowledge that the fear is not petty or vestigial but called for and warranted. We must know when and how to acknowledge, in the company of others, that our explanations, our myths, and our practical uses for things thin out quite close to us, and that then we must simply wait for meanings that come to us from outside.

We stood, sang, knelt, prayed in the tabernacle on late July nights and waited there together. In their prayer caps and wide, garish ties, these people had made a cultural triumph by paying attention first of all to other things. They had built according to an ideal of plainness—light, dark, the wooden roof, the grove. What the plainness meant was: the intention to *be plain*, with yourself and others; directness of purpose; the long establishment of languages in which spiritual things could be spoken of directly, plainly, in which spiritual business could be done. I would go back and sit there again, if I could—if the tabernacle had not been torn down and the people gone elsewhere—and absorb the preacher's words, the songs, watch the night and the rain wait on the threshold, smell the dense unflowered sweetness of the northern woods. I know that place for what it was: Immanuel's ground.

GOD AND WOMAN AT HARVARD

I went back to grad school ten years after college. I hadn't been idle in the meantime; I'd earned two master's degrees, published three books, and given birth to three babies. But I hadn't gotten around to that final Ph.D. I had lots of good reasons for going back to school. I enjoyed teaching, I had begun to feel the lack of critical grounding in my work, and I thought a few Ph.D. seminars might improve my writing. But mostly I wanted to get out of Office 4B.

I was teaching English as an adjunct instructor at the College of William & Mary. We adjunct English flunkies were a nomadic lot, shifting from office to office every year. In my fourth year of teaching, I drew Office 4B: the former supply closet in the bottom of Tucker Hall. Three adjuncts shared it, working out a careful schedule so that our office hours didn't overlap. My students, creeping down into the pipe-lined spaces of the basement, squeezed into the tiny room through the badly fitted door and sat on my student chair, their knees brushing awkwardly against mine when I swiveled my desk chair toward them. "What did you do to get stuck down here?" one freshman asked, his eyes wide at the barbaric university punishment system he'd conjured up.

One day I went upstairs in time to hear the department secretary correct a caller: "Dr. Bauer? She's in 4B. But it isn't *doctor* or *professor*—just Mrs. Bauer."

Wounded pride is much stronger than ambition. Egalitarian that I am, I went home and dumped all my motives, selfish and admirable, into my husband's lap. "What do you think I should do?" I asked.

"I think you should go finish your Ph.D.," he said.

And so I trotted off to register for my sixth year of full-time graduate study.

I found myself barraged, in seminar after seminar, by constant criticism of American Christianity. I was hearing many of the same themes from both inside and outside the evangelical tradition: Richard Hays and George Chauncey taught me that homosexual identity is a political, not a biblical, category. Kenneth Karst and Ed Dobson convinced me that right-wing politics is morally bankrupt. Judith Plaskow and Stanley Hauerwas introduced me to the problem of the Other, and I learned that I too often use the language of the West as though it were the language of Christ.

Yet I came back from my classes feeling bruised, sick, physically sore. On the long drive home, I would tune in the local Christian radio station and listen with nostalgic ease to the theological pap coming over the airwaves. The teaching was shallow and the music was terrible, but it was familiar, and it didn't pick away at the very foundations of my identity.

At school, I grimly held on to the evangelical label. There is much about evangelical culture that I loathe, however—especially its unthinking boosting of truth, rationality, and the American market-way—and whenever I criticized some prominent voice of evangelicalism—Jerry Falwell or Pat Robertson, for example—my classmates became visibly more comfortable with my presence. My willingness to find fault made me respectable. But to reject the evangelical label altogether, in a place where Christianity was so embattled, seemed like a betrayal.

I took three seminars from a brilliant lesbian activist historian who still calls herself Catholic. I sat in her office one day and told her all my troubles. I told her about growing up in evangelicalism, about the childhood church that had exalted masculinity and put women and children, weak and beautiful, in a safe, protected space; I told her about the years of watching my parents struggle free, and talked about how their rejection of that power-dynamic as they still held firm to their faith had helped me understand that a person might criticize a faith and yet still identify with it.

"I used to say that I was an ex-Catholic," she said. "But then I stopped, because when I said that, people reacted as though I had come to my senses. So now I just say that I'm Catholic. I don't want them to assume that to be secular is to be reasonable."

"Yes," I said. "That's exactly it. That's why I don't want to say that I used to be an evangelical."

The faculty, as a whole, didn't particularly care what I believed; I wasn't discriminated against. I found myself, rather, in a reasonably good position. "You're an important graduate student to the program," one professor told me. "Excellent, as expected," was a common remark on my papers. "A model essay," wrote my adviser.

But there were some things I learned not to talk about. Abortion, for example. Or really, anything having to do with reproduction.

Reading Cornelia Hughes Dayton's *Women Before the Bar*, I encountered stories of desperate colonial women trapped in virtual slavery by abusive marriages. I read of one woman who reacted to the unwanted child of such a marriage by dismembering the newborn and stuffing it into her chamber pot. Her black servant helped her conceal the evidence. The seminar discussion of that book centered around the helplessness of women who were unable to control pregnancy, addressing the ways that this helplessness created bonds between women of different race and social position. All well and good, but after two and a half hours of discussion I burst out, "Don't any of you want to say that it's wrong? That it's evil to dismember a newborn and stuff it into a jar?" And to my surprise, the other members of the class began to nod, one by one.

But this was infanticide, understandable but a little beyond the pale. The right to abortion continued to be an off-limits topic. (After all, we were meeting in the Women's Studies conference room.) Nor could I discuss my deepest questions with my evangelical colleagues. I wondered whether the termination of a first-trimester pregnancy was morally on a different plane than the termination of a viable child, but I didn't think I'd get much dispassionate analysis of this problem with those who were digging in their toes at the top of the slippery slope.

In my Ph.D. seminars, I read and discussed Plaskow, Margaret Bendroth, Carol Christ, Nancy Cott, Jeanne Boydston. I found much to admire: these were historians who believed that religion was explosively powerful and that women had too often been denied their character as daughters of God. Yet I had to compare all that I was reading against Christian truth on my own time, without any aid. All I found from the Christian side was evangelical rhetoric about how feminists want absolute and unbiblical freedom, yet I had already discovered that feminism is as nuanced as Christianity, that to speak of some blanket "feminist" ideology is akin to pairing Benny Hinn and Gary North together under the fundamentalist label.

So when I saw a notice in *Christianity Today* for Elizabeth Fox-Genovese's two-week graduate seminar in feminism and Christianity, I took the clipping in to one of my professors, in hopes that she might write me the required recommendation. Predictably, she wasn't enthusiastic. "You'll get a very odd take on feminism," she warned me. "Why don't I see if I can get you into this Harvard conference instead? There will be lots of evangelical women there, and you can hear a bunch of different points of view."

I suspected that an odd take on feminism was exactly what I needed at this point. On the other hand, the Harvard conference ("Core Connections: Women, Religion, & Public Policy") was only a weekend in Cambridge in November; the Fox-Genovese seminar was in Texas, in August, and I would have to spend two full weeks away from my three small children to do it. And Harvard would pay my way.

So I flew off to Cambridge, looking for a place to talk about abortion and Christianity and evangelicalism and feminism in a place where no one would foam at the mouth over any of these subjects.

The Harvard conference, I gathered from the materials sent to me, was intended to bring women together across academic and activist lines to discuss how women and women's involvement in religion affected policymaking. It was co-sponsored by the John F. Kennedy School of Government and the Harvard Divinity School, under the auspices of the U.S. Ambassador to Austria and the director of the Women and Public Policy Program at the Kennedy School.

The conference was designed as a whole series of small-group meetings, twelve to fourteen women at most; these groups were supposed to be safe places where we could all talk about the issues that divided us. It was supposed to be a series of conversations across lines of activism, practice, and scholarship; across religious and political divides; across religious traditions. It was supposed to be a time, the letter from the ambassador informed me, when we all would depart from normal conference procedure—the staking out and defense of positions—and instead try to find "unlikely" patches of common ground between us. Hallelujah, I thought.

I stayed with the daughter of a Westminster friend, an Inter-Varsity staffer who worked with Harvard undergrads. Her apartment was a ten-minute walk from the Kennedy School. I got up early the first morning and had coffee at a café where people wore black and talked about Foucault and read African poetry (at seven-thirty in the morning). I walked down Brattleboro Street and bought a book (Philip K. Dick's *The Divine Invasion*), circling back by the river to arrive for the opening continental breakfast in a mood of enlightened tolerance.

The ambassador had done herself proud, making connections across traditional religious lines; besides the usual representatives of Jewish and Protestant groups, she had invited women with aggressively secular agendas, Islamic activists and scholars, Asian Unitarian Universalist clergywomen, African-American Church of Christ ministers, lesbian clergy and public policy analysts, professional fundraisers and American Indian businesswomen, and a Buddhist nun who also held a Ph.D. from Yale.

I noticed, circling around with my coffee and bagel, that the tags we all wore were marked with our institutional affiliation. Slowly, I began to recognize names and faces, women I knew as evangelical because I had spoken to them, read their works, heard about what they were doing. Slowly, I began to realize that the evangelical women were all activists. And they all wore tags clearly identifying themselves with ministries: *Hope for the Heart, United Family Ministries, The Damaris Project,* even *The Beverly LaHaye Institute* (a move I rather admired; I wouldn't have had the nerve to parade into a Harvard Divinity School gathering of feminists with Beverly on my chest).

Slowly, I began to realize that not a single academic shared an evangelical theology that I recognized. And something else odd was happening; when I was introduced to women I didn't know—women with institutional tags that read *Harvard Divinity School* or *Yale University* or *National Women's Political Caucus* or NOW or ERA *Summit*—they greeted me as a friend. I was slightly startled by this, seeing myself as the outsider. And yet here I was an assumed insider, so that one woman drew me aside and asked me in a half-whisper if I'd seen "those scary conservatives" yet. I realized, late, that my tag said *College of William & Mary* and that this gave me some sort of automatic credibility. Obviously, I was no evangelical.

The first plenary session was full of jockeying for position. At its conclusion an African-American woman stood up and demanded to know why her name tag didn't bear the title "Reverend." "Here, of all places," she boomed, "surrounded by other women! Sojourner Truth asked 'Ain't I a woman?'; here I ask you all, 'Ain't I a woman pastor?' Why here don't I get the full respect I deserve?"

Everyone clapped, uncomfortably, and we were directed to head for the art museum, where the buffet supper and small-group meetings would be held. We walked across the Divinity School campus in the cold dark, through wrappers of mist and wisps of conversation. I found myself beside a woman wearing the name tag of an evangelical ministry, listening to her talk about the opportunities for witness and reaching out to those in darkness that the conference presented. No doubt there was plenty of darkness around; but this habit of seeing every opportunity for dialogue as an opportunity to shine a light into someone else's benightedness bothered me. No wonder they accuse us of close-mindedness, I thought, feeling pleasantly superior. We're not willing to learn anything; we're always trying to stand on our own superior Sinais and reveal the truth.

I ate salmon and lobster and drank white wine and mingled until the small-group meetings were called and we drifted away, one at a time, to our "safe places" to air our opinions and ask our questions and forge our unlikely alliances. I chose a workshop called "Fundamentalism and Reproductive Rights: Are They Incompatible?" The group's leader was a well-known lawyer and crusader for reproductive rights, a woman who (I found out later) had been recognized by the *National Law Journal* as one of "the 100 Most Influential Lawyers in America" and who made her living by opposing restrictions to abortion and the censoring of any sex education program.

"This seminar title is a question," she announced, to the fourteen women in a circle of folding chairs in the Dutch Masters room of the Fogg. "Let's go around and each of us begin by saying our answer to the question to open the discussion. I'll start out now by saying that my answer is 'No, definitely not.'"

None of the other women in the circle was wearing an evangelical ministry ID tag, but I was willing to entertain the idea that a few of them might nevertheless share some of my own concerns; after all, I wasn't wearing a ministry-type tag either. But everyone agreed, all the way around the circle, that fundamentalism and reproductive rights were incompatible. I ventured, when the loaded question got to me, "I think I'd want to know how we're defining fundamentalism, and how we're defining reproductive rights."

"Quite right," said the leader, approvingly. "Here's the definition I'm working from."

Fundamentalism, it turned out, was any religious system that depended on enforcing clear-cut gender roles as part of its essential order. Reproductive rights were seen as the complete power of every woman over all aspects of pregnancy and birth control. Thus any religious system that suggested any ethical restrictions to abortion or birth control was fundamentalist (and any system that refrained from making ethical pronouncements was nonfundamentalist). Naturally, then, fundamentalism and reproductive rights were incompatible.

It took me about half an hour to figure out this circular reasoning, and another ten minutes or so to add the obvious
implication in my head: the only reason any religious system
would make ethical restrictions on pregnancy is in order to
enforce clear-cut gender roles. The abortion issue is never
about life; it is always about power. More to the point, *religion*
is always about power, never about God; it is only horizontal,
never vertical.

I'd heard this before, of course, but it startled me a little to
hear it at a conference where people kept saying that they were
taking religion seriously. I ventured, twenty minutes before the
session's end, "What about a fetus at eight or nine months?
Should it have any rights to good treatment? Can it be abused? Is
there an ethical difficulty in aborting a child that could also be
saved through medical technology? And couldn't a religious system be concerned about the life of a child who is viable without
being motivated only by a desire to control women?"

I thought that this was a mild way to introduce the problem;
at least I wasn't shouting noisily about the moment of conception. But immediately all the women turned their chairs toward
me, so that I became the focal point of a suddenly triangular
group; and they all set to work to show me the error of my ways.

"What are you saying?" one woman demanded. "That late-
term abortions should be illegal?"

"I just wonder what the ethical problems are."

"Ethical problems should be regulated by religious organizations, not by government."

"But all laws take positions on ethical problems," I said, hardly
able to believe that I was having here (on the hallowed ground of
Harvard) a Philosophy 101 sort of discussion in response to such
a complex question.

"I don't think you've completely thought through your position on this," the group leader said severely.

"But I haven't taken a position," I protested. "I just asked a question."

"Let me tell you a story," she said, ignoring my point, and wound herself up into a passion telling the story of a twelve-year-old girl forced by law to bear a baby produced by incestuous rape. "And that," she declared, "is the reason why the law should take *no* position on late-term abortions. I can see that you haven't considered all the implications of saying that the fetus has rights at all. You're making a very dangerous argument!"

"Let me tell *you* a story," I said. "I have a much-loved relative—adopted—who can't seem to make any connections with her family. She doesn't love us. She doesn't identify with us. We've lived through thirty years of pain with her. And we've always suspected that this might have to do with alcohol abuse during her time in the womb. Didn't she have any rights? She has to live with the effects of what her mother did during pregnancy for the rest of her life. Can't I suggest that the law should be able to regulate what someone else inflicted on her before she could defend herself?"

And at this point I acted out a regrettable feminine stereotype and burst into tears.

Instantly the whole group produced tissues and made soothing noises and stopped attempting to change my mind. Apparently I was acceptable if I could justify my odd concern for fetal rights by telling a personal story. They could make allowances for my point of view. This was much more understandable than some strange and abstract idea about the personhood of an unborn baby and what God might think about such a thing, and whether that should have any effect on law. They didn't agree with me, of course, but they understood me. To understand is to cease to fear. This irritated the hell out of me, but my nose was running and my eyes were all red, so I was scarcely in a position to start a new debate on the difference between the personal and the political.

With order restored, the workshop leader produced her Leader's Checksheet and said brightly, "I need to ask now whether you all felt that this was a safe place where you could share exactly what you thought with others."

I blew my nose and said, "I didn't."

She looked at me, shocked.

"You all started trying to convert me to your point of view, instead of listening to the argument I was making."

She fixed me with a severe stare. "You may have felt that," she said, "but that's not what actually happened. Your view of reality is skewed." She turned to the NOW member next to me. "How about you? Did you feel that this was a safe place to express your point of view?"

"Oh, yes," my neighbor said, offering me another tissue.

I took myself and my skewed reality back to Harvard Square and located the hotel where a number of conference participants were staying for the night; an evangelical woman acquaintance had invited me back to her room, and I felt beaten-up and in need of some company who wouldn't tell me that my mind was being controlled by (male) fundamentalist forces. In the elevator I met another evangelical woman, high with delight because a secular feminist had just told her how reasonable her point of view was. "You know," she said, leaning toward me, "if these feminists would just recognize the need for authority, and understand their own need for submission, so many of these problems would resolve themselves. Are you going up to Elaine's room? Good. We're going to have a war meeting."

I sat on the carpet in the war meeting and listened to my allies talk. I thought: What would happen if I told them that I think Paul would be appalled if he could see the way the church has wielded male headship? What would happen if I told them that I think we're obsessed by homosexuality? What would they say if I told them that I think there's an ethical difference between an abortion at six weeks and one at six months? Why do I have to pretend that I agree with the fact that all their husbands are in charge of their lives?

But I didn't say any of it. I was feeling too bruised, and these were my friends, the women I would (I assumed) spend eternity with. But I was uncomfortable. I was uncomfortable with the easy assumption of truth, with the mouthing of martial language. I didn't want to fight a holy war; I wanted to hear what the other side had to say. I didn't want to think of the other side as the Other Side. I excused myself early and walked back down to my friend's cold apartment. Finding an Edith Wharton novel on her shelf, I read myself to sleep.

The next morning the ambassador cornered me at the continental breakfast in the Littauer Building's penthouse and asked me which workshop I'd attended.

"The one about fundamentalism and reproductive freedom," I said.

"How was it?"

"Well," I said cautiously, "it wasn't a safe space and all that. I wondered if we could talk about fetal viability and fetal rights at all, but the group didn't seem receptive. Frankly, I felt attacked."

She laid her hand on my shoulder and looked at me with great compassion.

"I'm so sorry you didn't feel that your voice got heard," she said. "I didn't realize that you were the only one of Them in that workshop. You must have felt terribly outnumbered."

In the hallway, heading for the last plenary session, I heard my name called. I recognized the name on the tag, but not the face: another evangelical woman. She said, "I saw you in Elaine's room last night, but I didn't get a chance to talk to you. How was your workshop? Mine was terrible. All the feminists in it were so confrontational and so loud that I finally just stopped talking. I couldn't make myself heard at all. They ruled the floor."

I made my way down to the plenary session and sat down next to a woman who looked like my Aunt Myrtle; she was wearing a twin set and pearl earrings, and she had soft silver hair in waves and wore a ladylike dusting of scented powder. The plenary speaker was a tall, elegant woman who leaned over the lectern and looked at us. "I am concerned," she said. "I am concerned because I have heard you all speaking to each other about public policy in the language of religion. You are presenting each other with fully formed policies and ideas, and demanding that each other 'get it' in a blinding flash before the conversation can continue. This is the language of conversion, of testimony, of faith. But deliberation is the natural language of political democracy."

The silver-haired woman beside me glanced at my *College of William & Mary* tag and leaned over toward me confidentially. "How was your workshop last night?" she breathed.

"Very confrontational," I said.

"So was mine. It was full of those evangelical women. They were so loud and angry and argumentative I finally just gave up. I felt so attacked."

I no longer call myself evangelical.

It isn't because of the women I met at Harvard, on either side of the rhetorical divide. It's because I learned, at Harvard, the extent to which we all lean on absolute truths. Even the most postmodern of academics has her feet on an absolute truth. Reproductive freedom is an easy one, but I heard half a dozen others mouthed at the plenary sessions in Cambridge. We may launch constantly from absolutes into the zero-gravity of subjectivity, yet we always settle back to them to regain our conviction.

The evangelical label has become my absolute; I'm afraid, somewhere deep down, that if I call myself simply a Christian someone
might identify me with the United Methodists down the road, or
with John Shelby Spong, or with (God forbid) Bill Clinton's version
of Baptist holiness. The word *evangelical* has become my way of
claiming an absolute truth. I am an evangelical; I am faithful.

And even as I've used it in this way, I've fallen into the trap of
playing academic power games with the word. "In my tradition,
the evangelical tradition," I said to my seminar group a few weeks
ago, "the Bible is central to piety." And then I heard what I had
done; I had called myself, not a Christian—that awkward identity that can never be fully defined—but someone who lived in
the "evangelical tradition," someone who had been born into a
way of life and both held to it and recognized it for what it is: a
cultural, time-bound phenomenon. Traditions are quaint and
charming. Traditions don't make demands on anyone from the
outside. Traditions don't even have to make sense, as long as they
fill the cold corners of your world with fuzzy warmth.

By the end of that Harvard conference, I wanted only to go
home. Not back to evangelicalism, but back to my family, to my
church, to those believers who are part of my community of faith
and who walk with me on a road that keeps bending. I wanted to
go back where I would be neither a William & Mary Ph.D. candidate nor a Useful Evangelical Spokeswoman, but simply myself,
living in the assurance of God my Father, the assurance of Christ
my Brother, and the presence of the Holy Spirit, my Comforter.

I suppose that means that I want simply to be a Christian; and
that I'm finally willing to let go of the label that assures me I'm on
the right side. Which is a relinquishment of power, after all; so
perhaps Harvard has brought me that much closer to the reality
of the crucified Christ. Although I'm not sure that's what the
ambassador had in mind.

TOM BEAUDOIN

SECOND THOUGHTS

(From *America*)

When that nostalgic softening of the lines around middle-aged eyes joins the voice of resignation, disappointment, and old-fashioned scolding—that's when I know the criticism is coming: "Your generation." (Pursed lips, both of us.) "What happened? Why don't you care about politics, like we did?"

For good reasons, many of our parents and mentors wonder if today's young adults inherited their passion for—or even literacy about—national political causes. They rightly wonder if the torch of activism for civil rights and feminism (and church reform) is being passed on.

For many of us in the post-boomer generations, the campaign to close the School of the Americas is a prime opportunity to redeem ourselves and cancel the popular image of us as self-centered materialists. Many young Catholics are risking this stance almost anonymously, in the midst of a post-Vietnam generation that has never had to commit itself en masse to a serious public political decision.

In attempting to inform my conscience better on this issue, I recently visited the school at Fort Benning, Georgia, in the flesh and without fanfare or placard, bullhorn or camera crew. In doing so, I confronted the shadow side of my self-satisfaction with my stance in the SOA debate. The clarity and certainty of my conscience were disrupted by meeting SOA employees, human beings whom I had been prepared to revile, and by walking inside the halls I had wanted to condemn with a prophetic, dramatic gesture, a condescending blessing, a smug Sign of the Cross. Face to face with real people, not devils, I was up against the knowledge that despite my conviction that I was on the "right" side of the issue—or because of it—my conscience could be enticed to cloak righteousness in self-righteousness. As I entered the building my raised pulse rate registered an impending sense that I could not reduce this experience, and maybe the larger debate over the SOA, to a matter of The Brave Priest versus Cowardly Colonels, David versus Goliath, or even Good (Us) versus Evil (Them).

The school, which had the self-important, muted bustle of an academic building, was brightly polished and studded with the symbol system of the U.S. and Latin American militaries. Under the courteous—and not at all sinister—eye of my chaperone, I toured classes in which soldiers from Latin American countries plotted military strategy, learned about human rights, and studied first aid. Everyone was real, not demonic; human, not Government Automaton. I had to admit that SOA staffers were other than what I needed them to be in order to feel confident about my own politics.

The undramatic details worked on me: the gentle drawl of the long-haired SOA librarian who spent several minutes explaining a loan system only a librarian could love; the faces of the Latin American soldiers, in their countries' uniforms, revealing pride, acid roughness, world-weariness, and even thin, deep trenches engraved in the most rugged brown face by years of laughter. I am embarrassed to report that I noticed I did not sense objective evil in anyone. And yet, I thought, the memory of every violently interrupted life at the hands of SOA-trained soldiers demands that I not allow seductive dehumanization entry into my imagination, no matter how prophetic I consider my stance to be.

This dehumanization is too easy to come by. I fear that, like myself, both sides in this debate could be tempted to it. One "Frequently Asked Questions" document published by the school alleges that "many critics [of the SOA] supported Marxism—Liberation Theology—in Latin America—which was defeated with the assistance of the U.S. Army." It is hard to know what is more execrable, the simple equation of Marxism with liberation theology, or the Army's reported defeat of this theology. Thus are the school's critics cast as Marxists, Others, Not Like Us. Although the school's major critics at School of the Americas Watch (SOAW) do not typically stoop so low, I have attended many talks in which the SOA is referred to repeatedly—often in a disarming but condescendingly loving tone—as the "School of the Assassins," and the SOAW Web site features a distorted SOA logo displaying a human skull wearing a beret with a dangling noose. Thus do SOAW staffers risk being cast as Assassins, Others, Not Like Us.

Dehumanization thrives when dialogue withers. For various reasons, attempts at dialogue between the two sides have been abandoned several times. Yet a series of dialogues is exactly what is needed to clear the fog of charges, countercharges, and insinuations that lead to demonization and that now cover this debate like the summer smog over Atlanta, just northeast of Fort Benning.

Facing the shadow side of my convictions gave rise to difficult questions. How much of my desire to shut down SOA is motivated by a thirst for revenge—surely an unacceptable motive—against those who killed or caused the disappearance of thousands of Latin Americans, including some of my own Catholic heroes? Such necessary soul-searching on the part of critics like myself, however, does not absolve the SOA. The school cannot continue to point to the good their graduates do while disclaiming any ability to "track" graduates after they're gone. If they claim the successes of their alumni, they must also take some responsibility for their failures. While I must check my thirst for revenge and my temptation to deny the human dignity of SOA supporters, the SOA must fully and publicly make an act of apology and repentance for sins of commission or, especially, omission in preparing the ground for past graduates to commit atrocities. The failure to make this act only quickens the determination of those of us who work to shut down the school.

Imagine with me the scandalous possibility of the SOA staff and its critics sharing a eucharistic celebration. If denominational limitations keep us from celebrating the Eucharist formally together, both sides are still free to adopt a eucharistic spirit toward this debate, imaging those Not Like Us as fully dignified members of the body of Christ. It is the only appropriately Christian spirit I can conceive in these tense days of threatened funding, mutual suspicion, and the impending protest in November 1999.

As of this writing, SOAW has proposed two debates for November, one at Columbus University in Georgia and one at Fort Benning. I hope the SOA will accept the offer and that the participants will strive to make the debate a eucharistic dialogue. It is up to all of us who sympathize with SOAW to make sure that, at least for "our side," that happens.

I will be at the School of the Americas Watch protest this November at the gates of the SOA. I will be just one member of my generation trying to find the right tenor for my Christian political voice, not so shrill that I become more confident of my salvation than that of those across the fence—but not so humble that I refuse to act with justice, to speak with and for those whose voices have been amputated from history. "I came not to call the righteous, but sinners"—protestors, defenders, and assassins.

ROBERT N. BELLAH

RELIGION AND THE SHAPE
OF NATIONAL CULTURE

(From *America*)

David Hollenbach, in a recent paper entitled "Is Tolerance Enough? The Catholic University and the Common Good," suggests why the idea of the common good is so important for public discussion in the United States today and why Catholics have a special responsibility for putting it forward. He emphasizes the virtue of solidarity as Pope John Paul II defines it, "a firm and persevering determination to commit oneself to the common good, that is to say, to the good of all and of each individual," and argues that such a position is not one to be merely tolerated, which is to say ignored, in the public sphere, but one that is rightfully central to the common civic project. And he argues that "engaged conversation about the good life," while central to the Catholic tradition, can reach out "across the boundaries of diverse communities" and actually lead to the development of larger, more inclusive communities as well.

I want to take up Hollenbach's suggestion and ask why it is so hard for Americans to understand the idea of the common good, much less engage in conversation about it. Then I want to tackle the really hard question: How could we change this situation so that concern for the common good might become more central in our society and beyond? I will speak frankly about the specifically Catholic contribution to a revitalized commitment to the common good and why Protestants often have a hard time even understanding the idea. Since I am not a Catholic, but a Protestant layman, one raised in the Presbyterian Church but presently an Episcopalian, perhaps I can be forgiven if I put the issue sharply and critically: The dominance of Protestantism, for historical reasons, in what I will be calling the American cultural code is responsible for many of our present difficulties. We badly need an infusion of what Andrew Greeley in *The Catholic Myth* (1991) calls the Catholic imagination if we are to overcome those difficulties. (See also his *The Catholic Imagination*, forthcoming.) Greeley speaks of a Catholic imagination in a way that is congruent with what I mean by a cultural code and he argues that it is different from the Protestant imagination. He paints the contrast in stark terms:

> The Catholic tends to see society as a "sacrament" of God, a set of ordered relationships, governed by both justice and love, that reveal, however imperfectly, the presence of God. Society is "natural" and "good," therefore, for humans, and their "natural" response to God is social. The Protestant tends to see society as "God-forsaken" and therefore unnatural and oppressive. The individual stands over against society and not integrated into it. The human becomes fully human only when he is able to break away from social oppression and relate to the absent God as a completely free individual.

This is not entirely fair, as it overlooks the community-forming capacity of Protestantism so evident earlier in our history, but it does help us understand Margaret Thatcher's otherwise nearly unintelligible remark, "There is no such thing as society," a quintessentially Protestant thing to say.

The Protestant Imagination

I want to take the argument of *Habits of the Heart* and *The Good Society* about American individualism and put it in the context of a Protestant-Catholic contrast, left implicit but perhaps evident to the discerning reader of those books. But before pursuing this line of argument further I want to make more explicit the general argument about the contribution of religion to the shape of national cultures. David Vogel in an as yet unpublished article argues that, in the formation of a national culture, a historical Protestant heritage may override the presence of a large number of Catholics in the society. As examples he cites Germany, the Netherlands and the United States. Drawing on Ronald Inglehart's values studies for corroboration, Vogel argues that historically Protestant culture overrides religious pluralism. As Vogel puts it, "for the purpose of my analysis *all* Americans are Protestants regardless of what particular religion they practice, just as are all Germans." Vogel seems to be confirming G. K. Chesterton's famous remark that "in America, even the Catholics are Protestants." Conversely, Vogel quotes Inglehart as saying, "The societies that are historically Catholic still show very distinct values from those that are historically Protestant—even among segments of the population who have no contact with the church today. These values persist as part of the cultural heritage of given nations. . . ." With the help of Andrew Greeley, I will have to qualify the notion that all Americans are Protestants, but it is part of the truth.

To sum up what I think to be the connection between Protestantism and our national cultural code, let me quote the historian Donald Worster: "Protestantism, like any religion, lays its hold on people's imagination in diverse, contradictory ways and that hold can be tenacious long after the explicit theology or doctrine has gone dead. Surely it cannot be surprising that in a culture deeply rooted in Protestantism, we should find ourselves speaking its language, expressing its temperament, even when we thought we were free of all that" (*The Wealth of Nature*, 1993, p. 200). I think what Worster is pointing to here is what Greeley would call the Protestant imagination.

Flaw in the Cultural Code: Radical Individualism

Far be it from me to condemn the Protestant cultural code altogether. It has contributed to many of our greatest achievements. But the idea of a deep cultural code is not without its ominous side. A genetic code can produce a highly successful species, successful because specialized for a particular environment. But then, even at its moment of greatest success, because of a dramatic change in that environment, the code can lead to rapid extinction. In the same way, a cultural code that has long enjoyed remarkable success in many fields can lead a civilization into abrupt decline if it disables society from solving central problems, problems perhaps created by its own success. And yet the cultural code, however deep, is not a genetic code: It can be changed, although sometimes it takes a catastrophe to change it.

What, then, is the flaw in the cultural code that could produce, perhaps is already producing, the gravest consequences?

The flaw in our cultural code was really the primary subject of both *Habits of the Heart* and *The Good Society*, although we did not call it that. In *Habits* we used the metaphor of "language" rather than "cultural code," and we argued that America has a first language, composed of two complementary aspects, utilitarian and expressive individualism, and also second languages, namely biblical and civic republican languages. These second languages have tended to get pushed to the margins. Already in the introduction to the 1996 paperback edition of *Habits*, my coauthors and I suggested that the individualism that forms America's dominant cultural orientation was not solely derived from 18th-century Utilitarianism and 19th-century Romanticism, but had roots in both of our second languages as well. In my November 1997 address to the American Academy of Religion, titled "Is There a Common American Culture?" (published in the academy's journal in summer 1998), I took the argument a step further. There I argued that beyond the homogenizing effect of television, education and consumerism, and deeper even than utilitarian and expressive individualism, there was a still, small voice, a tiny seed, from which our current cultural orientation derives.

Nestled in the very core of utilitarian and expressive individualism is something very deep, very genuine, very old, very American, something we did not quite see or say in *Habits*. Its core is religious. In *Habits* we quoted a famous passage in Alexis de Tocqueville's *Democracy in America:* "I think I can see the whole destiny of America contained in the first Puritan who landed on those shores." Then we went on to name John Winthrop, following de Tocqueville's own predilection, as the likeliest candidate for being that first Puritan. Now I am ready to admit, although regretfully, that we and de Tocqueville were probably wrong. That first Puritan who contained our whole destiny might have been, as we also half intimated in *Habits*, Anne Hutchinson; but the stronger candidate, because we know so much more about him, is Roger Williams.

Roger Williams, banished from the Massachusetts Bay Colony by John Winthrop and founder of Providence and of the Rhode Island Colony, was a Baptist. The Baptists in 17th-century New England were a distinct minority, but they went on to become, together with other dissenting Protestants, a majority in American religious culture from the early 19th century on. As Seymour Martin Lipset has recently pointed out, we are the only North Atlantic society whose predominant religious tradition is sectarian rather than an established church (*American Exceptionalism*, 1996, pp. 19–20). I think this is something enormously important for our culture.

What was so important about the Baptists, and other sectarians such as the Quakers, was the absolute centrality of religious freedom, of the sacredness of individual conscience in matters of religious belief. We generally think of religious freedom as one of many kinds of freedom, many kinds of human rights, first voiced in the European Enlightenment and echoing around the world ever since. But Georg Jellinek, Max Weber's friend and, on these matters, his teacher, published a book in 1895 called *The Declaration of the Rights of Man and of Citizens*, which argued that the ultimate source of all modern notions of human rights is to be found in the radical sects of the Protestant Reformation, particularly the Quakers and Baptists. Of this development Weber writes: "Thus the consistent sect gives rise to an inalienable personal right of the governed as against any power, whether political, hierocratic or patriarchal. Such freedom of conscience may be the oldest Right of Man—as Jellinek has argued convincingly; at any rate it is the most basic Right of Man because it comprises all ethically conditioned action and guarantees freedom from compulsion, especially from the power of the state. In this sense the concept was as unknown to antiquity and the Middle Ages as it was to Rousseau. . . ." Weber then goes on to say that the other rights of man were later joined to this basic right, "especially the right to pursue one's own economic interests, which includes the inviolability of individual property, the freedom of contract, and vocational choice."

My fellow sociologist of religion, Phillip E. Hammond, has written a remarkable book, *With Liberty for All: Freedom of Religion in the United States* (1998), detailing the vicissitudes of this sectarian Protestant concern for the sacredness of the individual conscience as it got embodied in the First Amendment to the Constitution and has been given ever wider meaning by the judicial system, especially the Supreme Court, ever since.

Roger Williams was a moral genius, but he was a sociological catastrophe. After he founded the First Baptist Church, he left it for a smaller and purer one. That, too, he found inadequate, so he founded a church that consisted only of himself, his wife and one other person. One wonders how he stood even those two. Since Williams ignored secular society, money took over in Rhode Island in a way that would not be true in Massachusetts or Connecticut for a long time. Rhode Island under Williams gives us an early and local example of what happens when the sacredness of the individual is not balanced by any sense of the whole or concern for the common good.

Predestination and the Divinization of the Self

Let me make two suggestions about how certain central Protestant beliefs have strengthened our radical individualism. The Reformers, fearing idolatry and magic, attacked the doctrine of transubstantiation and other Catholic practices. Afraid of the idea of the sacred in the world, they, in effect, pushed God out of the world into radical transcendence. With the doctrine of predestination Calvin (or if not Calvin, as some scholars now believe, then some of his followers) described a God who had preordained everything that can occur before the beginning of time. It was natural for some philosophers and scientists to move from that idea to a deterministic physical universe without a personal God at all: "I have no need of that hypothesis," as one of them said. So Calvin's powerful doctrine of divine transcendence paradoxically opened the door to atheistic naturalism. Even more ominously, into the empty space left by the absence of God came an understanding of the self as absolutely autonomous that borrows an essential attribute of God to apply to the self. Since Calvinism as a consistent doctrine hardly survived the 18th century, I am arguing that this aspect of the Protestant cultural code made its ambiguous contribution quite some time ago.

There is a second Protestant religious source of our problem that is, however, very much alive and well today. This is the near exclusive focus on the relation between Jesus and the individual, where accepting Jesus Christ as one's personal lord and savior becomes almost the whole of piety. When this happens, then the doctrine of the God-Man easily slips into the doctrine of the Man-God. The divinization of the self is often called Gnosticism, and Harold Bloom, in *The American Religion* (1993), sees Gnosticism as the quintessentially American religion. He says so not as a critic but as a believer, for he proclaims himself a Gnostic. He sees the evangelical Protestant focus on the personal relation of the believer to Jesus as one of the major sources of American Gnosticism.

If I may trace the downward spiral of this particular Protestant distortion, let me say that it begins with the statement, "If I'm all right with Jesus, then I don't need the church," which we heard from some of the people we interviewed for *Habits of the Heart*. It progresses, then, to the "Sheilaism" that we described in that book. A woman named Sheila Larson defined her faith thus: "It's Sheilaism. Just my own little voice." But Sheilaism seems positively benign compared to the end of the road in this direction that comes out with remarkable force in an interview recounted in Robert Wuthnow's *Loose Connections* (1998). A man in his late 20's who works as a financial analyst describes the individualism that "you're just brought up to believe in" as follows: "The individual is the preeminent being in the universe. There's always a distinction between me and you. Comity, sharing, cannot truly exist. What I have is mine, and it's mine because I deserve it, and I have a right to it." Let us hope he knows not what he says. The general tendency of American evangelicalism toward a private piety pulls everyone influenced by it very much in this direction. Some may think that Jesus-and-me piety is quite different from the individual as the preeminent being in the universe, but I am suggesting that they are only a hair apart.

Loose Connections and Porous Institutions

The flaw in our cultural code becomes most evident when the radical religious individualism I have just described is joined with a notion of economic freedom that holds that the unrestrained free market can solve all problems. Through much of our history a variety of associations, often created by Protestant or Catholic initiative, together with still vibrant extended families, provided a protective barrier against the creative destruction of the market economy. But since the early 70's many of these groups and associations have fallen into sharp decline, the churches themselves holding out the longest, but even they are now beginning to show signs of weakening. One recent study reported by Wuthnow found that 75 percent of the public said that the "breakdown of communities" is a serious national problem. Although 90 percent said it is important to participate in community organizations, only 21 percent said they did so, according to Wuthnow. What has been happening to us can be summed up in the title of Wuthnow's book: *Loose Connections*. People are not plugged in very tightly to groups and associations. They may volunteer a few hours a week for a while, but they will not join an organization that expects their loyalty and commitment for the long haul, or at least they are much more reluctant to do so than they once were. Loose connections is a powerful metaphor and I cannot help drawing a conclusion from it that Wuthnow does not stress: Loose connections can be dangerous, can lead to a fire, can lead to catastrophe.

Wuthnow pairs the metaphor of loose connections with another metaphor that partly explains it: porous institutions. Porous institutions are institutions that do not hold individuals very securely; porous institutions leak. In a world of porous institutions it is hard to have any connections that are not loose. One thinks of the family. Whereas in 1960 one in four marriages would fail, today one in two will. And a lot of things go along with that. The fastest growing category of households is those with one member, which now amount to 25 percent of all households. Families, as we know, do not necessarily consist of two parents and their children. Husbands and wives drift in and out, often bringing children from a former marriage with them, resulting in what is called "blended families." However successfully families are coping with these conditions, there is always the uncertainty: Will this marriage last? Will my parents divorce?

Work, the other great source of personal identity besides family for most Americans, has also become increasingly porous. Arlie Hochschild, in her book *The Time Bind* (1997), reports the statement of a factory worker in a corporation she studied: "In the last 30 years while I've had this job, I have had two marriages, both of which broke up, and several girlfriends in between. This job is my family." Unfortunately, Hochschild reports, this man was about to be downsized. In *Habits of the Heart* we talked about jobs, careers and callings as three increasingly engaged ways of thinking about work. But not only have jobs become transient and insecure; careers are increasingly vulnerable to change. Wuthnow writes: "The median number of different careers listed by people aged 45 or over in the U.S. labor force is now three; the traditional pattern of working in only one career now typifies only 21 percent of all workers aged 45 or over." If job and career are uncertain, then we may wonder how many people actually find a calling.

These symptoms suggest that there may be aspects of our deep cultural code that are a significant part of the problem. Just when we are in many ways moving to an ever greater validation of the sacredness of the individual person, our capacity to imagine a social fabric that would hold individuals together is vanishing. This is in part because of the fact that our ethical individualism, deriving, as I have argued, from the Protestant religious tradition in America, is linked to an economic individualism that, ironically,

knows nothing of the sacredness of the individual. Its only standard is money, and the only thing more sacred than money is
more money. What economic individualism destroys and what
our kind of religious individualism cannot restore is solidarity, a
sense of being members of the same body. In most other North
Atlantic societies, including other Protestant societies, a tradition
of an established church, however secularized, provides some
notion that we are in this thing together, that we need each
other, that our precious and unique selves are not going to make
it all alone.

The Catholic Contribution: Solidarity/Communion

It is in this context that, I believe, we can turn to a Catholic cultural tradition in America that has never been completely Protes-
tantized after all. If our deep cultural code in its Protestant
version combines privatized piety with economic freedom in a
way that leads to loose connections and porous institutions and
has inundated us with the incessant language of freedom and
responsibility but is virtually inarticulate about the common
good, how can an alternative Catholic code help us? The
resources of the Catholic tradition of the virtues and Catholic
social teaching as embodied in papal encyclicals are invaluable.
David Hollenbach and other Catholic ethicists are right to bring
these traditions into public discussion. But the cultural code that
we need to change is deeper than ideology or policy analysis; it is
rooted in what Greeley calls the religious imagination, which
operates on a partly unconscious level. I believe we need at this
moment to reconstitute our cultural code by giving much greater
salience to the sacramental life (Greeley uses the terms "Catholic
imagination" and "sacramental imagination" interchangeably),
and, in particular, to the Eucharist.

The most fundamental practice that tells us who we are as
Christians is worship. The very concreteness of the sacramental

tradition is difficult for free-floating middle-class Americans, even Catholics, to understand. If I find that I live in porous institutions with loose connections, how can I understand that this bread and this wine is the actual body and blood of Christ and that by participating in the Eucharist I become immediately and physically one with the body of Christ, and so one with the whole of God's creation? Yet for Protestants, as for Catholics, not only the word but the sacraments are necessary for our salvation. The sacraments pull us into an embodied world of relationships and connections, a world in which, to quote Greeley, "humans [are] integrated into networks, networks that reveal God," rather than a world in which individuals attempt to escape from society.

Some concrete examples and the voices of Catholic believers will illustrate my point better than abstract analysis. I would like to turn first to a parish where the sacramental imagination has been enacted. David Roozen and his associates in their book *Varieties of Religious Presence* describe a Catholic parish, St. Margaret's, largely made up of Puerto Ricans, in the poorest neighborhood of Hartford, Conn., which was deeply involved in a justice ministry. Here a sacramental theology has formed the life and worship of the whole parish. As one of the members put it:

> The Mass is the reenactment of the moment of Redemption. In every Mass, the Cross of Calvary is transplanted into every corner of the world, and humanity is taking sides, either sharing in that Redemption or rejecting it, by the way we live. We are not meant to sit and watch the cross as something done and ended. What was done on Calvary avails for us only in the degree that we repeat it in our lives. All that has been said and done and acted during Holy Mass is to be taken away with us, lived, practiced, and woven into all the circumstances and conditions of our daily lives. (p. 161)

"Life at St. Margaret's," in the words of a deacon, "begins and ends with the Mass." Priests and parishioners share a common eucharistic theology. "Mass is the center of everything," the senior priest states emphatically.

> The Eucharist is the living presence of Christ. In sharing that presence, the call is to go out to make that presence operational, living in the world. That going out wears us out, so the Eucharist is both the beginning and the end. It draws us to it, pushes us out into the world, and then draws us back. It is an overflow of the Lord's presence. The Mass is part of the world and the world is part of the Lord. (p. 162)

Roozen sums up his account of this parish as follows:

> The expressed goal of the leadership—clerical and lay—is to work within the world to make it Christian, a world in which love toward God and neighbor is the maxim. Energy for this task, in the St. Margaret's view, comes from the Mass. The model is Christ on the cross, and there is a firm belief that human nature can be shaped into the formations of love. (p. 176)

The Roozen book is some 20 years old now, but just last year I learned of things going on near my home that confirm the current vitality of that sacramental understanding of life. I was fortunate to sit on the Graduate Theological Union doctoral dissertation committee of a Jesuit from India named Matthew Jayanth, whose thesis was entitled "Eucharist and Social Ethics." While conducting interviews in several East Bay communities, he found lay persons whose understanding was quite similar to that of the parishioners at St. Margaret's. A number of them, not necessarily aware of one another, had adopted a simple mode of life in which they worked only to maintain their necessities and spent most of their time in the voluntary service of the destitute. They are a kind of contemporary third order Franciscans without the formality of it. Several of them used a phrase with which I was not previously familiar: They spoke of "being eucharist for others." One of them said, "That's what life is for me, being eucharist for others. It is not about martyrdom, it's about life; it's about giving life to others." Another put it this way:

> The commission to "go in the peace of Christ to love and serve one another" means that this is what the Mass has nourished us to do. And yet, when he says the Mass is ended, that is only true in one sense. . . . It is not ended, it is continuing. It is an invitation to go out and put it into practice now. To do what you said you were going to do. What you tried to focus yourself on so that you can function as a whole person, united with Christ and then as the whole body of Christ. So now you have to go out and incarnate that, that is what life is about.

And a final voice:

> To become eucharist. I mean to become willing to give ourselves, to be willing to risk all that we have, willing to bring new life to others, willing to break open our bodies. . . . The full sense of the Eucharist would be to understand the totality of our lives as eucharist. . . . The major connection between Eucharist and the life of commitment to justice is that in the eucharistic celebration we are nourished and empowered and we are sent forth to become eucharist for others.

What these people are talking about is that tangible, physical act of participating in the body and blood of the crucified and risen Christ. It is in that moment that we become members one of another, that we not only partake of the Eucharist but can actually become eucharist, ourselves completing "what is lacking in Christ's afflictions," as Paul says in Colossians, by self-giving love for the whole world.

Because the Catholic and the Protestant imaginations are rooted in a common tradition, they are both available to all American Christians. But our most urgent need at the moment is to open up our deep cultural code so that the sacramental imagination will have a more pervasive influence over our lives. That would probably require a severe reality-challenge to our present apparently successful way of life, something like a major depression, and, in response, a combination of the Catholic imagination with a kind of evangelical revivalism, Catholic content in a Protestant form if you will. It is that improbable but not impossible scenario that I have attempted to describe.

HARVEY COX

THE MARKET AS GOD

(From *The Atlantic Monthly*)

A few years ago a friend advised me that if I wanted to know what was going on in the real world, I should read the business pages. Although my lifelong interest has been in the study of religion, I am always willing to expand my horizons; so I took the advice, vaguely fearful that I would have to cope with a new and baffling vocabulary. Instead I was surprised to discover that most of the concepts I ran across were quite familiar.

Expecting a terra incognita, I found myself instead in the land of déjà vu. The lexicon of *The Wall Street Journal* and the business sections of *Time* and *Newsweek* turned out to bear a striking resemblance to Genesis, the Epistle to the Romans, and Saint Augustine's *City of God*. Behind descriptions of market reforms, monetary policy, and the convolutions of the Dow, I gradually made out the pieces of a grand narrative about the inner meaning of human history, why things had gone wrong, and how to put them right. Theologians call these myths of origin, legends of the fall, and doctrines of sin and redemption. But here they were again, and in only thin disguise: chronicles about the creation of wealth, the seductive temptations of statism, captivity to faceless economic cycles, and, ultimately, salvation through the advent of free markets, with a small dose of ascetic belt tightening along the way, especially for the East Asian economies.

The East Asians' troubles, votaries argue, derive from their heretical deviation from free-market orthodoxy—they were practitioners of "crony capitalism," of "ethnocapitalism," of "statist capitalism," not of the one true faith. The East Asian financial panics, the Russian debt repudiations, the Brazilian economic turmoil, and the U.S. stock market's $1.5 trillion "correction" momentarily shook belief in the new dispensation. But faith is strengthened by adversity, and the Market God is emerging renewed from its trial by financial "contagion." Since the argument from design no longer proves its existence, it is fast becoming a postmodern deity—believed in despite the evidence. Alan Greenspan vindicated this tempered faith in testimony before Congress last October. A leading hedge fund had just lost billions of dollars, shaking market confidence and precipitating calls for new federal regulation. Greenspan, usually Delphic in his comments, was decisive. He believed that regulation would only impede these markets, and that they should continue to be self-regulated. True faith, Saint Paul tells us, is the evidence of things unseen.

Soon I began to marvel at just how comprehensive the business theology is. There were even sacraments to convey salvific power to the lost, a calendar of entrepreneurial saints, and what theologians call an "eschatology"—a teaching about the "end of history." My curiosity was piqued. I began cataloguing these strangely familiar doctrines, and I saw that in fact there lies embedded in the business pages an entire theology, which is comparable in scope if not in profundity to that of Thomas Aquinas or Karl Barth. It needed only to be systematized for a whole new *Summa* to take shape.

At the apex of any theological system, of course, is its doctrine of God. In the new theology this celestial pinnacle is occupied by The Market, which I capitalize to signify both the mystery that enshrouds it and the reverence it inspires in business folk. Different faiths have, of course, different views of the divine attributes. In Christianity, God has sometimes been defined as omnipotent (possessing all power), omniscient (having all knowledge), and omnipresent (existing everywhere). Most Christian theologies, it is true, hedge a bit. They teach that these qualities of the divinity are indeed *there*, but are hidden from human eyes both by human sin and by the transcendence of the divine itself. In "light inaccessible" they are, as the old hymn puts it, "hid from our eyes." Likewise, although The Market, we are assured, possesses these divine attributes, they are not always completely evident to mortals but must be trusted and affirmed by faith. "Further along," as another old gospel song says, "we'll understand why."

As I tried to follow the arguments and explanations of the economist-theologians who justify The Market's ways to men, I spotted the same dialectics I have grown fond of in the many years I have pondered the Thomists, the Calvinists, and the various schools of modern religious thought. In particular, the econologians' rhetoric resembles what is sometimes called "process theology," a relatively contemporary trend influenced by the philosophy of Alfred North Whitehead. In this school although God *wills* to possess the classic attributes, He does not yet possess them in full, but is definitely moving in that direction. This conjecture is of immense help to theologians for obvious reasons. It answers the bothersome puzzle of theodicy: why a lot of bad things happen that an omnipotent, omnipresent, and omniscient God—especially a benevolent one—would not countenance. Process theology also seems to offer considerable comfort to the theologians of The Market. It helps to explain the dislocation, pain, and disorientation that are the result of transitions from economic heterodoxy to free markets.

• • •

Since the earliest stages of human history, of course, there have
been bazaars, rialtos, and trading posts—all markets. But The
Market was never God, because there were other centers of
value and meaning, other "gods." The Market operated within a
plethora of other institutions that restrained it. As Karl Polanyi
has demonstrated in his classic work *The Great Transformation*,
only in the past two centuries has The Market risen above
these demigods and chthonic spirits to become today's First
Cause.

Initially The Market's rise to Olympic supremacy replicated the
gradual ascent of Zeus above all the other divinities of the ancient
Greek pantheon, an ascent that was never quite secure. Zeus, it
will be recalled, had to keep storming down from Olympus to
quell this or that threat to his sovereignty. Recently, however, The
Market is becoming more like the Yahweh of the Old Testament—not just one superior deity contending with others but the
Supreme Deity, the only true God, whose reign must now be universally accepted and who allows for no rivals.

Divine *omnipotence* means the capacity to define what is real. It
is the power to make something out of nothing and nothing out
of something. The willed-but-not-yet-achieved omnipotence of
The Market means that there is no conceivable limit to its inex-
orable ability to convert creation into commodities. But again,
this is hardly a new idea, though it has a new twist. In Catholic
theology, through what is called "transubstantiation," ordinary
bread and wine become vehicles of the holy. In the mass of The
Market a reverse process occurs. Things that have been held
sacred transmute into interchangeable items for sale. Land is a
good example. For millennia it has held various meanings, many
of them numinous. It has been Mother Earth, ancestral resting
place, holy mountain, enchanted forest, tribal homeland, aesthetic inspiration, sacred turf, and much more. But when The
Market's Sanctus bell rings and the elements are elevated, all

these complex meanings of land melt into one: real estate. At the right price no land is not for sale, and this includes everything from burial grounds to the cove of the local fertility sprite. This radical desacralization dramatically alters the human relationship to land; the same happens with water, air, space, and soon (it is predicted) the heavenly bodies.

At the high moment of the mass the priest says, "This is my body," meaning the body of Christ and, by extension, the bodies of all the faithful people. Christianity and Judaism both teach that the human body is made "in the image of God." Now, however, in a dazzling display of reverse transubstantiation, the human body has become the latest sacred vessel to be converted into a commodity. The process began, fittingly enough, with blood. But now, or soon, all bodily organs—kidneys, skin, bone marrow, sperm, the heart itself—will be miraculously changed into purchasable items.

Still, the liturgy of The Market is not proceeding without some opposition from the pews. A considerable battle is shaping up in the United States, for example, over the attempt to merchandise human genes. A few years ago, banding together for the first time in memory, virtually all the religious institutions in the country, from the liberal National Council of Churches to the Catholic bishops to the Christian Coalition, opposed the gene mart, the newest theophany of The Market. But these critics are followers of what are now "old religions," which, like the goddess cults that were thriving when the worship of the vigorous young Apollo began sweeping ancient Greece, may not have the strength to slow the spread of the new devotion.

Occasionally backsliders try to bite the Invisible Hand that feeds them. On October 26, 1996, the German government ran an ad offering the entire village of Liebenberg, in what used to be East Germany, for sale—with no previous notice to its some 350

residents. Liebenberg's citizens, many of them elderly or unemployed, stared at the notice in disbelief. They had certainly
loathed communism, but when they opted for the market economy that reunification promised, they hardly expected this.
Liebenberg includes a thirteenth-century church, a Baroque
castle, a lake, a hunting lodge, two restaurants, and 3,000 acres
of meadow and forest. Once a favorite site for boar hunting by
the old German nobility, it was obviously entirely too valuable
a parcel of real estate to overlook. Besides, having been expro-
priated by the East German Communist government, it was
now legally eligible for sale under the terms of German reunification. Overnight Liebenberg became a living parable, providing an invaluable glimpse of the Kingdom in which The
Market's will is indeed done. But the outraged burghers of the
town did not feel particularly blessed. They complained loudly,
and the sale was finally postponed. Everyone in town realized,
however, that it was not really a victory. The Market, like Yahweh,
may lose a skirmish, but in a war of attrition it will always win
in the end.

Of course, religion in the past has not been reluctant to
charge for its services. Prayers, masses, blessings, healings, bap-
tisms, funerals, and amulets have been hawked, and still are. Nor
has religion always been sensitive to what the traffic would bear.
When, in the early sixteenth century, Johann Tetzel jacked up
the price of indulgences and even had one of the first singing
commercials composed to push sales ("When the coin into the
platter pings, the soul out of purgatory springs"), he failed to realize that he was overreaching. The customers balked, and a young
Augustinian monk brought the traffic to a standstill with a placard tacked to a church door.

It would be a lot harder for a Luther to interrupt sales of The
Market's amulets today. As the people of Liebenberg discovered,

everything can now be bought. Lakes, meadows, church build-ings—everything carries a sticker price. But this practice itself exacts a cost. As everything in what used to be called creation becomes a commodity, human beings begin to look at one another, and at themselves, in a funny way, and they see colored price tags. There was a time when people spoke, at least occasionally, of "inherent worth"—if not of things, then at least of persons. The Liebenberg principle changes all that. One wonders what would become of a modern Luther who tried to post his theses on the church door, only to find that the whole edifice had been bought by an American billionaire who reckoned it might look nicer on his estate.

It is comforting to note that the *citizens* of Liebenberg, at least, were not put on the block. But that raises a good question. What *is* the value of a human life in the theology of The Market? Here the new deity pauses, but not for long. The computation may be complex, but it is not impossible. We should not believe, for example, that if a child is born severely handicapped, unable to be "productive," The Market will decree its death. One must remember that the profits derived from medications, leg braces, and CAT-scan equipment should also be figured into the equation. Such a cost analysis might result in a close call—but the inherent worth of the child's life, since it cannot be quantified, would be hard to include in the calculation.

It is sometimes said that since everything is for sale under the rule of The Market, nothing is sacred. But this is not quite true. About three years ago a nasty controversy erupted in Great Britain when a railway pension fund that owned the small jeweled casket in which the remains of Saint Thomas à Becket are said to have rested decided to auction it off through Sotheby's. The casket dates from the twelfth century and is revered as both a sacred relic and a national treasure. The British Museum made an effort to buy it but lacked the funds, so the casket was sold to a Canadian. Only last-minute measures by the British government prevented removal of the casket from the United Kingdom. In principle, however, in the theology of The Market, there is no reason why any relic, coffin, body, or national monument—including the Statue of Liberty and Westminster Abbey—should not be listed. Does anyone doubt that if the True Cross were ever really discovered, it would eventually find its way to Sotheby's? The Market is not omnipotent—yet. But the process is under way and it is gaining momentum.

Omniscience is a little harder to gauge than omnipotence. Maybe The Market has already achieved it but is unable—temporarily—to apply its gnosis until its Kingdom and Power come in their fullness. Nonetheless, current thinking already assigns to The Market a comprehensive wisdom that in the past only the gods have known. The Market, we are taught, is able to determine what human needs are, what copper and capital should cost, how much barbers and CEOs should be paid, and how much jet planes, running shoes, and hysterectomies should sell for. But how do we know The Market's will?

In days of old, seers entered a trance state and then informed anxious seekers what kind of mood the gods were in, and whether this was an auspicious time to begin a journey, get married, or start a war. The prophets of Israel repaired to the desert and then returned to announce whether Yahweh was feeling benevolent or wrathful. Today The Market's fickle will is clarified by daily reports from Wall Street and other sensory organs of finance. Thus we can learn on a day-to-day basis that The Market is "apprehensive," "relieved," "nervous," or even at times "jubilant." On the basis of this revelation awed adepts make critical decisions about whether to buy or sell. Like one of the devouring gods of old, The Market—aptly embodied in a bull or a bear—

must be fed and kept happy under all circumstances. True, at times its appetite may seem excessive—a $35 billion bailout here, a $50 billion one there—but the alternative to assuaging its hunger is too terrible to contemplate.

The diviners and seers of The Market's moods are the high priests of its mysteries. To act against their admonitions is to risk excommunication and possibly damnation. Today, for example, if any government's policy vexes The Market, those responsible for the irreverence will be made to suffer. That The Market is not at all displeased by downsizing or a growing income gap, or can be gleeful about the expansion of cigarette sales to Asian young people, should not cause anyone to question its ultimate omniscience. Like Calvin's inscrutable deity, The Market may work in mysterious ways, "hid from our eyes," but ultimately it knows best.

Omniscience can sometimes seem a bit intrusive. The traditional God of the Episcopal *Book of Common Prayer* is invoked as one "unto whom all hearts are open, all desires known, and from whom no secrets are hid." Like Him, The Market already knows the deepest secrets and darkest desires of our hearts—or at least would like to know them. But one suspects that divine motivation differs in these two cases. Clearly The Market wants this kind of x-ray omniscience because by probing our inmost fears and desires and then dispensing across-the-board solutions, it can further extend its reach. Like the gods of the past, whose priests offered up the fervent prayers and petitions of the people, The Market relies on its own intermediaries: motivational researchers. Trained in the advanced art of psychology, which has long since replaced theology as the true "science of the soul," the modern heirs of the medieval confessors delve into the hidden fantasies, insecurities, and hopes of the populace.

One sometimes wonders, in this era of Market religion, where the skeptics and freethinkers have gone. What has happened to the Voltaires who once exposed bogus miracles, and the H. L. Menckens who blew shrill whistles on pious humbuggery? Such is the grip of current orthodoxy that to question the omniscience of The Market is to question the inscrutable wisdom of Providence. The metaphysical principle is obvious: If you *say* it's the real thing, then it must *be* the real thing. As the early Christian theologian Tertullian once remarked, "*Credo quia absurdum est*" ("I believe because it is absurd").

Finally, there is the divinity's will to be *omnipresent*. Virtually every religion teaches this idea in one way or another, and the new religion is no exception. The latest trend in economic theory is the attempt to apply market calculations to areas that once appeared to be exempt, such as dating, family life, marital relations, and child-rearing. Henri Lepage, an enthusiastic advocate of globalization, now speaks about a "total market." Saint Paul reminded the Athenians that their own poets sang of a God "in whom we live and move and have our being"; so now The Market is not only around us but inside us, informing our senses and our feelings. There seems to be nowhere left to flee from its untiring quest. Like the Hound of Heaven, it pursues us home from the mall and into the nursery and the bedroom.

It used to be thought—mistakenly, as it turns out—that at least the innermost, or "spiritual," dimension of life was resistant to The Market. It seemed unlikely that the interior castle would ever be listed by Century 21. But as the markets for material goods become increasingly glutted, such previously unmarketable states of grace as serenity and tranquillity are now appearing in the catalogues. Your personal vision quest can take place in unspoiled wildernesses that are pictured as virtually unreachable—except, presumably, by the other people who read the same catalogue. Furthermore, ecstasy and spirituality are now offered in a convenient generic form. Thus The Market makes available the religious benefits that once required prayer and fasting, without the awkwardness of denominational commitment or the tedious ascetic discipline that once limited their accessibility. All can now handily be bought without an unrealistic demand on one's time, in a weekend workshop at a Caribbean resort with a sensitive psychological consultant replacing the crotchety retreat master.

Discovering the theology of The Market made me begin to think in a different way about the conflict among religions. Violence between Catholics and Protestants in Ulster or Hindus and Muslims in India often dominates the headlines. But I have come to wonder whether the real clash of religions (or even of civilizations) may be going unnoticed. I am beginning to think that for all the religions of the world, however they may differ from one another, the religion of The Market has become the most formidable rival, the more so because it is rarely recognized as a religion. The traditional religions and the religion of the global market, as we have seen, hold radically different views of nature. In Christianity and Judaism, for example, "the earth is the Lord's and the fullness thereof, the world and all that dwell therein." The Creator appoints human beings as stewards and gardeners but, as it were, retains title to the earth. Other faiths have similar ideas. In the Market religion, however, human beings, more particularly those with money, own anything they buy and—within certain limits—can dispose of anything as they choose. Other contradictions can be seen in ideas about the human body, the nature of human community, and the purpose of life. The older religions encourage archaic attachments to particular places. But in The Market's eyes all places are interchangeable. The Market prefers a homogenized world culture with as few inconvenient particularities as possible.

Disagreements among the traditional religions become pica-
yune in comparison with the fundamental differences they all
have with the religion of The Market. Will this lead to a new
jihad or crusade? I doubt it. It seems unlikely that traditional religions will rise to the occasion and challenge the doctrines of the
new dispensation. Most of them seem content to become its
acolytes or to be absorbed into its pantheon, much as the old
Nordic deities, after putting up a game fight, eventually settled
for a diminished but secure status as Christian saints. I am usually
a keen supporter of ecumenism. But the contradictions between
the world views of the traditional religions on the one hand and
the world view of the Market religion on the other are so basic
that no compromise seems possible, and I am secretly hoping for
a rebirth of polemics.

No religion, new or old, is subject to empirical proof, so
what we have is a contest between faiths. Much is at stake. The
Market, for example, strongly prefers individualism and mobil-
ity. Since it needs to shift people to wherever production
requires them, it becomes wrathful when people cling to local
traditions. These belong to the older dispensations and—like
the high places of the Baalim—should be plowed under. But
maybe not. Like previous religions, the new one has ingenious
ways of incorporating pre-existing ones. Hindu temples, Buddhist festivals, and Catholic saints' shrines can look forward to
new incarnations. Along with native costumes and spicy food,
they will be allowed to provide local color and authenticity in
what could otherwise turn out to be an extremely bland Beulah
Land.

There is, however, one contradiction between the religion of
The Market and the traditional religions that seems to be insur-
mountable. All of the traditional religions teach that human
beings are finite creatures and that there are limits to any earthly
enterprise. A Japanese Zen master once said to his disciples as he

was dying, "I have learned only one thing in life: how much is enough." He would find no niche in the chapel of The Market, for whom the First Commandment is "There is *never* enough." Like the proverbial shark that stops moving, The Market that stops expanding dies. That could happen. If it does, then Nietzsche will have been right after all. He will just have had the wrong God in mind.

JEAN BETHKE ELSHTAIN

ABRAHAM LINCOLN AND THE LAST BEST HOPE

(From *First Things*)

The beginning of the nineteenth century of the millennium now almost past was promising enough. The Congress of Vienna in 1815 marked, at long last, the end of the Napoleonic wars and heralded a period of enduring peace—peace under the auspices of emperors and monarchs of dubious legitimacy and stability, to be sure, but peace nonetheless. The settlement was far from complete. The Balkans remained a tinderbox and, indeed, the entire Austro-Hungarian Empire seemed an improbable thing to hold together indefinitely, composed as it was of a tension-ridden mix of languages, peoples, religions, and ethnic allegiances. Yet the Hapsburg crown, although loosely fixed on typically ineffectual royal heads, appeared more or less secure. In Russia, the Romanov autocracy was holding its own, despite rumblings of discontent connected, not least of all, with the continuing system of serfdom. France was—after Revolution, Terror, and Napoleon—a volatile mix of the autocratic and republican, but posed no immediate threat to others. The German-speaking peoples were scattered among multiple principalities, and spilled over into Russia, Central Europe, and—a point of major contention for France—Alsace-Lorraine. Only England appeared to have put together a workable combination of monarchy and constitutionalism.

The calendar notwithstanding, the real nineteenth century began in 1815, and the story of that century has often been depicted as one of Europe's outward expansion through territorial grabs ranging from Africa and Southeast Asia to the Indian subcontinent. Another story is that of "people's nationalism" within Europe, which erupted in the "springtime of the peoples" in 1848. Patriots such as Giuseppe Mazzini in Italy erected people's republics all over Europe, most of which were soon crushed by the old order. These reversals left in their aftermath nationalist frustrations that exploded sporadically—and most fatefully with the assassin's bullets that struck down Archduke Francis Ferdinand on June 28, 1914, precipitating the end of the century that began in 1815, and with it the end of the promise that was Europe.

But of course there was another nineteenth century, and there, too, promise and tragedy contended. A still young American republic strained outward in what seemed a limitless possibility of expansion driven by almost every human passion imaginable— ambition, greed, patriotism, desperation, curiosity, and a simple desire to better one's lot. Whatever the western pioneers were looking for, they usually found hard work and, for those with a little luck and the toughness to stick with it, a modest reward. It was a hard-scrabble frontier existence into which, on February 12, 1809, was born a figure about whom so much has been written that I'm not sure I, or anyone else for that matter, can say much that is new. But one need never apologize for thinking again about Abraham Lincoln.

Thomas Lincoln had managed to scrape together enough money to buy a small tract in Kentucky, and, as his son would later write, they moved when he was still a little boy to a larger tract "in the valley of Knob Creek, surrounded by high hills and deep gorges." It was rocky, unfruitful soil where the furious washing of a "big rain in the hills" would sweep new planting "clear off the field." The American frontier was called a new world, but it was a peasant subsistence very much like what had been known for centuries in the old. It seems that the mother, Nancy Hanks Lincoln, was able to read but could not write. Life was nonstop work from dawn to dusk, and "book learning" was held in slight regard.

Separating as best we can fact from legend, we know that the Lincolns set out for Indiana in 1816, crossing the Ohio River in search of better land titles and—at least according to recent biographer David Herbert Donald—in order to get away from slavery. Thomas Lincoln, who favored the Separate Baptist Church, apparently opposed slavery on both religious and economic grounds. Slave labor, he believed, was unfair competition to "free labor," and that argument was carried forward by Abraham, who was a free labor advocate throughout his years as a Whig and, later, as a Republican. From his mother's early death, it is said, began the spells of melancholia that would never leave him. In 1817 she succumbed to what was called "milk sickness," and a year later was succeeded by a stepmother, Sarah, who trailed in her wake three children and elegant domestic furnishings, such as were previously unknown to the Lincoln household. Sarah's liveliness did not end young Abraham's descents into melancholy, but we are told that the ungainly youth became sprightlier. Although Sarah was illiterate, Lincoln was now introduced to schooling for the first time, which quickly sparked his famous passion for book learning.

Lincoln's education, which may strike us as haphazard, was largely a matter of being drilled in the basics of grammar, spelling, composition, and ciphering, as it was called. Donald notes that Lincoln's contemporaries "attributed prodigies of reading to him, but books were scarce on the frontier and he had to read carefully rather than extensively. He memorized a great deal of what he read." Today, of course, memorization is routinely dismissed as "rote learning," and priority is given to "self-expression" in the service of "authenticity" and other presumed goods. Reflecting on the experience of Lincoln (and innumerable others subjected to "rote learning") may lead one to suspect that there is much to be said for having one's mind formed by the best that others have thought and said before giving it unbridled expression. All those hours spent reading by dim firelight the same book over and over (the way little children still like to be read to) were to contribute to Lincoln's being the foremost master of prose among our presidents. Indeed, he has few peers in our entire history.

For young Lincoln, as for so many others of the time, an inescapable book was John Bunyan's *Pilgrim's Progress*, first published in 1678. It is difficult for us today to appreciate the pervasive power and influence of Bunyan's tale, told "in the similitude of a Dream." In that sustained religious allegory of moral heroism and imagery both vivid and frightening, the reader lives through Christian's travails and all-too-human backsliding, until finally tasting his victory as one's own. Bunyan's biting commentary on human folly, joined to an inspiring account of human possibility, must have played an important part in shaping Lincoln's complexity of mind through a life of action and of reflection, often mordant reflection, on that action.

With the teenage years, Lincoln set out to escape the hard life he had known and became something of a drifter—trying on, as it were, different tasks, vocations, and identities. Settling in New Salem, Illinois, he took up the practice of law and began "politicking." The Lincoln legend has this "fresh breeze from off the prairie" (as Jane Addams called him) going from splitting rails to the White House, but neglects the many years in between when he was refining his craft as a speaker, writer, and politician. Despite distractions, setbacks, and uncertainties, his course was steadily upward: the move to Springfield, marriage with Mary Todd, election to the state legislature. As a politician he was mainly preoccupied with routine questions of domestic improvements, currency, and contract law. He was, in short, the familiar Whig politician, although a Whig with a growing reputation for straightforwardness, rough-hewn honesty, mental agility (with a streak of ironic humor), and a capacity for getting things done.

On the great question, Lincoln had never been pro-slavery, but his early pronouncements addressed it almost entirely in terms of free labor. Importing slaves into the new territories, he contended, would create unfair competition for nonslave labor. Under the force of circumstances and his own reflection, however, his public statements slowly began to change. The great question heated up with the passage of the Kansas-Nebraska Act of 1854, which opened the western territories to slavery. The question was being recast in terms of a constitutional and moral crisis, with Northern calls for emancipation becoming ever more adamant. In response, Lincoln delivered a speech in Peoria, Illinois, on October 16, 1854, that may fairly be said to have put him on the course to his place in history.

He acknowledged the extraordinary difficulties in extirpating an established social institution, even when that institution is as pernicious as slavery. He allowed that his Southern contemporaries had not created the institution, and that "it is very difficult to get rid of it, in any satisfactory way." His own preference was to "free all the slaves, and send them to Liberia," but he knew the "sudden execution" of such a plan to be "impossible." Even if it were possible to send all the slaves there, most of them would likely perish without a means of support. Also unacceptable, he said, was the alternative of freeing the slaves and then keeping them here as "underlings." Because of a "universal feeling, whether well- or ill-founded" (a feeling that Lincoln confessed he shared), the option of making freed slaves "politically and socially our equals" was also excluded. His position was that slaves did have constitutional rights that must be respected, "not grudgingly, but fully and fairly." This left him with the proposal that the best to be done at present was to prevent the extension of slavery and to look forward to the possibility of "gradual emancipation." Even in the Peoria speech that gained him national attention, however, he left no doubt that his opposition to Kansas-Nebraska was based on the conviction that the "new free states are places for poor people to go to and better their condition." He frankly admitted that his chief concern was the welfare of poor whites.

Readers today may think the speech tepid, even repugnantly cautious. This is no clarion call for abolition. It is a thoughtful reflection on the relationship between moral duty and political possibility in the recognition that the two are not always nicely matched. Yet in the same speech he declared that there is no "moral right in the enslaving of one man by another." Slavery is a form of theft that violates the basic principle that none should live by the fruits of another's forced labor. In a manner both earthy and clear, Lincoln preached a "labor theory of value" not entirely unlike the theory advanced with such obtuse complexity by Karl Marx. He drew on a naturalistic morality, not entirely unlike natural law, rather than invoking doctrines of revealed religion. Slavery, he believed, is a consequence of our most base natural drives and is incompatible with a "love of justice" that is also natural. First principles are involved, and those principles can be known through reason. In 1858 he wrote a three-sentence summary of his thought "On Slavery and Democracy": "As I would not be a *slave*, so I would not be a *master*. This expresses my idea of democracy. Whatever differs from this, to the extent of the difference, is no democracy."

To the extent that it countenanced the institution of slavery, it would seem to follow, his country was not a democracy. Lincoln did not reach that conclusion lightly, such was his piety toward the American Founders. But he came to the view that their preeminent task had been to forge the federal union. They had no choice but to leave the slavery question to a future generation—to his generation. In this way of thinking, the Framers had not resolved but had only postponed the question of slavery, and Lincoln's sense that the time had come to move, however cautiously, toward a resolution had about it a force of obligation that he did not hesitate to call sacred.

In his 1858 debates with Stephen Douglas, the argument was extended: Slavery is not only wrong, it also "threatens the Union." While Lincoln continued to play to the race fears that were part of the free labor platform, he was also clear on what should have to give when popular sovereignty clashes with moral right. His devotion to democracy did not include the idolatrous doctrine that the voice of the people is the voice of God. What is true for the voice of the people applied also to the voice of courts. By ruling that slaves had no rights that white men were required to respect, the infamous Dred Scott decision of 1857, said Lincoln, was responsible for "blowing out the moral lights." The "real issue in this controversy," he contended against Douglas, is slavery and whether it should be treated as a "moral, social, and political wrong" or whether it should be made "perpetual and national."

While Lincoln lost the senatorial election of 1858, his campaign laid the foundation for his nomination and election as president in 1860. It was now clear to him that his task was the "repurifying" of the republic, to cleanse it "in the spirit, if not the blood, of the Revolution." "Let us," he declared, "readopt the Declaration of Independence, and with it, the practices and policy which harmonize with it." He had accused Douglas of distorting the views of the Founders; there is not, he insisted, a shred of evidence that "the Negro was not included in the Declaration of Independence." That being said, the new president was not at all clear about what was to be done—meaning what was to be done without spilling rivers of blood and abandoning the American experiment in self-government.

The debate over the Civil War and Lincoln's part in precipitating, pursuing, and concluding it will continue as long as the American republic. That conflict is our defining tragedy. Yet Lincoln's words and conduct as war leader and definer of the conflict runs against the usual definition of the American character. He never minimized the costs or exaggerated what the war would achieve; his language was at once prophetic and tragic. If the defining American myth is that of Progress, the belief that each new time will be an improvement over what went before, Lincoln did not subscribe to it. He resisted also the temptation to depict opponents as wholly evil while casting oneself and one's allies as the "children of light." Much of American politics has been in the mode of moral crusade. Earlier in this century we fought a war to end all wars and make the world safe for democracy. The prohibition of liquor promised a nation restored to righteousness. Women's suffrage was not a matter of simple justice but what Elizabeth Cady Stanton called a "new evangel of womanhood." Examples of the crusading credo in action can readily be multiplied.

In *the* great conflict of American history, Lincoln seems almost un-American in his refusal to embrace that credo. A terrible duty had to be done and a terrible price had to be paid, and, in doing that duty and paying that price, good and evil were to be found on both sides of the conflict. In his resistance to the pattern of American "triumphalism," it is not too much to say that Lincoln reflected an Augustinian perspective on the ambiguities of history. Politics is a severely limited instrument, and the task of bringing about a social order approximately more just is always an unfinished task. All this is evident, above all, in Lincoln's own words—words that American school children, at least outside the deep South, were once required to memorize. Lincoln's words bear the weight of his awareness that he was, in ways not of his own desire or design, authoring and thereby authorizing the future of a republic "purified" by the blood of both North and South. Purified of the great wrong of slavery but not yet, perhaps not ever, pure.

The sense of dedication to an unfinished task comes through most powerfully in the Gettysburg Address. As all know, the featured speaker of the day was Edward Everett, the most famous orator of the time, a spellbinder who took two hours to say the many things appropriate to say upon the dedication of a military cemetery. Not until many years later did the public pay much attention to the few words of the president that followed. "Four score and seven years ago," and then it was "shall not perish from the earth," and the president had sat down before many in the crowd realized he was speaking. Those few words, barely mentioned at the time in the inside pages of the newspapers, have likely occasioned more reflection than any other text among people who would understand the genius of the American experiment. He spoke of consecration and hallowing, of a new birth of freedom and of a nation under God, but all without explicit reference to Divine agency or scriptural text. There is no doubt about the piety, but it is not piety on parade.

Setting aside the much discussed question of Lincoln's religion, there can be no doubt about his deep immersion in the cadences and parables of the Bible. His impatience with those who presumed to know the purposes of God has frequently been remarked. The proper human stance before the ways of the Lord, he believed, is that of deep humility. Thus he writes to Albert G. Hodges on April 4, 1864, a year before his own death, "I claim not to have controlled events, but confess plainly that events have controlled me." American political historian John Diggins says that Lincoln helped heal the "Machiavellian wound" that resulted from the separation of politics and morality. Lincoln, he believes, renewed the theory of statecraft by insisting that "ulti-mate moral questions did not admit of relativistic interpretations," while knowing at the same time that the attempt to right moral wrongs may have tragic consequences and almost certainly will not achieve unqualified success.

But again, our best course is to attend to the words of Lincoln. Recall the Second Inaugural Address of March 4, 1865, little more than a month before his death. There are two paragraphs on the war and the imperative to save the Union, moving directly in the next paragraph, the heart of the speech, to slavery. One side, he observes, wanted to strengthen and perpetuate the institution, the other to restrict its enlargement. (And, although he does not say so, many on the Northern side were determined to abolish it.) In any event, nobody expected a war of such magnitude and dura-tion. Each hoped for an "easier triumph, and a result less funda-mental and astounding." Then come the extraordinary words that better educated Americans know almost by heart:

> Both read the same Bible, and pray to the same God; and each invokes His aid against the other. It may seem strange that any men should dare to ask a just God's assistance in wringing their bread from the sweat of other men's faces; but let us judge not that we be not judged. The prayers of both could not be answered; that of neither has been answered fully. The Almighty has His own purposes. "Woe unto the world because of offenses; for it must needs be that offenses come, but woe to that man by whom the offense cometh!" If we shall suppose that American slavery is one of those offenses which, in the providence of God, must needs come, but which, having continued through His appointed time, He now wills to remove, and that He gives to both North and South this terrible war as the woe due to those by whom the offense came, shall we discern therein any departure from

those divine attributes which the believers in a living God always ascribe to Him?

The form changes now to that of supplication:

Fondly do we hope—fervently do we pray—that this mighty scourge of war may speedily pass away. Yet, if God wills that it continue, until all the wealth piled up by the bondsman's two hundred and fifty years of unrequited toil shall be sunk, and until every drop of blood drawn with the lash shall be paid by another drawn with the sword, as was said three thousand years ago, so still it must be said, "The judgments of the Lord are true and righteous altogether."

Of course, Southerners would for generations deride these words as an indulgence in unctuous self-righteousness, and it is obvious that Lincoln was not "above" the conflict he is discussing. The description of the conflict is not, as it is said today, nonpartisan. His duty, reluctantly accepted, had been to be a partisan and a leader of partisans, but the import of the address is that now that time is past. More remarkable in the words of a victorious party is the refusal to recruit God as a partisan. The war and its outcome do not vindicate a grand narrative of historical inevitability but bring all parties under Divine judgment. We are united as a bleeding and wounded people, and it is on the basis of that experience, not on victory parades and rallies, that a nation is to be renewed. With Augustine, Lincoln recognized the lust to dominate that is so inextricably entangled with yearnings for peace and justice. No one walks away even from a justifiable war morally unscathed.

Lincoln offers words that are, at the same time, benediction, his own epitaph, and a continuing inspiration to a more worthy politics:

With malice toward none, with charity for all, with firmness in the right as God gives us to see the right, let us strive on to finish the work we are in, to bind up the nation's wounds, to care for him who shall have borne the battle and for his widow and his orphan, to do all which may achieve and cherish a just and a lasting peace among ourselves and with all nations.

The reference to other nations is by no means incidental to Lincoln's understanding of what was at stake in America's conflict. In history's ongoing struggle between despotism and self-government, he was prepared to believe that America was earth's "last best hope"—not as the world's economic colossus or imperial hegemon but as an exemplar of what politics, with all its limitations, can accomplish.

A poem to which Lincoln often returned was "Oh, Why Should the Spirit of Mortal Be Proud?" written by one William Knox. Forget that it is not great poetry, indeed that it descends to doggerel. It says something important about the man who thought it wise:

> Oh, why should the spirit of mortal be proud?
> Like a swift fleeting meteor, a fast-flying cloud,
> A flash of the lightning, a break of the wave,
> Man passeth from life to his rest in the grave. . . .
> The hand of the king that the sceptre hath borne;
> The brow of the priest that the mitre hath worn;
> The eye of the sage and the heart of the brave,
> Are hidden and lost in the depth of the grave. . . .
> The saint who enjoyed the communion of heaven,
> The sinner who dared to remain unforgiven,
> The wise and the foolish, the guilty and just,
> Have quietly mingled their bones in the dust. . . .

'Tis the wink of an eye, 'tis the draught of a breath,
From the blossom of health to the paleness of death,
From the gilded saloon to the bier and the shroud—
Oh, why should the spirit of mortal be proud?

Perhaps it is too obvious to observe that, in an era of sound bites, poll-driven politicians, plausible deniability, single-interest PACs, and media spin-meisters, Lincoln seems to exist in a different moral and political universe. And it is both true and a very good thing that other presidents did not have such momentous events by which they were controlled and made candidates for comparable greatness. That being said, however, Lincoln is by no means irrelevant. He was in most respects a politician like other politicians. He knew all about interests and power, was a master of clever ripostes, well-placed barbs, and the tricks of outwitting opponents. In short, he played the game and played it very well.

The difference is that he never forgot that politics is one way in which very imperfect human beings can enact projects based on moral reasoning; that politics is a theater of both comedy and tragedy, relentless in the teaching of humility. It is cause for both amazement and gratitude that, in a century when the promise of Europe migrated to a New World which, or so we are told, offers the prospect of the nearest thing there has ever been to a universal history of freedom and justice, Abraham Lincoln was president of these United States of America. More than a hundred years later, there is no point in hoping for another Abraham Lincoln. But one may hope that we have not entirely forgotten the possibilities of political and moral leadership that he exemplified.

VIGEN GUROIAN

INHERITING PARADISE

(From *Books & Culture*)

I am an Armenian Orthodox believer and theologian. The Orthodox faith is a sacramental faith. When Orthodox Christians perform the great rite of the blessing of the water by ocean beach or riverbank, they behave, as the Armenian liturgy says, like the holy apostles who became "cleansers of the whole world." While God might have driven Adam and Eve out of the Garden of Paradise, God still ensured that the living waters issuing from the garden continued to irrigate the whole earth and cleanse its polluted streams and lakes. When we bless water, we acknowledge God's grace and desire to cleanse the world and make it paradise.

Water is the blood of creation. Our own bodies are 80 percent water. Water is also the element of baptism. Saint Thomas Aquinas said: "Because water is transparent, it can receive light; and so it is fitting that it should be used in baptism, inasmuch as it is the sacrament of faith." By cleansing the water we make it clear again. By expelling the demonic pollutants we ready it for greater service to God. We tend not only the garden that we call nature but also the garden that is ourselves, insofar as we are constituted of water and are born anew by it.

We ought not to draw a line that neatly marks off nature from humankind. This is a modern heresy that we have inherited from the Enlightenment. Contrary to environmentalists' accusations of anthropocentrism, Christians believe that human beings are especially responsible for tending the creation. This is no less a responsibility than the duty to care for our own bodies as temples of the Holy Spirit. God has given human beings this responsibility as an emblem of his own great love for all of creation. The fourth-century church father Saint Ephrem the Syrian says in his *Hymns on Paradise:*

> The fool, who is unwilling to realize
> his honorable state,
> prefers to become just an animal,
> rather than a man,
> so that, without incurring judgment,
> he may serve naught but his lusts.
> But had there been sown in animals
> just a little
> of the sense of discernment,
> then long ago would the wild asses
> have lamented
> and wept at their not
> having been human.

Saint Ephrem does not condone an ecologically destructive anthropocentrism. He does not say that human beings are masters over creation with the right to use it solely for their own selfish purposes or comfort. Rather, he reminds us that everything comes from God, and that without God's constant nurture, nothing would be and nothing could grow. "It is not the gardeners with their planting and watering who count," writes Saint Paul, "but God who makes it grow." Indeed, we are not only "fellow workers" in God's great garden; we ourselves are God's garden (1 Cor. 3:7–9, REB). This is the ground of our humility as mere creatures among all other creatures loved by God.

Our Christian living ought to reflect an "oikic" ethos. The Greek word *oikos* means a dwelling or a place to live. The words *economy* and *ecology* come from this same Greek word. The *oikumene,* the whole creation, is the church's ethical concern. Our incarnational faith inspires a vision of humankind's relationship to creation that is sacramental, ecological, and ethical. In its elevation of bread and wine, the liturgy of the Eucharist makes this connection clear.

The Armenian writer Teotig tells a story about the genocide of the Armenians during World War I. Father Ashod Avedian was a priest of a village near the city of Erzeroum in eastern Turkey. During the deportations, 4,000 Armenian men of that village were separated from their families and driven on a forced march into desolate regions. On their march to death, when food supplies had given out, Father Ashod instructed the men to pray in unison, "Lord have mercy," then led them in taking the "cursed" soil and swallowing it as communion. The ancient Armenian catechism called the *Teaching of Saint Gregory* says that "this dry earth is our habitation, and all assistance and nourishment for our lives [comes] from it and grows on it, and food for our growth, like milk from a mother, comes to us from it."

Teotig's story is a reminder that we belong to the earth and that our redemption includes the earth from which we and all the creatures have come, by which we are sustained, and through which God continues to act for our salvation. If water is the blood of creation, then earth is its flesh and air is its breath, and all things are purified by the fiery love of God.

For the earth to bring forth fruit there must be water and air and the light and heat of the sun. Every gardener knows this, and so recognizes that the right combination of these elements lies beyond the control of science or contrivance. That is the wisdom and agony of gardening. God's creation cannot subsist without God's abundant grace. God has given human beings the sacred responsibility of mediating God's grace and, by offering blessings, of lifting the ancient curse of Adam and expelling the demons from every living thing and from the earth and its waters and from the air. No human science or technology can accomplish this, although we are constantly tempted to think so.

So let us be good gardeners and teach our children to be the same. Modern Christians have spoken a lot about "stewardship" of the earth. But I think we are overly practiced at the kind of management that this word easily connotes. We need another perspective, another metaphor. Scripture gives us the symbol of the garden. Adam and Eve were placed in a garden where they walked together with God and did not need to labor. But when they sinned and were expelled, gardening began. Gardening symbolizes our race's primal acceptance of a responsibility and role in rectifying the harm done to the creation through sin.

The Armenian liturgy speaks of human beings as "cocreators" with God. But what is meant by this expression? Certainly not any kind of equality with God. God alone is the creator. We are not *literally* cocreators, but sacramental gardeners. We garden in order to provide sustenance for ourselves and the other creatures. But we also use the fruit of our gardens to prepare the bread of the sacrament. In a petitionary prayer of the Armenian Rite of Washing the Cross, the priest asks: "Bless, Lord, this water with the holy cross, so that it may impart to the fields, where it is sprinkled, harvests, wherefrom we have fine flour as an offering of holiness unto thy Lordship."

The fruit of the garden is not restricted to what we eat. Every garden lends something more to the imagination—beauty. The beauty of a turnip garden may be more homely than the beauty of a tulip garden, but there is beauty in it nevertheless. Every garden holds the potential of giving us a taste of paradise. Sometimes this comes as a grace that does not exact one's personal labor, but somewhere someone has labored with the sweat of the brow to make the garden grow.

Jesus prayed in a garden and agonized there, watering it with his tears. His body, which was torn on the cross, was also buried in a garden. And three days after his crucifixion, the women who wept as he hung on the cross and anointed our Lord's body returned to that garden to find that the seed that they had lovingly prepared for planting had already borne a sweet and fragrant fruit. Every garden is an intimation of the Garden that is Christ's, that he himself tends in the hearts of those who welcome him in.

God also has planted within each human being a seed of hope that, if properly nurtured, grows into a confidence that all will be well, all manner of things shall be well. The breath of God reaches into even the smallest and most remote garden and human heart and infuses life. Even more, it brings salvation. The anemone and the rose grow in the earthly garden, but in the Garden of Paradise the anemone grows without the blood of the cross, and the rose has no thorns. The Armenian Epiphany hymn of the blessing of the water declares: "Today the garden appears to mankind, / let us rejoice in righteousness unto eternal life. . . . / Today the shut and barred gate of the garden is opened to mankind."

Let every Christian be a gardener so that he and she and the whole of creation, which groans in expectation of the Spirit's final harvest, may inherit paradise. If we Christians truly treasure the hope that one day we, like Adam and the penitent thief, will walk alongside the One who caused even the dead wood of the cross to blossom with flowers, then we must also imitate the Master's art and make the desolate earth grow green.

THE RECOVERY OF MORAL AGENCY?

(From *Harvard Divinity Bulletin*)

The overall argument of this lecture will move through three stages. In the first I identify two contrasting styles of moral utterance that dominate our present public discourse and spell out their shared presuppositions, remarking that both modes are characterized by an absence of self-questioning, a certain type of thoughtlessness. This, I'll suggest, renders those whose modes of utterance they are responsive to vulnerable to a range of nonrational influences that operate upon desire, influences that make us, unless we have acquired certain powers of practical discrimination, victims of our own desires and of those influences rather than genuine moral agents.

Those same powers of practical discrimination, powers exhibited in self-knowledge and self-directedness, are, I shall argue, generally to be acquired only through training in and engagement with certain kinds of disciplined practice through which moral character is formed. And in the second part of this lecture I'll discuss what kinds of practice those are and offer two examples. Finally and briefly, I shall contrast the styles of moral utterance characteristic of those whose moral character has been formed through this kind of practice with the culturally dominant styles of moral utterance.

It is because we still do engage in types of practice that do provide resources for recovering from the afflictions of contemporary morality that I speak in my title of the recovery of moral agency. And it's because it is far from clear that we are able to give those types of practice anything like their due place in our common life that I speak of the recovery of moral agency only with a question mark.

I

Consider two very different modes of and attitudes to moral judgment, both characteristic of present-day North American public debate. One is self-confidently assertive and apparently innocent of any sense of moral complexity. The other is characteristically tentative in its expression and, even when not so, often presents its judgments on particular acts or choices without giving determinate form to whatever universal and general principles might be presupposed by those judgments.

For these latter, complexity often seems to be a refuge from finality of judgment, a warrant for hesitation and qualification. By contrast, the speech-acts characteristic of those whose mode is confidently assertive are generally those of either unproblematic condemnation or unproblematic confession. Moral indignation or moral self-laceration are its emotions of choice, while the practitioners of the tentative mode, bent as they are on finding some way of judging without being what they're apt to call judgmental, often seem to exhibit in their feelings the same cloudy indefiniteness that their judgments betray. For the one, a sense of outrage is instantly available; for the other, when some act—a lie, for example—is allowed to be wrong, the word "wrong" is uttered almost as if it were a word from some imperfectly known foreign language.

Neither of these psychological modes is to be identified with any particular point on the political spectrum. And indeed, sometimes within one and the same individual both attitudes are found, so that dogmatism and assertiveness about issues of, say, distributive justice or individual rights may coexist with tentative and indeterminate attitudes to issues of truth-telling and lying. Yet, on any particular subject of moral controversy, those who judge in the one mode generally identify those who judge in the other as among their antagonists. And each, in rejecting the other, tends to see its rival as the only alternative to itself. Neither seems open to the thought that a moral culture in which choice is so often defined by these two alternative types of attitude might itself be defective. And this is perhaps unsurprising. For both modes generally provide a terminus for thought. Neither seems open to self-questioning, to entertaining doubt about, in the one case, their certainties or, in the other, their uncertainties and qualifications. So, generally neither appears willing to undertake the work of identifying, let alone putting in question, their shared presuppositions.

Part of the work of disclosing those presuppositions, so that they can be put to the question, is historical. For both sets of attitudes seem to have been generated, at least in part, as responses to predicaments characteristic of post-Enlightenment moral cultures. Those predicaments are the effect of combining a continuing allegiance to Enlightenment standards for the justification of moral judgments with an awareness of the outcome of the moral debates of the Enlightenment.

Enlightenment standards require of those who give them their allegiance that they should be able to justify their particular moral judgments by appeal to some unique set of universal and general principles, principles such that they couldn't reasonably be rejected by *any* rational agent. Enlightenment inquiries, however, have provided us with just too many different and rival conclusions as to what those principles should be: principles enjoining the maximization of utility, principles enjoining the exceptionless prescriptions and prohibitions of the categorical imperative, principles ascribing universal and inalienable natural rights, principles appealing to contractarian considerations. And Enlightenment debates, both debates between different and rival protagonists of Enlightenment—Diderot, Bentham, Rousseau, Kant, and not only these—and debates between the protagonists of the Enlightenment and its critics, resulted in an uneasy awareness that, although none of these positions was, or is liable to be, anything like conclusive refutation by its rivals, none had been able to provide resources for the refutation of those rivals, except in its own terms and by its own standards.

Consequently, the self-aware inhabitants of a post-Enlightenment moral culture have had to combine a claim to the rational superiority of their own positions over against those advanced by rival claimants with a recognition that those same rival claimants are, by and large, as intelligent and well-informed and morally self-aware—that is, as rational—as they are. And this isn't just a predicament of philosophers. For the thought of plain persons, to some large degree, is in the same condition. For them, too, when they're confronted by large issues of principle, implicit or explicit claims to the rational superiority of their own positions coexist with a similar awareness of disagreements with others who are advancing claims to the superiority of rival and incompatible positions. And this in a situation in which each party, while judging itself to be argumentatively victorious in its own terms and by its own standards, is nonetheless recurrently reminded that its rivals also, and in just the same way, take themselves to be the victors.

It is not surprising that those who find themselves in this type of situation should tend to respond either with self-confident and adversarial reiterations of the superiority of their own standpoint or else with a certain distancing of themselves from all contending points of view, so their judgments become tentative expressions of unsure and indefinite commitments. But there's another feature of their situation that needs to be remarked. It's not only that both contending parties exclude from view the historical roots of their situation. Neither seems able to engage with questions about the social and psychological factors that are at work in making them what they are.

The setting of limits to self-questioning is reinforced by another feature of our social order. Our institutions provide a number of different kinds of forum for moral debate. But it is very rare indeed—outside academic, and that's to say, in this respect irrelevant, contexts—that there are opportunities for ordinary citizens, for plain persons, to engage together in systematic and extended inquiry into the issues posed for them by debate. So, for example, there are recurrent occasions on which public debate takes place over a lie told by some official person, over whether that lie was or was not justified—or if not justified, was at least excusable, or if not excusable, was perhaps too trivial to censure. And there are a range of opportunities, both for political and religious spokespersons, and for plain persons, to express judgments on such occasions. But these are judgments that must, in very many cases, be mindless, just because those who express them have, like the vast majority of their fellow citizens, never been afforded any opportunity to consider, together with others, in any systematic and extended way, what different and alternative views have been taken and might be taken of what rules ought to govern truth-telling and lying and why, and of how the virtue of truthfulness is to be conceived.

Absent such opportunity, what we're bound to have is, to a significant extent, a morality of public thoughtlessness—a thoughtlessness too often evident in both the mode of moral dogmatism and the mode of moral indeterminacy.

When I speak of thoughtlessness here I refer to a lack of will to carry reflection beyond a certain point. It is exemplified in a type of debate that is inescapable in many areas in which adjudication between rival claims of certain types is central to our decision-making. Those claims concern, on the one hand, rights; on the other, utility. And there are therefore three different kinds of conflict that require adjudication: conflict in which the rights of one contending party can only be upheld if someone else's rights are violated; conflicts in which the utility of this or that set of individual or corporate persons can only be maximized at the expense of the utility of some other set of individual or corporate persons, and conflicts in which the decision must be either to give priority to someone's rights over someone else's utility or vice versa.

Let's attend for the moment only to conflicts of this third kind, supposing, even if only for the sake of the argument, that we're in fact in possession of some rational method for assigning priorities to rights, so that we can decide whose rights should prevail over whose, and some rational method for maximizing utilities, so that we can decide which out of alternative courses of action will genuinely maximize the general utility. How then are conflicts between rights-based claims and utility-based claims adjudicated?

When those who adjudicate such conflicts report upon how in fact they make their decisions, they almost invariably speak in terms of the weight to be given to each of the relevant considerations and of balancing one set of considerations against another. That is, they resort to metaphor. But how is this metaphor to be understood? What plays the part of the scales that provide some measure of weight and balance? And how are those scales calibrated? The short answer is: there are no such scales. There is no rationally justifiable method for making such decisions. And the mind that allows thought to terminate with this metaphor disguises this fact from itself. What is also disguised is the nature of the nonrational influences that are at work in the making of such decisions—the influences concealed by the metaphor. And an unwillingness or an inability to recognize and to understand those influences is an unwillingness or inability to confront the sources and the inequalities of power.

For at those points at which agents for no further reason give weight to this set of reasons rather than to that—something that characterizes *all* the types of moral attitude that I've so far identified—we always need to ask: To what particular influences are they being responsive? Whose power is at work in making them responsive to those influences and not to these? And what are the distributions of power that determine whose power is effective and whose ineffective in this particular area of decision-making?

It is only through asking and answering these questions that we become able to identify the otherwise often unrecognized pressures exerted on individual agents to become what the social order needs them to become if they are to enact the roles presented for them in this or that area of social life in a way that doesn't call into question those distributions of power, and to engage in those debates that define what had been socially determined to be the range of acceptable attitudes and choices. If we leave these questions unasked, we deprive ourselves of a crucial dimension of self-knowledge. And what I've called thoughtlessness is a quality of minds so deprived.

What's the effect of this kind of thoughtlessness? It is that individuals without being adequately aware of it are molded by forces at work in their social environment, so that their judgments express uncritically attitudes that they've never had an opportunity to make genuinely their own. They don't exhibit bad character so much as lack of character. They are no longer fully responsible agents, having become too responsive to this or that set of pressures. Thoughtlessness is then a mark of loss of moral agency. And the types of moral judgment that I've described are symptoms of that loss.

What then is it instead to be thoughtful? It is to be unwilling to allow thought to rest content with unscrutinized metaphors or unidentified presuppositions, especially when these function as obstacles to further moral inquiry. But at this point there's a mistake that would be easy to make. For we might suppose that in order to deal with those nonrational influences that have, for the most part without our recognizing it, molded our character and set limits to the alternatives between which we choose in our decision-making, we need to embark on sociological and psychological inquiries—inquiries whose end product would be a set of generalizations about how power is distributed and about how nonrational influences are exerted in contemporary social and cultural orders.

But while such inquiries are certainly of value, it is possible for someone to be very well-informed about their findings without having moved in any way toward the kind of self-knowledge without which we'll be able to understand our own habits and choices adequately and to distinguish that in them which is genuinely directed toward our good as rational agents and that in them which derives from a variety of unacknowledged nonrational influences.

The knowledge that we need for moral agency is not theoretical, but practical. And practical knowledge is not applied theoretical knowledge. The relevant practical knowledge is the knowledge of how to discriminate among the various objects of attention presented to us by our desires. And it's in the first instance our own desires of which we have to learn to beware. For the nonrational influences that may make us, for example, responsive to advertising rather than to reliable sources of information, or that render us vulnerable to the selectivity of television news programs because we are not aware of the principles governing that selectivity, or that lead us to form our ambitions in response to the aura of prestige and glamour surrounding the rich and the powerful, those influences, all of them, operate on our desires. Arousing them, magnetizing them, focusing them, strengthening them, and determining what is taken to be frustration or deprivation in respect of desire, so that in an important way those passions are no longer wholly ours but have become in part a medium by which we are possessed, so that desire desires through us, so that what have become the objects of our strongest desires dictate to us. The Japanese have a saying about alcohol: "First the man takes a drink, then the drink takes a drink, then the drink takes the man." This, I take it, captures very well the way in which we may more generally become victims of a variety of forms of desire that operate upon us as though they were impersonal forces.

The condition of victims of dictatorial desire is one that we're all able to recognize easily enough when it takes the extreme form of an addition, but of which we're much less often aware in other cases. There's a whole range of influences upon character and decision that, even when we acknowledge their power at the level of theory and generalization, we largely and often entirely ignore in the particularities of practice. The questions then are: What kind of a human being would I have to become in order not to be so influenced? And what would I have to do or what would have to happen to me for me to become such a human being?

The aim isn't, of course, to arrive at a point at which one's desires are no longer subject to external influences. That would be an impossible, even a silly, aim. It is instead to aim to make one's desires truly one's own, by making them, so far as possible, responsive only to those influences to which it is for the agent's good to be responsive. It is to aim at educating one's desires, so that they are discriminatingly responsive, giving expression to those powers of rational discrimination that are one mark of moral agency. So how then should we proceed?

II

Here I might, as a certain kind of Aristotelian, a Thomist Aristotelian, be tempted to make another mistake: that of turning to the texts and developing answers to these questions based on what is said by Aristotle, and by Aquinas in his commentaries on Aristotle. But to proceed in this way would tend to preserve the illusion that such questions can be addressed adequately at the level of theory. And by introducing Aristotle's moral theory as one more contribution to contemporary moral debate, I would be transforming Aristotle into one more post-Enlightenment moral philosopher, so enlarging the controversies of post-Enlightenment moral philosophy by adding yet another contending standpoint, but not changing their character. So, Aristotelian ethics would become understood, as too often it has been understood, as just one more set of theoretical positions whose adherents are engaged in one more set of inconclusive debates with utilitarians, Kantians, and contractarians. But theory of and by itself, reasoning of and by itself, good theory just as much as bad theory, never made anyone a better human being. Indeed, Aristotle suggested that theorizing is sometimes a device of those anxious to avoid habituation into the virtues: "They take refuge in discourse and think that they are philosophizing and in this way will become good."

We need instead to begin with practice, for theory is the articulation of practice and good theory of good practice. Moral debate is therefore not primarily between theories as such, but rather between theories that afford expression to rival forms of practice. And we do not understand any theory adequately until we've understood in concrete detail the form of practice of which it's an articulation. Note that I'm not at all suggesting that theory has no practical relevance. There are types of practice that are atheoretical, forms of practice from which theory is absent or even excluded, and that thereby set narrow limits to the possibilities of reflection upon practice, limits that inevitably themselves produce what I have called thoughtlessness. Theory, when it is recognized to be the articulation of practice, enables practice to be reflectively thoughtful and so to remedy what have been its defects and limitations.

One function of such theory is to enable those who engage in relevant forms of practice to address questions to themselves about their practice—questions posed by theory, but to be answered in practice, by acting in one way rather than in another. So that what theory may provide—what good theory should provide—is an agenda for practical reflection. Hence what we need to take from Aristotle's texts are not primarily theses, but rather questions, questions whose answers would enable us first to reformulate and then to address in practice those issues that concern the transformation of our desires and of our attitudes to our desires, so that we may no longer be victimized by them. Consider four such Aristotelian sets of questions.

A first set concerns how I am to make the distinction between those objects of desire that I seek to attain just because they are objects of my desire, and I want my desire to be satisfied, and those objects of desire that I seek to obtain because I judge it to be good in general for human beings to obtain this kind of object, and good in particular for me here now to do so. In the former case I value the object just because and insofar as it's an object of my desire. In the latter, I take the desire to provide a good reason for action just because and insofar as it's a desire for what is good and in these circumstances best. So a form of practice that's to educate the desires will be one that enables those engaged in it to make this distinction in their practice. (And here, of course, at the level of theory Aristotle has to be able to provide resources for a reply to Hume, who allows no place for this distinction.)

A second set of Aristotelian questions concerns how we are to acquire the ability to act for the best here and now, in situations in which there isn't enough time for deliberation, so that the agent has to draw upon past deliberations that have prepared her or him to act spontaneously and immediately in this type of situation. The agent needs to have learned how to act with good reasons and from good reasons without making those reasons explicit. And the agent's appetites and passions have to be such that the agent is moved only by the desire to act immediately for the best and is not distracted by irrelevant fearful or hopeful wishes. So that when the agent is presented with someone else's gross and urgent need—a child needs to be rescued from imminent danger, a persecuted individual or group is threatened with death—she or he does not have to calculate, but finds it unproblematic to respond, even when the risk may be to her or his own life. What matters is whether such an agent has embodied in her or his dispositions to feel, to judge, and to act a rank ordering of goods, a conception of human flourishing that issues in this kind of response to gross and urgent need. It matters not at all whether she or he is able to articulate that rank ordering, that conception, in theoretical terms. It does matter, of course, that it should be articulatable, that it should be expressible in the form of theses and arguments, so that it can be put to critical question. But an inability of any particular agent to do this on some particular occasion is never of itself a moral defect. (And here, of course, at the level of theory Aristotle has to be able to reply to Kant, who denies that the concept of human flourishing can have this kind of place in our rational practice.)

To these two marks of adequate practice conceived in Aristotelian terms—an ability to discriminate those objects of my desire that it is here and now good for me to pursue from those that solicit my desires simply as objects of desire, and an ability on occasion to act when there is good reason to act without having to remind myself of what that good reason is—a third must be added. For we also need to ask questions about how an agent's practice is to embody features that belong to the overall unity of that agent's life. The episodes through which these and other abilities are developed must be understood as part of a narrative that the agent is enacting, in which the agent's success or failure in understanding at the level of practice what it would be to complete that narrative well or badly is itself one important aspect of completing that narrative well or badly. The agent's life, thus, should exhibit and exhibit increasingly some degree of overall directedness, a certain narrative unity, so that retrospectively earlier stages in that life can be understood as just that, stages on the way to something not yet adequately but increasingly characterizable.

The agent progresses toward making her or his activities intelligible, both to her or himself and to others, through her or his emerging conception of a final telos toward which those activities are directed and from which they get not their *only* point and purpose, but *further* point and purpose. Desire, that is to say, will have been directed toward a further and ultimate object, one in which, were it to be achieved, it could rest satisfied, and one in which, were it not to be achieved, it would be permanently unsatisfied. (And here, of course, at the level of theory Aristotle has to be able to reply to Hobbes, who holds that there is no such object.)

A fourth mark of good practice in an Aristotelian view is supplied by answering questions about the types of social relationship in and through which the goods of such practice are achieved. We can only initially engage in good practice through putting ourselves into the hands of others who will be able to teach us what we need to learn. And we can generally achieve the goods of practice only in systematic and structured cooperation with others who also recognize that only insofar as we and they achieve our common good can we achieve our individual goods.

My actions are to contribute to activities and projects that are not only mine, but ours, so that we have to deliberate with others. And on this view, insofar as I think of the actions to be engaged in and the goods to be achieved as primarily mine, I will tend to act in such a way as to frustrate my achievement of important types of good.

Any kind of competitiveness that encourages egoistic thinking is therefore an enemy of good practice. So we have to learn that while it is important to care about excelling, it's corrupting to care about who is ranked higher than whom in respective excellence. Desire has to be detached from the badges of such rank ordering—prizes, fame, money—while directed toward those achievements of excellence for which, ostensibly at least, such badges are awarded.

We need then to be educated into the relevant kind of relationship with those others who participate with us in particular practices. And to be so educated we have to entrust ourselves to others who will act both as instructors and exemplars. Note that they won't so instruct us by professing to teach us something whose name is "ethics." Practical moral instruction is incidental to instruction in the tasks of many types of practice— farming and fishing, building houses and staging plays, playing football and conducting scientific inquiries. It is in such contexts that desires that we initially bring to these tasks—often desires to please parents or teachers and to obtain goods that are the external rewards for success in this or that particular activity, prizes, fame, money—are displaced by and transformed into desires for the goods internal to each particular activity, and more especially, for the good of excellence in performing those tasks.

This displacement and transformation of desire is then also something achieved incidentally and not by being directly aimed at. And it is generally achieved only by those whose teachers have themselves, at some earlier period, experienced just such a displacement and transformation. If those teachers are successful, they make of their students or apprentices future teachers. Having entrusted themselves to the authority of their teachers, those students or apprentices become able to exercise authority as teachers of others. Having had exemplars, role models, they in turn become exemplars. Good practices are transmitted through traditions of good teaching.

So far, then, I've tried to supply, from within a generally Aristotelian framework, proposals for an outline account—a very bare outline account—of some of the conditions that would have to be satisfied by our practice, if we were to become able to direct desires toward our goods and our good, so that we would no longer be rendered vulnerable to the nonrational solicitations and influences that are determined by distributions of power. Earlier I suggested that the dominant forms of contemporary morality do not rescue those who give them their allegiance from this vulnerability, and I tried to identify some sources of that vulnerability. Now I add the suggestion that the dominant forms of our culture may provide too few opportunities for education into the kind of practice through which the desires become directed in such a way that they are less liable to be responsive to and perhaps corrupted by the stimuli of nonrational influences. But my discussion, as I noticed earlier, has remained, could not but have remained, at the level of theory. What I can do, however, is to identify examples of the type of practice articulated by this kind of Aristotelian theorizing and in so doing allow theory to direct our attention beyond theory to practice. What then are one or two relevant contemporary examples of practice?

III

Every stable form of human life within which goods are achieved depends for its continuing existence, let alone its flourishing, upon there being those who provide it with security from external and internal aggression and who therefore must be prepared to sacrifice their lives, if necessary, in that cause. And one measure of the moral substance of a way of life is what answer it gives in practice to the question: What do the rest of us owe in justice to those who are so prepared? Our attitudes to police officers, firefighters, prison guards, and the military are therefore significant, and not only because we have entrusted our lives and our security to them. For in trusting them we have to recognize that, if they are to perform their duties adequately, they have to be authorized to use coercive violence of a kind forbidden to the rest of us. But this power can very easily be misused. So those who are so authorized have to be trained, so that they use their power for the sake of achieving the relevant goods rather than misusing it. And we have to trust not only in them but also in the effectiveness of their training.

It is obvious that the training of such individuals will have to involve just that kind of redirection of the desires about which I've been speaking. They will have to become disposed to act, so that they unhesitatingly prefer on occasion the safety of the community to their own safety, and also so that of the opportunities afforded to them by their power they avail themselves of those that involve no misuse of it. What kind of training inculcates such dispositions? The answer to this question given by the United States Marine Corps in the 11 weeks of basic training is among the most interesting answers ever given.

The recruits who receive this training are, by the standard of our society, generally very unpromising material: often those with whom their high school teachers have failed, nearly half of whom have used drugs, had brushes with the law or experienced other problems. (For the data here, particularly the statistical data, I am relying heavily on Thomas E. Ricks's splendid 1998 book *Making the Corps*, published by Touchstone.) At the end, those who have survived their basic training are not only excellent at what they do, but some at least have made significant initial progress toward becoming the future noncommissioned leadership of the Corps, including those who, as drill instructors, will train future recruits. How did they make this transition? It could not have happened without strenuously enforced discipline throughout their working hours, without their being screamed at, harassed, and subjected to the pains of punishment, until they had become self-directed toward and narrowly focused upon succeeding at each successive task.

But during this period they will also have learned both that they will be given every assistance possible to succeed and also that they are capable of high levels of practical achievement that they had for the most part never realized. They will also have learned that these achievements were made possible only by the contributions of others and that their value lies in enabling them to achieve shared tasks with the rest of their platoon—that it is, in the end, the shared success or failure that counts and not just their own. So they'll have learned that they're accountable to others for their actions and especially for their failures. Why does it matter so much that they shouldn't fail? Because others have put their lives in their hands, and this in two ways.

First, the people of the United States have put their lives and their security into the hands of, among others, the Marines. There have been perhaps 15 serious attempts to abolish the Corps. All have failed, and all failed because of public opinion. "You know why America has a Marine Corps?" the recruit training regiment commander is quoted as saying to recruits. "Because she wants one." And their training is designed to make marines aware of how they serve the needs of the wider society. But secondly, all marines will have learned that if their own lives are at risk, then any other marine at hand is bound to come to their aid, even at the possible cost of life, and that in turn each of them is under the same obligation.

These two bonds of responsibility—to their fellow marines, and to the wider society—are both formed by their training, but they are, of course, very different types of bond. And it is difficult to resist the conclusion, even from the most favorable accounts of marine attitudes and actions, that the strength of the first bond is to some extent achieved by means that weaken the second. Solidarity with one's fellow marines is at the expense of solidarity with the wider society. For becoming a marine, at the same time as it inculcates some sense of a responsibility to the wider society, seems to alienate marines, not only from those aspects of the wider society about which they may be quite right to be dismissive, but also from any external standpoint that might put their own values seriously in question. A narrow limit to the possibility of moral reflection has been imposed. And from a military standpoint this may be all to the good. Battlefields are generally not places for reflection, moral or otherwise. But the limitations of marine culture are as instructive as its achievements.

Earlier I identified four distinguishing characteristics of the kind of practice participation in which would provide individuals with the ability to discriminate among and to transform and redirect their desires, so that they would, as far as possible, no longer be open to being influenced by nonrational solicitations. The practice that is the outcome of Marine Corps training exhibits three of these four, although not all to the same degree. What it signally lacks, however, is one of these characteristics, the kind of directedness that has to inform not merely a term in or a career in the military, but a whole life, and this not only because time spent as a marine is only an episode, even if sometimes a prolonged episode, within a more extended narrative of a marine's life, but also because there are such important areas of human activity that fall outside the scope of marine training. Principal among them are those activities that are crucial to participation in the life of family and household and the life of a local community. What marine training doesn't provide is the discipline of reflection upon what part each of these types of activities should play in an overall human life—that is, reflection upon a wider range of goods, upon how those goods relate to one another, and upon how the importance each of them is accorded by a particular individual in her or his life answers at the level of practice the question of what that agent takes human flourishing to consist in.

An adequate moral education, then, will have some of the features of marine training, but it will unite these with education into a capacity for reflection upon goods that provides those engaged in the tasks of redirecting and transforming their desires with an additional resource. What kind of practice might provide this? Like marine training, it will have to be demanding and to enable its practitioners both to extend their powers and to test themselves against high standards. It will have to teach individuals to excel without making them value winning over others rather than excelling. It will have to do this while inculcating a strong sense of dependence on others, of having had to put your life into the hands of others, thus warranting in others an expectation that they'll be able to depend on you. And yet, unlike marine training, it will not merely leave one open to reflect on how goods should be ordered, and upon whether they are ordered rightly within this kind of training, but will provide a stimulus for such reflection and, if possible, make such reflection inescapable.

One salutary example of just such an education is that provided by the experience of members of some types of fishing crews who are at home in local communities where fishing has been a or the primary occupation through several generations. I could have taken examples from the northeast of Scotland or the northwest of Ireland or from Newfoundland. If I focus attention on fishing crews from New England towns to the south and north of Boston, and among them on some of those crews who fish for giant bluefin tuna, it's because Douglas Whynott's remarkable 1995 book, *Giant Bluefin* (Farrar, Straus & Giroux), asks and provides a starting point for answering more of the relevant questions than do most books on fishing. But first let me make a more general point about deep-sea fishing as an activity.

It is the most dangerous of American industries, with a death rate of 178 workers per 100,000 per year—significantly more dangerous than logging (155 deaths per 100,000 workers a year), and generally a good deal more dangerous than being a marine. Members of fishing crews, therefore, have to be able to rely on one another, on other fishing crews, and on the Coast Guard. They have to develop a range of skills, a capacity for hard manual labor, and a temperament that allows them to live at close quarters with others without friction that would be damaging to the enterprise.

What makes the recent history of tuna fishing really interesting is the way in which extreme and unpredicted changes made it more difficult than usual to resolve issues about the relationship between competitiveness and cooperativeness in the lives of crews. Both the extreme of prosperity, as Japanese markets opened up from the 1970s onward, and the extreme of restriction, due to the imposition of quotas in the early 1990s, fostered competitiveness. In the early times of prosperity, fortunes could be made or lost. In the later times of restriction, "reduced quotas, the shortened season, an increase in participants, migratory patterns that favored one region over another and the abuse of the rules all brought conflicts."

Both kinds of competitiveness put two kinds of strain on those engaged in fishing. On the one hand, cooperation was endangered. On the other, the question arose for many individuals of whether to stay with fishing or to engage in some other occupation. And these are questions with large import not only for those engaged in fishing, but also for their families and their communities. So for those engaged in fishing problems about how a variety of goods are to be rank-ordered arise inescapably from time to time. And it's difficult to remain a member of a fishing crew for any length of time without becoming to some extent reflective. What the outcome of such reflection is depends in key part upon varying qualities of character as well as of intelligence that individuals bring to the tasks of reflection and what those qualities of character are depends in turn upon how each particular individual has resolved the tensions between competition and cooperation.

Whynott reports on the view of those qualities taken by one Cape Cod fisherman, Robert Sampson. The danger for a tuna fisherman is an egotism that is generated by the need to have confidence in his or her own decisions, but that, by fostering a lack of confidence in others, "doom[s] cooperative ventures from the start because of lack of trust." What has to replace egotism is a confidence grounded in self-knowledge of one's individual strengths and weaknesses—a self-knowledge that not only makes one independent but enables one to contribute to cooperative enterprises and not to allow competitiveness to undermine cooperation. So envy and greed are viewed as threats. Bob Sampson's thought about what lack of such self-knowledge and lack of such independence entails is summarized by Whynott: "Otherwise you watched other people and you made your decisions according to what they were doing. . . . You became a blend of what others had thought and decided."

I am not of course suggesting—Sampson doesn't suggest, Whynott doesn't suggest—that the experiences and activities of fishing crews always have so admirable an outcome. What can go well can always go badly, and this is as true of fishing as it is of marine training. To engage in such a mode of life is never sufficient for the formation of the kind of character that enables individuals to stand back from and reflect on their desires, so that they are not, through lack of self-knowledge and self-directedness, the victims of those desires and of the influences that mold them. The question is: How difficult is it to acquire the virtues without some such mode of life?

Aristotle would have been astonished and appalled by this line of argument. Fishermen were, in his view, laborers whose banausic occupation made them unfit for citizenship and so for any part in public deliberation. And he would more generally have found it difficult to acknowledge any close connection between the nature of the occupation in which someone engages and that individual's likelihood of developing the virtues. Jefferson, by contrast, would not have been surprised: he took it that, by and large, a society of virtuous individuals, a society capable of sustaining the politics of a republic, would be a society of independent farmers. His farmers were also to act as a citizen militia, willing to put their lives on the line for the sake of their community. And in their ability to recognize the importance of both independence from and dependence upon others in their lives, the farmers envisaged by Jefferson resemble in important ways the marines described by Thomas Ricks and the fishermen described by Douglas Whynott.

If we ask what relevant features are and were shared in these three ways of life, we will soon recognize that they can be found, although with varying degrees of salience, in a considerably wider range of occupations. Those features include an ability and a willingness to take risks, possibly at great cost

to oneself, for the sake of others; the kind of integrity that jus-
tifies others in trusting one; an ability to recognize common
goods through which one's individual good is to be achieved
and to contribute to shared enterprises designed to achieve
those goods; justice in recognizing such contributions and fair-
ness in assigning merit; a desire to excel, rather than to win; an
ability to reflect upon one's own judgments and those of others, so that one becomes capable of the reflective correction of
errors of judgment; and—what I've been principally concerned
with here—an ability to focus one's desire on the relevant
common and individual goods, so that one is neither dis-
tractible nor seducible by agencies seeking to attract and focus
one's desires at the expense of one's self-knowledge and one's
independence.

It therefore becomes possible for us to ask more systemati-
cally which types of work in our society, through their structures
of training and apprenticeship and through the social relationships that engagement in them requires, provide systematic
opportunity for education into the relevant virtues; which, by
contrast, provide a setting that leaves it open to the individual
and those immediately around her or him whether or not to make
of the workplace a place of moral education; and which are, by
their nature, inimical to growth in the virtues and favorable,
therefore, to the acquisition of those vices that leave us open to
the deformation of our desires. And of course, it is not only the
activities and relationships of the workplace that conduce to or
fail to conduce to character formation. The activities and relationships of households and families are also such as to favor or
disfavor the development of character. So our inquiry will have to
widen its scope. But, having noticed the importance of proceeding with such inquiry, I put it for the moment on one side, to ask
further about the characteristics of those whose education into
some practical discipline of the relevant kind has resulted in the

self-knowledge and self-directedness that are prerequisites for independent moral agency. What kinds of moral judgments do such individuals make? What do they take to be the point and purpose of the actions of moral judgment? And what is their style of utterance?

When such individuals of character remark to themselves or to others that it is wrong to act in such and such a way, either in some particular occasion or generally, they remind themselves or those others that, by so acting, the possibility of achieving some recognized good has been obstructed or frustrated and that the individual responsible for such a wrong has defected from, has excluded her- or himself from, any relationship that is informed by such a shared recognition of goods. A moral judgment gives expression to self-criticism or to action or potential change in relationships. The utterance of such judgments presupposes that those who utter them, and those to whom they're addressed, are both able to recognize that this is how moral judgments function, just because they share, to some large degree, the same abilities and the same dispositions to recognize goods, to distinguish between objects that are desired simply qua objects of desire and objects that are desired qua goods, to rank-order goods, and to direct themselves toward the achievement of the common good. There will always, of course, be room for some measure of disagreement, but such disagreement presupposes a background of more fundamental agreement, including agreement on those means by which disagreement is, if possible, to be resolved.

Such agreement is practical, and it is, so I have claimed, the expression of the kind of character that is generally and characteristically formed only by participation in those kinds of apprenticeship and training I've attempted to characterize. Where in some particular culture such participation is widespread, there will be correspondingly widespread agreement, not only on the content of moral judgment, but also on how its point and purpose is to be understood.

Where, however, this isn't so, or is no longer so, where such widespread agreement is now lacking, we should expect to find not only diversity and disagreement in the content of moral judgments, but also a transformation in the modes of their utterance. To utter a moral judgment can no longer have the purpose of reminding ourselves, or others who share our moral dispositions and recognitions, of what it is that we share, when we have come to share too little. Instead, the utterance of moral judgments will tend to acquire just those characteristics that I identified at the beginning of this lecture. In the mouths of those whose modes of utterance are, for whatever psychological reasons, assertive and adversarial, judgment will receive its characteristic expression in speech acts of condemnation. Their utterances will become in this way acts of self-expression, the striking of individual attitudes. Others, for whom disagreement is not a stimulus to self-assertion, but instead an occasion for puzzlement and reconsideration, will, in consequence, be increasingly apt to resort to tentative modes of speech and to hedging their judgments around with qualifications. To them, those who speak in the first mode will appear unwarrantedly and intolerably dogmatic, while those who are aggressive in their judgments will take this latter mode of utterance to exhibit a reprehensible failure to stand fast on moral issues. But in neither case will moral judgment function as the expression of well-formed moral character, but rather of lack of character, a sign of thoughtlessness. And those of us who find both modes of utterance inappropriate will do best perhaps to fall silent.

For I have tried to suggest that the unhappy condition of a culture dominated by these two modes of moral utterance is not to be remedied by further pursuit of those recurrent and inconclusive debates between rival and alternative points of view that have been so central to our moral thinking since the Enlightenment, either at the level of philosophy or that of everyday moral judgment. The recovery of moral agency depends rather upon what types of practice it is in which we and others find ourselves engaging, and not on what type of theoretical standpoint we adopt. Moral theorizing does, of course, have distinctive and valuable functions, but there are times at which it may have the effect of distracting us from our practical responsibilities. And perhaps this is one of those times. Perhaps what I should have learned from my own theorizing in this lecture, and elsewhere, is no longer to give such lectures. And what you should have learned is no longer to listen to them.

A COLD DAY IN DECEMBER

(From beliefnet.com)

On a cold day in December a mother gave birth to a baby boy. Seventeen years later he sat in her kitchen with a towel around his neck while she trimmed his hair. When a boy reaches a certain age he doesn't like his mother to touch him anymore. This is as close as she's likely to get, circling him, nipping behind his pink ears with scissors.

An hour earlier Nancy hadn't known if he was alive or dead. He'd been arrested with a baggie full of drugs and swore he'd either flee to Mexico or kill himself. But on his trial date he came home one last time, to borrow his brother's shoes and have his mom trim his hair. She circles him, sifting through his hair with measuring fingers, and dark broken wisps drift to her arms like jumbled dashes.

A couple of hours later he is in the back of a police car. They must leave for the state school immediately. The boy stares stonily ahead as his parents stand outside the car, leaning together like wind-battered trees. "Say goodbye," the officer instructs. "I don't know them," the boy mutters. The car door slams and he is gone.

On a cold day in December a mother gave birth to a baby boy. Have you heard that story before?

Perhaps too many times before; it is so old, so worn, so overly familiar we can't hear it anymore. It is blunt, irrelevant. At best, it's merely cute. A friend told me about a Christmas display she saw at the mall: giant plush bears robed as Mary and Joseph, beaming at a swaddled Baby Jesus bear in the manger. If there was once grand mystery around the Incarnation, it has long since dispersed. Three jolly bears now convey everything we know or expect to know. It is a scene that is plump with stupidity. Jesus as a cookie. God as a pet.

This is very bad news.

For one thing, a circle of cuddly bears is useless at helping us deal with pain. It cannot help us grasp searing heartbreak; it cannot deflect the hard, sharp reeling pain of a car door slamming and then tail lights at the end of the road. We want a just-my-size God, fluffy and approachable, without all those picky commandments. But once we get him down to teddy-bear size we find that he is powerless. He is not able to ease our suffering or comprehend our dark confusions; he does not have strength equal to our grief. A reduced God is no God at all.

God cannot be less than we are; he must be more. Our understanding is partial and dim, but we know at least that he is greater than we are. We grasp for analogies: Some people are artists, but God is the greatest artist. Some are wise, but he is wisdom itself. Most frequently, however, we say that God is love, because love is the best thing we know.

We're more likely to say he loves like a parent than like a lover. Romantic love is dazzling, but parental love wins the prize for endurance. When we have seen heroic love, it has most likely been the love of a parent for a wandering child. Suffering parents love in the face of contempt, give despite ingratitude, keep vigil despite rejection. If fallible humans can sometimes do this, God must do it more.

On a cold, star-pierced night a frightened girl gave birth in a stable. When she carried her baby into the temple a few weeks later, an old man stopped her to say: "This child will be a sign that is spoken against. And a sword will pierce through your own soul, also."

A hidden theme of the Christmas story is suffering parental love. We recognize and understand the love Nancy has for her son, the love the Virgin Mary has for hers, and stand in awe of what mothers are prepared to endure.

But these loves are really reflections of a much vaster love, that of God the Father for all his wandering children. The greatest, most self-sacrificing earthly loves are comparatively fragile blooms sprouting from that underlying soil.

Maybe this crazy thing happened: God came down in a suit of skin and bones, and walked and talked, and offended people, and finally they tortured him to death. And by that death he destroyed death; he rescued us and gave life everlasting and every other good thing. Into this universe crammed with pain we say that God came down, because he loves us with the kind of love that we can only understand by thinking of how a parent loves.

He longs over us as over a lost and contemptuous child, a child at the edge of gaping danger, ignorant, sulky, and rude. We spurn, laugh, ignore him, pinch each other, boast "I don't know him," slam the door. And he waits.

We ridicule him, trivialize his gifts, preen and bicker. And he waits.

Maybe none of this is true. Maybe a giant hand spun us into motion and then turned away. Maybe all the cruelty of a thousand bloody centuries will never be made right, because no one outside our globe cares. Maybe the raw material of visible life is all there is—a world bursting with stunning detail but meaningless, a glove meticulously made for no warm hand. The stars are far and cold.

Later that evening Nancy looked up at the stars and thought, He's getting there about now. It's hard to come to a new place in the dark; so many buildings lined up side by side with their windows black. She thought of him lying awake in a strange bed, wondering what lay ahead. She wondered if he was scared.

She thought about her little boy.

R I C H A R D   J O H N   N E U H A U S

THE IDEA OF MORAL PROGRESS

(From *First Things*)

Almost everybody agrees that progress is a good thing. But most self-evidently good things, when examined more closely, have a way of generating disagreements. And so it is with the idea of progress, of which the idea of moral progress is part.

Thinkers arguing from the most diverse perspectives have agreed that no one thing is so characteristic, indeed constitutive, of modernity as the idea of progress. To be modern is to believe that history is "getting somewhere" in overcoming the problems and limitations of the human condition. Although muted among the secular-minded, there is also the implicit belief that getting somewhere means that history is going somewhere. Progress is more than change; it is change with a purpose. Change is the undeniable experience; the idea of progress is a way of explaining that experience. Change, it is observed, is the only thing that doesn't change. It might almost be said that change is the component of continuity that makes it possible to speak of "history" at all, and to speak of it as one thing. Without this happening and then that happening and then the other thing happening—in other words, without change—there would be no history. At the same time, it is said that history is necessarily contingent, which means that what happens does not happen necessarily. Such are among the conceptual oddities caught up in the idea of progress.

We are routinely told that ours is an age of unprecedented rapidity of change. In ethics and almost every other field, it is said that new questions require new answers. The same was likely said at the time about every age. One imagines Adam remarking to Eve as they are leaving the garden, "My dear, we are living in an age of transition." The modern assumption is that the transition is to something better. The modern sensibility unbounded is that of the neophiliac, the lover of the new. I noticed on a New York City bus an advertisement for a telecommunications company that bluntly proclaims the neophiliac creed: "Change is Good!" The unarticulated, and perhaps unconscious, assumption is that change is going somewhere; it has an end, or what the Greeks called a *telos*. In the language of philosophers, change is teleological. Change is good because it is a move to the better on the way of history toward some unspecified, and perhaps unspecifiable, good. Such is the faith of modernity.

While sensible people have problems with the simplistic proposition that change is good, they have equal difficulty with the counter-proposition that change is bad. Leaning toward one proposition or the other marks the difference between dispositions usually called conservative and liberal—or, as some prefer, progressive. Even the most progressive, however, allow that there are setbacks in history, that time is not the vehicle of smoothly incremental progress. And the most determined conservative, while suspicious of change, will nonetheless allow that there are instances of undoubted progress. To the question of whether there is progress in history, a conservative friend, a distinguished social scientist, responds with what he thinks is a decisive answer: Up until about a hundred years ago, most people went through at least half of their lives with a toothache. In our society today, few people born after 1960 know what a toothache is.

Progress in medical care, while often exaggerated, is frequently cited as the most irrefutable evidence for faith in progress itself. Also cited, with considerable justice, is economic improvement. It is no little thing that the thirty million Americans who are today officially counted as living in "poverty" have, with relatively few exceptions, a standard of living that was considered "average" only twenty-five years ago. Moreover, there is hardly a product that we buy—from cars to razor blades to a bed mattress—that, controlling for inflation, is not cheaper and better today than twenty-five years ago. And that is not to mention the many products that were not available then. I was in Cuba a while back, and walking down one of the decaying streets of Havana I tried to place this puzzling sound—a persistent clacking noise coming from a government office. It was the sound of someone using a manual typewriter, an apt symbol of what progress has left behind.

Nor need we content ourselves with medical, economic, and technological evidence of historical advance. Is there not also a phenomenon that is rightly called moral progress? In the history of our own country, we have put slavery and legally imposed racial segregation behind us, and almost nobody doubts that this counts as moral progress. More ambiguously, there are the recent decades of changing sex roles and redefinitions of the family. The proponents of such changes express confidence that their recognition as progress is only a matter of time. Also in the realm of what we might call political morality, it would seem that we have learned from the catastrophes of the past. Outside the weekend militias, very few people today advocate a regime based upon the superiority of Aryan blood; and outside our universities, very few propose the state collectivization of private property. Moreover, it is surely great progress that, at least in the West, we do not kill one another in wars of religion. Whether this is because of a decline in religious commitment or because we have come to recognize that it is the will of God that we not kill one another over our disagreements about the will of God, it is undoubtedly a very good thing. I will be returning to the claim that all such instances of moral progress are a development or unfolding of received moral wisdom—wisdom that counts as knowledge.

But the immediate point is that those who adhere to the gospel of progress are not without considerable evidence to support their faith. Yet there is no denying that faith in progress is not so robust as it once was. Apart from corporate advertisers declaring that they are in various ways "making things better," full-throated boosterism of the gospel of progress is rare today. Perhaps the most quoted poem of our time is W. B. Yeats's 1921 reflection on "The Second Coming," in which he observes that "Things fall apart; the center cannot hold." The real or imagined prospect of impending ecological collapse and the all too real proliferation of nuclear, chemical, and biological weaponry, among other things, cast a pall over the future, suggesting that, to paraphrase Eliot, the world may end with both a bang *and* a whimper.

The casting of the pall, in one telling of the story, goes back to the guns of August 1914, when it was said that the lights were going out all over the world. As a college student reading the memoirs of British philosopher Bertrand Russell, I recall being deeply impressed by his assertion that nobody who was not a child before 1914 could know what real happiness is. In his privileged and enlightened world, all good things then seemed possible, indeed inevitable. It was only a matter of time. Of the French Revolution, more than a century earlier, Wordsworth could exclaim, "Bliss was it in that dawn to be alive, / But to be young was very heaven!" Humankind seems much older now.

To be sure, in recent decades we witnessed a counterculture that, in a spasm of historical amnesia, had flower children announcing the Age of Aquarius to the tune of "the times they are a-changing." Grownups knew better, even if many felt obliged to indulge the youthful trashing of the world that they had made and that their children held in contempt. Yet those same children, now the middle-aged establishment in charge of almost everything, seem not to believe that the doctrine of historical progress has been vindicated. The Woodstock Nation was a youthful high, but it is now nostalgically remembered as a "time out" from the real world.

How can one seriously believe in progress at the end of what is undeniably the bloodiest century in history—the century of the Battle of the Somme, of Auschwitz, of the Gulag Archipelago, of Maoism, of obliteration bombing, and of mass starvation as government policy? In this century, so many people have been deliberately killed by other people that the estimates of historians vary by the tens of millions, and they end up by agreeing to split the difference or to round off the victim count at the nearest ten million. One might conclude that it has not been a good century for the idea of progress in general, and of moral progress in particular.

Shortly after World War I turned out the lights all over the world, Oswald Spengler published his two-volume *Der Untergang des Abendlandes*, known in English as *The Decline of the West*. Professional historians pilloried his scholarship, but many of the brightest and best of a generation suspected he was telling the truth, as they also succumbed to the mood of Eliot's *The Waste Land*, published in the same year as Spengler's second volume. A great depression and another world war later, after Henry Luce's "American Century" had been proclaimed and then debunked by Vietnam and all that, Robert Nisbet published, in 1980, his *History of the Idea of Progress*. Nisbet believed that, despite spasmodic eruptions of an ever more desperate optimism, the idea of progress was moribund or dead.

The idea of progress, Nisbet wrote, began with classical Greece and its fascination with knowledge, a fascination that was appropriated and put to intellectual and practical use by Christianity. From the early church fathers through the high Middle Ages and into the Puritan seventeenth century of Isaac Newton and Robert Boyle, there was a confidence that ever-expanding knowledge held the promise of something like a golden age. Although often in militantly secular form, this confidence drove also the Enlightenment, which was living off the capital of Christian faith in historical purpose. The assumed link between knowledge and progress explains what Nisbet described as the liberal belief in "education" as the panacea for human problems, paving the road to utopia. But by the 1970s, said Nisbet, all the talk was about the limits of knowledge, the end of scientific inquiry, the unreliability of claims to objective truth. The curtain was falling on the long-running show of modernity and progress. What would come to be called "postmodernity" was waiting in the wings.

For many centuries, the argument was that knowledge equals progress, and now—or at least many were saying—advances in real knowledge were coming to an end. In 1978 an entire issue of the journal *Daedalus* was devoted to articles by scientists on "The Limits of Scientific Inquiry." Not only does science no longer have the cultural and even moral authority that it once enjoyed, the contributors noted, but many scientists are filled with doubts about their own enterprise. Some went so far as to suggest that we may be witnessing a reversal of roles between science and religion, with the ascendancy of the latter in providing a stable definition of our historical circumstance.

Some years earlier, the distinguished molecular biologist Gunther Stent published under the auspices of the American Museum of Natural History a widely read little book, *The Coming of the Golden Age: A View of the End of Progress.* There is irony in his reference to a "golden age," for what he discerned was a decline or *stasis* in almost every aspect of scientific, social, and artistic life. His critique is much more subtle than just another lament about growing license and decadence. He noted, for instance, that the progress of art in modernity has been accompanied by a freedom from accepted canons and limits, and that this freedom is undoing art itself. "The artist's accession to near-total freedom of expression now presents very great cognitive difficulties for the appreciation of his work. The absence of recognizable canons reduces his act of creation to near-randomness for the perceiver. In other words, artistic evolution along the one-way street to freedom embodies an element of self-limitation."

Stent noted that a similar sense of limits, of an end of progress, is evident in the so-called hard sciences, and in his own field of molecular biology. We may view such claims with a certain skepticism. When the Sumerians invented the wheel, there were perhaps those who observed that that was the end of progress. The French historian Charles Perrault wrote in 1687: "Our age is . . . arrived at the very summit of perfection. And since for some years the rate of progress has been much slower and appears almost insensible—as the days seem to cease lengthening when the summer solstice draws near—it is pleasant to think that there are probably not many things for which we need envy future generations." History's destination had been reached, he concluded, or was close at hand.

Gunther Stent, however, spoke not from such smug complacency but from a keen appreciation of scientific facts. He traces the various stages of the ascendancy of scientific progress in understanding ever more complex phenomena. We have now, he says, arrived at "the end of progress" because we have come up against the "mind-matter paradox." Stent asks, "Is it in fact likely that consciousness, the unique attribute of the brain that appears to endow its ensemble of atoms with self-awareness, will ever be explained?" He answers that question in the negative. He suggests that the search for a "molecular" explanation of consciousness is "a waste of time." "Thus, as far as consciousness is concerned, it is possible that the quest for its physical nature is bringing us to the limits of human understanding, in that the brain may not be capable, in the last analysis, of providing [an] explanation of itself."

Today, the connections between brain, mind, and consciousness are the subject of heated debate among scientists, philosophers, and theologians. One elementary problem may be put this way: The human brain would have to be a great deal more simple than it is in order for us to understand it; but if our brain were simple enough for us to understand it, our brain would be too simple to understand it. It is something of a quandary, and that quandary hardly begins to touch on the deeper questions about the relationship between brain, mind, and consciousness.

Similar limits are becoming evident in other sciences. To cite but one obvious instance, cosmologists who study the structure of space-time relationships in the universe note that the billions of light years between ourselves and the reception of the data that we can examine mean that we never know what is happening *now* billions of light years away (or even what "now" means in this context). And the very logic of the circumstance means that it will not, it cannot, change in the future. Scientists a billion years from now, if we can imagine such a thing, will still be billions of light years away from the data accessible to their scrutiny. Even if, in ways that are not now imagined, we were able to leapfrog, so to speak, over vast spaces of time, there would always be beyond any point reached an infinity of points not reached. In other words, there is no end, and it is that realization that is at the heart of the idea of the end of progress.

I am not an astronomer or physicist or molecular biologist, but one cannot help but follow these discussions with great interest. Of most particular interest to the theologian and philosopher is the discussion of the mind-matter connection that, especially in light of what physicists call the "anthropic principle," is richly suggestive for the biblical understanding of humanity created in the image and likeness of God—we are participants, if you will, in the consciousness of God. But exploring these questions here would take us too far afield. The question at hand is the idea of progress, and how that idea is now challenged not only by events in politics, society, and culture, but also by science, which, following its own rigorous methodology, discovers that there are many things we do not know and can never know. One may object that these limits are at the margins, that there are still vast fields of discovery open to future generations. But that is the way it is with limits; they are, by definition, always at the margin. They define the margins. The crucial point is that the link between knowledge and progress that was forged in classical Greece and that, in the form we call scientific, has been both the motor and the guarantor of the modernity project has now been broken. Or so we are told by some of the more impressive thinkers of our time.

But there was something else driving the idea of progress as well. Returning to Nisbet's rather melancholic book on the subject, his epilogue asks the question, "What is the future of the idea of progress in the West?" He continues, "Any answer to that question requires answer to a prior question: What is the future of Judeo-Christianity in the West?" He notes that the great thinkers of the Enlightenment—for instance, Lessing, Kant, Herder, and Priestley—all recognized that the idea of progress is "closely and deeply united with Christianity." The same is true of the enormously influential prophets of progress. "The mature writings of Saint-Simon and Comte, both preeminent in the history of the idea of progress, bear this out. Even Mill, apparent atheist through much of his life, came in his final years to declare the indispensability of Christianity to both progress and order." As for Karl Marx, it is by now a commonplace to observe that his grand ideological structure of the dialectic of history was but a heretical variation on Christian themes.

Although Nisbet's melancholy goes deep, he expresses the hope, perhaps a wan hope, that something like a religious awakening might yet rescue the idea of progress. He saw signs of such an awakening, and twenty years later many think those signs are stronger. Nisbet quotes Yeats: "Surely some revelation is at hand?" Maybe. Maybe not. He concludes the book with this: "Only, it seems evident from the historical record, in the context of a true culture in which the core is a deep and wide sense of the *sacred* are we likely to regain the vital conditions of progress itself and of faith in progress—past, present, and future."

Progress as dogma. Progress as faith. It sounds very much like a religion—the Religion of Progress. That progress has become a false religion, indeed an idol, has been the worry of a number of Christian and Jewish thinkers in the modern era. Few have expressed that concern with such incisiveness and prophetic passion as Reinhold Niebuhr. No American theologian since Niebuhr, who died in 1971, has had such a wide influence in our intellectual culture. A champion of what was called "neoorthodoxy," Niebuhr attacked precisely the link between Judeo-Christian religion and the idea of progress that Nisbet and many others have wanted to revive. In his 1939 Gifford Lectures, *The Nature and Destiny of Man,* Niebuhr noted: "The idea of progress is possible only upon the ground of a Christian culture. It is a secularized version of biblical apocalypse and of the Hebraic sense of a meaningful history, in contrast to the meaningless history of the Greeks."

Niebuhr did not intend that as a compliment to Christian culture. His point is that the idea of progress is a cultural distortion of authentic Christianity. A staunch Protestant writing in an era before the full flowering of ecumenical etiquette, Niebuhr blamed this distortion on what he called the "Catholic synthesis" of nature and grace as that synthesis was secularized in the Renaissance and then in subsequent modernity. The secularized idea of progress emerged from the biblical understanding of purpose in history, said Niebuhr, but it broke away from the biblical truth that the fulfillment of history transcends history itself, as it also jettisoned any notion of divine judgment. The secularized story of history therefore ended up with "no consciousness of the ambiguous and tragic elements in history." It is true, said Niebuhr, that human history is filled with endless possibilities, but the idea of progress forgets that they are endless possibilities for both good and evil. "History, therefore, has no solution of its own problem."

Niebuhr was accused of offering a bleak or pessimistic view of history. He called his view "Christian realism." If, without the idea of progress, people might despair of the tasks of personal, social, and scientific advance, that too, said Niebuhr, might be to the good. There is such a thing as "creative despair" that induces faith, he said, and such faith "becomes the wisdom which makes 'sense' out of a life and history which would otherwise remain senseless." What we should have learned from the last two hundred years, and especially from the tragedies of this century, is that history is not the answer to the question that is history. Niebuhr puts the point nicely: "We have learned, in other words, that history is not its own redeemer."

One may be unpersuaded by some of Niebuhr's conclusions, but a Niebuhrian sensibility is an invaluable safeguard against the shallow sentimentalisms and utopian fantasies that have all too often afflicted thinking about history and its possibilities. Niebuhr rightly reminds us that history is not the uninterrupted triumphal march of progress. In the Christian view of things, experience both personal and social is cruciform; it is the way of the cross. At the same time, the cross is not the final word. There is resurrection, and it is both resurrection in history and resurrection of history. It is first the resurrection of the history of Jesus—and that is the foretaste, or preview, or promise of the resurrection of all things. That is surely the import of St. Paul's great cosmic hymns in, for instance, the first chapters of Ephesians and Colossians. To the Ephesians Paul writes, "For [God] has made known to us in all wisdom and insight the mystery of his will, according to his purpose which he set forth in Christ as a plan for the fullness of time, to unite all things in him, things in heaven and things on earth" (Ephesians 1:9–10).

This vision is inseparable from an emphatically Jewish understanding of the Messianic Age. The chief difference between Jews and Christians is over if, or in what way, that Messianic Age is anticipated in the person of Jesus, whom Christians call the Christ. For both Christians and Jews, past and present time participate in what Paul calls "the fullness of time." In the call of Abraham, the election of Israel, the promises given through the prophets, and (for Christians) the coming of the Christ, the plan of history is being fulfilled. Jews disagree with Jews and Christians disagree with Christians over the eschatological scenarios and apocalyptic details by which "the fullness of time" will be achieved, but all are agreed that history is not, in the words of the cynic, just one damn thing after another; history will be fulfilled in the Kingdom of God. Niebuhr is undoubtedly right to say that "history is not its own redeemer." But the biblical view— a view that is utterly formative for Western culture in both its religious and secular expressions—is that history does have a Redeemer, and that the Redeemer is, however veiled and sometimes hidden, present and active in history itself.

And, ecumenical etiquette notwithstanding, it must be admitted that Niebuhr's very Protestant reading of history is in tension, if not in conflict, with the "Catholic synthesis." In our own time, that synthesis is energetically set forth by the pontificate of John Paul II. In October 1998, the Pope issued his thirteenth encyclical, *Fides et Ratio* (Faith and Reason), in which he powerfully affirms that there can be no conflict between faith and reason, between science and religion, between philosophy and revelation; all truths are one because God, the source and end of all truth, is one. Human beings are by nature seekers after truth, and revelation provides the ultimate "horizon" of that search. The Word of God, or the *logos* that is the ordering reason of all things, is incarnate in history and is the guarantee that the search for truth is not in vain. Not until the final End Time will we know the truth perfectly, but along the way both believers and unbelievers who honestly seek for the truth according to the rules of science and reason will be vindicated.

This is surely an audacious vision, but is it a doctrine of progress? The answer is no and yes. If by progress we mean a smooth, incremental, and almost automatic movement in time from worse to better, from ignorance to enlightenment, the answer is certainly no. If, however, by progress we mean that human beings are free agents who are capable of participating in the transcendent purpose that is immanent in history and holds the certain promise of vindicating all that is true, good, and beautiful, then the answer is certainly yes.

Moral progress may be a quite different matter, however. We have already noted the events of this century that have so brutally battered the idea of moral progress. We should at least be open to the possibility that we are today witnessing not moral progress but a dramatic moral regression. While, as we have seen, practitioners in the hard sciences express a new humility about the limits of their knowledge and control, many who work in the field of ethical theory and practice exhibit an unbounded hubris. For instance, Princeton University recently gave a distinguished chair in ethics to the Australian ethicist Peter Singer. Singer is famous, or infamous, for his championing of animal rights as equal or superior to human rights, and for his proposal, among other things, that there should be a trial period of one month after the birth of human babies in which those who are defective may be legally killed. Because of his advocacy of infanticide and eugenics, Singer has been denied platforms in German universities, where there is a more vivid historical memory of such arguments and their consequences.

As the decision of Princeton suggests, Singer is no marginal figure in our intellectual culture. He is also author of the main article on ethics, a full twenty pages, in the fifteenth edition of the *Encyclopedia Britannica.* From Confucius and Aristotle, to Maimonides and Aquinas, through Hume and Kant to Peter Singer, the article traces the liberation of moral theory and practice from any truths that pose an obstacle to our will to power and control. The gist of it is caught in the title of Singer's 1995 book, *Rethinking Life and Death: The Collapse of Our Traditional Ethics* (St. Martin's). That Singer does not regret the collapse of what he dismissively refers to as traditional ethics is evident in the chilling conclusion of his *Britannica* article: "The culmination of such advances in human reproduction will be the mastery of genetic engineering. . . . Perhaps this will be the most challenging issue for twenty-first-century ethics." Singer leaves no doubt that he welcomes the challenge and the brave new world it portends. The cosmologists and molecular biologists—those who are bound by the disciplines of scientific method—reach the end of knowledge, at which point they fall silent in what might be viewed as a recognition of human creatureliness. Ethical theorists—bound by no such disciplines—reach the end of knowledge, at which point anything can be said, and anything can be done.

For a dramatically different account of the history of ethics and its progress or regress, we have Alasdair MacIntyre's much discussed and eminently readable little book, *After Virtue*—in my judgment, one of the most important books on moral philosophy published in this century. For MacIntyre, the account of moral theory and practice offered by people such as Singer, which is the dominant account in the academy today, results in a rationalized ethics that has broken loose from any tradition of virtue or truth—from our *knowledge* of virtue and truth. The stark choice facing us, MacIntyre says, is a choice between Aristotle or Nietzsche, between a tradition of virtue, on the one hand, and moral nihilism, on the other. The various intellectual dispositions that today run under the banner of "postmodernism" have quite consciously opted for nihilism. The hubris of Enlightenment rationalism that Niebuhr rightly criticized has given way to the hubris of postmodernity's irrationalism. Secular rationalism tried to do too much, but can rationally recognize when it fails. Irrationalism has no access to such humility.

In the view of MacIntyre and others, the Enlightenment project has failed on its own terms. Despite monumental efforts, perhaps the greatest of which is that of Immanuel Kant, it failed to produce an ethics to which any rational person, acting rationally, must give assent. Society was for a time able to live off the capital of earlier traditions of virtue, but now that capital has been depleted, the failure of the Enlightenment project has been widely advertised, and the time has come round at last for the triumph of nihilism. In this reading, postmodernity is the product of failed modernity, and the nihilistic avant garde is a regression to the rule of the barbarians. Barbarians today, as in classical Greece, are defined as those who are outside the civilizational circle of conversation about how we ought to order our life together, about the meaning of right and wrong, good and evil. They are those who know nothing, and insist that nothing can be known, about such matters.

Recall the concluding passage of *After Virtue.* MacIntyre draws the parallel between our time and the collapse of the Roman Empire when St. Benedict's monastic movement provided a refuge for civilization. "What matters [now] is the construction of local forms of community within which civility and the intellectual and moral life can be sustained through the new dark ages which are already upon us. And if the tradition of the virtues was able to survive the horrors of the last dark ages, we are not entirely without grounds for hope. This time, however, the barbarians are not waiting beyond the frontiers; they have already been governing us for quite some time. And it is our lack of consciousness of this that constitutes part of our predicament. We are waiting not for a Godot, but for another—doubtless very different—St. Benedict."

We may think that picture somewhat overdrawn. After all, those who are called barbarians are not primitives, they are not neanderthals; they are frequently those thought to be the "brightest and best" among us. But that is to miss the point. The new barbarians are barbarians not because they are unsophisticated but precisely because of the hyper-sophistication with which they have removed themselves from what I have called the civilizational circle of moral conversation. In simpler terms, that is called "traditional values." The barbarians refuse to be limited by what we know, by the wisdom we have received, about good and evil, right and wrong. For them, the past is *merely* prelude.

What, then, can we say about the future of moral progress? Within the civilizational circle, there is moral progress (and regress!) in how we live, but there is no progress in the sense of moving beyond the moral truths that constitute the circle itself. We can develop the further implications of those truths, or we can step outside the circle by denying that there is such a thing as moral truth. It has become the mark of hyper-sophistication in our time to echo the question of Pontius Pilate, "What is truth?" Pontius Pilate, an urbane Roman ever so much more sophisticated by worldly standards than the prisoner who stood before him, was a forerunner of the barbarians now in power.

Those permanent truths are sometimes called natural law. In the Declaration of Independence they are called the laws of nature and nature's God. Or they are called the first principles of ethics. First principles are, by definition, always first. Moral analysis cannot go beyond or behind them any more than human consciousness can go beyond or behind human consciousness. Fifty years ago, C. S. Lewis, borrowing from Confucianism, called these first principles the Tao. In *The Abolition of Man*, he anticipated with great prescience today's debates in biomedical ethics about reproductive technologies, genetic engineering, and eugenic progress. The Tao, Lewis said, draws support from all religious and moral traditions in inculcating certain rules such as: general beneficence toward others, special beneficence toward one's own community, duties to parents and ancestors, duties to children and posterity, the laws of justice, honesty, mercy, and magnanimity. Whether drawn from the Torah, the Sermon on the Mount, Chinese *Analects*, Cicero, or the *Bhagavad Gita*, these are the truths that constitute the civilizational circle.

Like all tradition, the Tao is vulnerable. Those who want to violate it ask, "Why not?" and it is not always possible to give a rationally convincing answer, or an answer that is convincing to everybody. In response to the assertion of rules that set limits, the avant garde offers the challenge, "Sez who?" and the invoking of authority, even of the most venerable authority, carries little weight in our time. Most corrosive is what is called the hermeneutics of suspicion, in which every rule or law or custom is perceived to have behind it some hidden purpose, some power protecting its own interests. Thus the Tao is debunked, we "see through" its supposed authority, and the force of its commands and limits is "explained away." The result is what Peter Singer approvingly calls the collapse of traditional ethics. Lewis had a keen appreciation of what was happening in our intellectual culture. Recall again that remarkable passage from *The Abolition of Man*:

But you cannot go on "explaining away" forever: you will find that you have explained explanation itself away. You cannot go on "seeing through" things forever. The whole point of seeing through something is to see something through it. It is good that the window should be transparent, because the street or garden beyond it is opaque. How if you saw through the garden too? It is no use trying to "see through" first principles. If you see through everything, then every-thing is transparent. But a wholly transparent world is an invisible world. To "see through" all things is the same as not to see.

To which many of our contemporaries say, "Precisely. To see through the first principles of ethics is to see nothing, which means to see that there is nothing except what *we will* to do; and, if there is nothing, all things are permitted." So speak the barbar-ians among us. Whether they rule us to the degree that MacIntyre suggests, I do not know. Whether they will rule us in the future depends upon our ability to argue—and to give public effect to the argument—that there is such a thing as moral *knowledge*. It is in the nature of knowledge that we can argue endlessly about what we know and how we know it. Or at least we can argue until, in the happy phrase of 1 Corinthians 13, we finally know even as we are known. Lewis's Tao provides one minimal founda-tion for such argument. My suspicion is that, while it is useful, it is too minimal; that a firmer and publicly effective understanding of natural law and first principles requires the specific acknowl-edgment of the God of Israel and the achievement of the Greeks, as these find expression in what is rightly called the Judeo-Christian moral tradition. That particularist tradition provides the most solid foundation for a truly universal ethic. But that is a discussion for another time.

The answer to the question of whether the barbarians will rule us in the future depends upon parents, religious leaders, edu-cators, scientists, politicians, artists, and writers who are not embarrassed to give public expression to what they know about right and wrong, good and evil. The first proponents of the idea of progress, including moral progress, were right to believe that knowledge and progress are inseparable. There can be no progress *beyond* but only *within* the civilizational circle of the moral truths into which we were born, by which we are tested, and to which we are duty bound, in the hope of sustaining the circle for those who come after us. The alternative is the willed ignorance of nihilism.

WINDOWS ON FIRE
(From *Books & Culture*)

Saturday, 2:19 P.M.
Saint Jean-Baptiste Church
76th & Lexington Avenue

I understand as soon as I walk through the door and see the enormous windows on either side of me: stained glass is one form of
art that should never be taken out of context. In a museum, it is
exquisite but empty. I can't understand it placed in front of a light
box with a printed caption tacked below. In a sacred place, it
takes on a new dimension; I can almost sense the thousands of
faithful who have prayed here, looking beyond the glowing
mosaic of color to the Truth that lies beneath.

This church is one of many in the city dating to an era when
a church without stained glass was almost unthinkable. Right
away, the four huge windows on each side draw me in. The central arch soars into a dome at the far end, with smaller circular
windows around its perimeter.

It's very quiet here. (I'm trying to take off my jacket with a
minimum of rustling.) A scattered handful of worshipers sit or
kneel in the vast expanse of the sanctuary. I walk to the rows of
votives to light one; much to my dismay, I find that they are elec-
tric. Little lightbulbs are fastened in the top of the red plastic,
and by pushing a button you can turn one on. How convenient.

The windows are a curious mix of biblical and contemporary scenes: "Piux X and Frequent Communion" faces the Annunciation. The former depicts the pope administering wafers and sips of wine to nine small children. The scene is not very realistic— they look awfully well behaved for little kids. I think of the children I've seen in church, the ones who wrinkle their noses or turn their heads and purse their lips when their parents hold them up to the chalice.

The faces of most of the people depicted in the windows are expressionless. It's a relief to come upon a scene charged with emotion: in "The Manna," a cloud hovers near the top of the window while Moses gestures with ferocity toward the ground, where the Israelites, grateful and fearful, gather up the bread. Perhaps he is warning them about taking more than they will use. In "The Washing of the Feet," Jesus bends low over the feet of one of his disciples. He and the disciple are intent, concentrating on each other. A rapport exists there, but nowhere else in the group.

There are mosaics on the wall under the windows, including one in which Jesus is condemned to death. Pilate is stone-faced, unmoving. "What is truth?" he asks defiantly. His eyes, though, reveal a deeper understanding of what he has tried to get around. "The Wedding Feast at Cana" is next. Jesus points at the jars, and Mary looks adoringly at him: "Do whatever He tells you." Here, as in many of the designs, the people look conspicuously unreal, especially the soldiers in the foreground; their stagy poses detract from the simple power of the design. And there seem to be too many colors in each window, crowding each other, as if the artist didn't trust himself or the power of his medium.

The silence is broken by a man entering the church; he makes a snippy remark to the homeless man slumped in a corner, dozing. I want to ask the scolder what he's here for. When he leaves, I take the dollar that I was going to use for a candle and leave it on the corner of the sleeping man's jacket.

3:51 P.M.
Marble Collegiate Church
3 West 29th Street

Entering this church is like entering a place of business; I have to go to the receptionist and ask to be shown into the sanctuary. She seems unwilling: "I'm sorry, but the man who gives the tours isn't here today." No, I explain, I don't need a tour; I just want to see the stained glass. She still doesn't trust me. Finally, after I'm reduced to begging, she calls the janitor and asks him to let me in.

He doesn't speak much English, but he tries anyway to give me the formal explanation of the history of the building. We enter the worship space; immediately, I don't like the layout. The chancel is laden with gaudy gold-painted figures, fake plants, and three of something that looks like an overly decorated throne. A balcony runs round the top of the church, cutting the windows—five on each side—about two-thirds down. Only three are of any interest: two were installed in 1900 by Tiffany Studios, and one was just unveiled last year. The most recent one is very Pentecostal: hootin', hollerin' worship.

There is much more emotion in this one piece than in the whole collection I just visited—but I'm not sure I like it. It's a little overdone. In the foreground, three children—one black, one white, one Asian—smile together in racial harmony. Okay, it's *much* too overdone.

The Tiffany windows are breathtaking; they display the artistry of a master. On the left is Joshua at the battle of Gibeon, where the sun stood still for 36 hours so that the Israelites could finish winning their battle. Here are fields of massacred soldiers, the heat and sweat of battle, and Joshua leading his men to victory. The design is in the color and texture of the glass, not in the painting behind it. There are many more colors than in the previous set, but they are so subtle that the design isn't choked by them. They are alive, rippling and full. Joshua has lots of yellows, oranges, browns, with a little purple and blue; next to him, Moses' colors are much cooler. They complement one another well.

The window on the right shows the burning bush: not an American bush, a fluffy ball of green, but a withered brown tree with blue flames shooting from it. Moses kneels, barefoot. Above him, the sky is a mixture of pink and royal blue, the trees as lush and verdant as the cave is dry and barren. "This is holy ground." I'm deeply absorbed in thought when the janitor suddenly claps his hands. "All right, your time has expired," he says with a cheerful smile. I look at my watch; it's been 15 minutes. "I have to go," he says, steering me to the door. I ask if I can have a few more minutes. "No, I can't leave you here alone," he says. Rules are rules, I suppose, even in God's house.

5:14 P.M.
Judson Memorial Baptist Church
Washington Square South & Thompson

After my last experience, I call first, but there is no answer. I decide to chance it anyway, and just as I'm about to stop ringing the bell, a man hollers at me from another door. "Miss?" I ask to see the La Farge stained glass, and he looks uneasy. As a last resort, I tell him I'm writing for a magazine. Finally, he opens the door. "You're making it tough on me, y'understand?" I thank him profusely, and he softens a bit. He even leaves me alone in the sanctuary.

As I enter, I inhale sharply: here is beauty. The area is dark and empty with a piano in the corner. The caretaker has turned the lights on for me, but after he leaves, I sneak back and turn them off. In the dark, the stacks of folding chairs and recording equipment become shapeless forms, and I can enjoy the vast emptiness of this sacred space.

There is something so much more churchlike about an empty floor like this one. On Sunday morning it will be littered with metal folding chairs, but for now there is wonderful solitude in the openness. I cough once, and the acoustics are so amazing that I'm tempted to throw the cover off the piano and launch into a Chopin prelude.

The sun is just about to set, and the windows are on fire. The colors are bursting out of the walls. The designs are simple, elegant, and very powerful: portraits from the Old and New Testaments, with rectangle-tiled patterns covering the bottom third of the panes. The colors are carefully chosen and clear; they mean something. The figures are haloed, in prayerful gesture; there is a silence about them that speaks much louder than all the emotion of the Bible-thumping revivalists.

The portrait of Samuel is especially touching. The caption reads: "Speak, Lord, for thy servant heareth." I imagine a young boy saying these words in the middle of the night to One he didn't know or understand. This window was donated in memory of "a friend of children."

I sit in the quiet darkness and drink in the burning colors until the light from the setting sun dwindles, and then I exit the way I came in. The man who admitted me reluctantly is friendly now and shakes my hand on the way out. "Take care."

WHAT SHALL WE DO WITH MOTHER?

(From *Books & Culture*)

One day a year or so ago, my father found my mother lying on the bedroom floor where she had fallen while tucking in a sheet. Her collarbone, they discovered at the emergency room, had snapped when she fell, an entirely predictable consequence of her combined ailments—Parkinson's disease and osteoporosis. Something else appeared to have broken in my mother as well, however. Confused and fearful, she took to wandering from room to room at night, looking for intruders. My father, 80 years old and profoundly deaf, felt helpless to deal with the rapidly deteriorating circumstances of their lives.

Since then, my husband and I have moved back to Texas and now live just down the road from my parents. During the past nine months, my father has had three operations, including a triple bypass. Between the two of them, they have seen a total of 12 different doctors over the past year. I have become an expert at reading medical billings, insurance claims, and Medicare statements. My computer's Web browser is bookmarked for a number of disease and medication sites. The learning curve for me has been Matterhorn-steep, however. At first I didn't even know the difference between Medicare and Medicaid.

My parents are scrupulous people who wanted to cause their children as little trouble as possible. Since I am the executor of their wills, they long ago gave me copies, as well as a key to their safety deposit box. They made sure I knew where to find their insurance policies. I was present when they planned and paid for their funerals. We had all prepared for death. What we hadn't prepared for was decline. I soon found that I needed a crash course in what is almost as inevitable as death—caring for aging parents. Kübler-Ross may have taught my generation the five stages of grief, but no one had told us about the long good-bye.

Nor was I alone in facing this largely ignored crisis ignorant and unarmed. Just last night, for instance, my friend Ted called me from Pennsylvania. He mentioned that while his stepfather and mother were visiting for the holidays, the stepfather had suffered a stroke. After his release from the hospital, the elderly couple returned to Georgia. Nevertheless, Ted doesn't think his stepfather is long for this world.

"So, what are you going to do then?" I ask.

"What do you mean?" he says after a long pause.

"I mean, what will your mother do then?"

No pause this time, just a long drawn-out "Wellll . . ." as Ted considers this, obviously for the first time. "I don't think she'd live in that house by herself. There's five acres to mow, and I'm not sure she'd be safe alone."

"Have you talked with your brother and sister about this?"

"No," he says, sounding a little uneasy. "But I don't think Mother would want to leave Georgia. All her friends are there." Ted's sister lives in Cleveland. His brother lives in Georgia, but, since he is on probation for transporting stolen pecans, he's not likely to be much help.

"Well?" I persist.

"Of course, my sister would be glad to have her. We would, too, for that matter, but," and again he speculates that his mother wouldn't want to leave Georgia.

I admonish him to talk the situation over with his sister and even his black-sheep brother before his stepfather's next stroke catches them all flat-footed. In fact, I now urge all my fiftysomething friends to ponder their parents' future. For, unless you are an orphan or thoroughly estranged from your parents—and those of your spouse—the chances are that you'll be facing such a crisis sooner or later, if you haven't already.

If you doubt this prediction, poll your own friends who are over 50. You will probably be as surprised as I was to discover how many of them are already wrestling with this problem. Of course, their stories will be as diverse as the individuals who tell them. The particulars are not predictable, only the overall pattern.

My friend Jessie, for instance, turned 60 this year. Twice divorced, she directs a small nonprofit foundation at a private college a thousand miles distant from the small town where she grew up. Jessie's father died in 1978, and her mother, at 95, still lives in the family home. Jessie's brother lives with her; he moved in after returning from combat in Vietnam. A bachelor, he spends a good part of every day drinking at the local VFW.

Jessie either flies or drives across three states to visit her mother several times a year. On her last visit, she found the house filthy and the yard overgrown with weeds. Stacks of bills mixed with advertising flyers spilled off the dining table. She had hardly set down her suitcase before the phone rang.

"Welcome home," her brother said. "I'm at a motel. There's an extra key on the window sill over the kitchen sink. Just put it back there when you leave. I need a break."

A neighbor confided to Jessie that her mother might not be getting enough to eat, so Jessie arranged for a woman to come in every day, do some cleaning, and make Jell-O and soup for her mother. Jessie did not discuss this arrangement with her brother. She fears he might resent her interference, and in the past he has refused to use his mother's money to hire help. So Jessie sends a check every month to the neighbor, who pays the housekeeper.

My friend Florence, also divorced, sees after the needs of her father and widowed stepfather, both in their eighties. Her father has, for the past 50 years, lived alone in Houston until last year. Long before his health and memory began to decline, he made both his daughters swear they would never take him into their homes. But after his second minor car accident, Florence moved him into an apartment about ten minutes from her house and hired a college student to drive for him and help him with shopping. On most days, her father still thinks he's living in Houston.

She has taken him to the hospital emergency room twice so far, both times for cuts he got in falls. For the past two weeks she has gone twice a day to change the dressing on an abscessed cyst on his back.

"Why not get a home health-care nurse to do that?" I ask.

"He wouldn't let a stranger in the door," she says. "And for Daddy, even the same nurse would be a stranger every time."

Florence pays the bills and arranges doctor appointments for both her father and her stepfather, who has survived a stroke. Florence has durable power-of-attorney for both her charges and keeps the documents handy in the glove compartment of her car, along with the "Directive to Physicians" specifying that they are not to be put on life-support systems.

I have similar papers now for both my parents. Jim, the rector at my church, advised me, soon after I returned to care for my parents, to arrange not only for durable power-of-attorney, which would allow me to handle their financial affairs, but also power-of-attorney for health care. As the elder of two sons, Jim had learned this lesson the hard way a decade earlier when his father, sinking into dementia, had to be admitted to a nursing home.

"But your mother is still alive. Why didn't she handle it?" I asked.

"She just refused to deal with it. She was simply overwhelmed, so she tried to ignore the situation, even though it was dangerous for both of them," he said, shaking his head. "I had to go before the judge to get my father declared incompetent before I could get him into a place where he'd be taken care of adequately. You don't want to have to go through that trauma if you can possibly avoid it."

Colleen and Carrie were schoolteachers who never married. In their fifties, the two women moved back to the family home to care for their widowed mother after she developed Parkinson's disease. A brother lives in the same town but has school-age children, a condition that exempted him from primary responsibility for his mother's care. Not long after their mother's disease began seriously to erode her functioning, Colleen was diagnosed with cancer. After a couple years of surgery, chemotherapy, and a desperate pursuit of alternative cures, she died.

Carrie continues to work to support herself and her mother. Since her mother cannot be left alone, Carrie first tried a combination of home health-care workers and "sitters," but their schedules proved too unreliable. Also, Medicare funds for home health care have recently been cut back.

After much agonizing over the decision, Carrie moved her mother to a local nursing home. A few weeks later she brought her mother home again. Both her mother and her brother had been unhappy with the arrangement, and the expense was eating up their combined resources. (Contrary to what many middle-aged innocents believe, Medicare does not pay for long-term nursing home care.) Recently Carrie has found a couple who care for six patients in their home. By supplementing her mother's social security checks, she can just afford this arrangement.

Thirteen million Americans presently care for their aging relatives in their homes. That number includes none of the friends I have mentioned above. Nor would I count in that official census of "caregivers." Thus, I figure that the number of people who have made major changes in their lives and spend a good part of the day helping with aging parents is at least twice that large. And I also suspect that their new role came to most of them as a complete surprise.

Very few parents, I suspect, actually sit down with their grown children and talk about what's going to become of them when they get old and infirm. Once they edge past 60, they find themselves using the stark words "old" or even "elderly" less frequently, even though they may still joke about failing memory and "senior moments." At 70, however, they often greet references to Alzheimer's and Depends with prickly rejoinders that old age comes to us all eventually. Their friends and children must tender offers of help with increasing diplomacy.

For their part, very few children are willing to face, much less force, the issue with either their parents or their siblings. And not simply because they fear being thought ghoulish or insensitive. What we fear goes much deeper. Parents—mothers especially— are the oldest things we know about the world. They are an archetypal necessity in the structure of our universe. When they begin to weaken, we feel the foundations tremble.

Faced with our parents' inevitable decline and mortality, we must choose then between causing pain by broaching unpleasant realities or conspiring in the dangerous illusion that everyone maintains good health and mental competence until the moment we draw our last breath.

But making the hard choice gets even more complicated if we must take into account the wishes and fears of our siblings—and perhaps those of our parents' siblings as well. Decades of accrued family history have already tangled the strings of attachment, preference, personalities. Finances, geographical proximity, spouses, and jobs must all be factored into decisions. The combinations of complications seem endless. And for the child who volunteers or is elected to care for an aging parent, always and at bottom lies the daunting prospect of an open-ended personal commitment that could last for decades. Middle-aged children remember all too clearly what it's like to be tied to toddlers and teenagers. Now the care of an ill and elderly parent could rob us of our last chance at personal autonomy and freedom.

On the other hand, we may remember how our grandparents were cared for within the extended family. Perhaps we've seen our own mothers take on this responsibility. Don't we owe them the same consideration? If they could do it, why shouldn't we?

The Cultural Context

In 1900, when the United States was still largely an agricultural society, two out of three men over 65 were still working and supporting a household. By 1984, that figure had dropped to only one in six. The other five have "retired." Obviously, men do not quit working at a younger age now because their jobs are more physically demanding than milking cows and plowing fields. A variety of economic and social forces brought about this change, most notably the Social Security Act, which specifies 65 as the age at which one can collect full benefits from the system. We may not have invented the concept of retirement in this century, but we have certainly defined it more dogmatically than any previous generation. But whereas retirement used to carry the stigma of "being put out to pasture," we have made it desirable, a goal to work toward. This shift in attitude has also altered the way elderly parents are cared for.

Agricultural economies are, of necessity, geographically stable. Grown children stick around instead of absconding to distant cities. Typically, families in agricultural societies care for their aging members, even when the patriarch is no longer able to do much but sit in the sun. To some extent, economics accounts for this age-friendly arrangement. In Ethiopia, where the Sidamo live by herding sheep and goats and cultivating maize and bananas, the older generation maintains such a tight grip on the means of production that their culture has been labeled "gerontocratic."

Such cultures, organized around the extended family, from Hellenistic Greece to prewar Japan, have generally been willing to support those members no longer able to work. Even the socialistic People's Republic of China, still largely dependent on agriculture, made it a legal requirement for children "to support and assist their parents."

During most of our country's history, family-owned farms operated somewhat like corporations, with grandfather as the CEO and chief stockholder, while his grown sons were upper-level managers and his grandchildren supplied much of the work force. Thus, aging landowners maintained some degree of legal and social control that today's retiree cannot command.

Ethical values derived from the Bible were shared by large segments of the agrarian population. The fifth of the Ten Commandments, for instance, links filial responsibility to the land: "Honor thy father and mother that thy days may be long upon the land which the Lord thy God giveth thee." Paul later pointed out to the Ephesians (as my mother often has to me) that this is the first commandment "with promise."

The Old Testament emphasizes that great age was a sign of special favor in the epoch before Noah, and many of Israel's early heroes achieved impressive feats in their latter days. Abram, for instance, was just setting out on his lifelong trek around Mesopotamia at the age of 75. Not until we reach the Psalms are we told that "three score years and ten"—or in exceptional cases, "fourscore"—marks the reasonable limit of life's expectancy.

Nevertheless, nowhere in the Old Testament, with the possible exception of the self-mocking Ecclesiastes, do we find the infirmity of old age ridiculed for its own sake the way it often is in Greek and Roman literature.

Remarkably little is said about old age in the New Testament, perhaps because so few of the chief players survived that long. The Gospel of Luke shows us Anna and Simeon, both exemplars of messianic hope, surviving into old age. From Jesus' picture of Peter's fate at the conclusion of John's gospel, we infer that the apostle lived to a ripe, if not particularly comfortable, old age. Jesus' own dilemma about what to do with Mother must have dogged him throughout his earthly career. As eldest son, he was responsible for his widowed mother's well-being, a duty that his younger siblings must have rebuked him for neglecting. And indeed, he was at pains to tie up this domestic loose thread, even as he hung dying on the cross.

Though the early church made provision for elderly widows, it was in the early Middle Ages that monasteries began to establish infirmaries for indigent old people. Some fiefdoms and parishes likewise provided pensions for the elderly. But as successive assaults of the bubonic plague carried off disproportionate numbers of children and young adults, the demographics of Europe became distorted (much as our own population will be in the next few decades by aging baby boomers). An overload of elderly citizens and a dearth of younger workers resulted in generational conflicts.

The medieval church tried to defend the elderly against the resentment of the young by insisting that old age was a valuable period of preparation for death, a time to review and rectify one's soul before presenting it to God. In his *Convivio*, Dante compares one's proper activity during these last years to that of a boat slipping peacefully into harbor following its long voyage. At the same time, he preserves the psalmist's upper lifespan limit of 80 years, claiming that Jesus, had he not been crucified, would nevertheless have been translated directly to heaven when he turned 81.

During the Renaissance, a "youth culture" every bit as pervasive as our own elevated the kind of strength and beauty that belongs only to the young. Old age was generally regarded as an aesthetic affront. Thomas More, one of the few Renaissance writers sympathetic to the aged and who supported a poorhouse for old men out of his own pocket, tried to find a suitable place for the elderly in his *Utopia*. In this ideal state where reason reigned, aged citizens were to be treated with respect and given suitable work to do. However, when they would become absolutely too decrepit to benefit the community, More, a Catholic so devout he died for his faith, nevertheless felt they should have the good grace to commit suicide!

Lorenzo Tonti, a Neapolitan banker of the seventeenth century, was more practical. He invented an age lottery that operated something like an office football pool—the precursor to our modern life insurance and annuity policies. The church, however, opposed this speculating on the life and death of human beings as a gross usurpation of divine privilege. But once the plague no longer decimated the population, the workforce swelled once more and annuities became a popular investment.

At about the same time, care for the aged infirm began to migrate from families to national governments. In 1601, the British Parliament passed the first Poor Law, which assigned to parishes the care of the elderly indigent within their geographical jurisdiction. In 1880, the first social security system was put in place by Germany to compensate infirm workers for loss of income. Great Britain adopted old-age pensions in 1908. A couple of decades later, in response to the Great Depression's effect on the elderly, the United States set up the Federal Old Age Insurance system. But social security checks, which now make up the major source of income for old people in the United States, are often inadequate to meet basic needs. Consequently, a disproportionate percentage of the nation's elderly live below the poverty line.

Lest we grow nostalgic for a land-based economy where older parents retained economic power and social control, it should be pointed out that the younger members not only of the Sidamo in Ethiopia but also the Chaggas of northern Tanzania, the Zulus of South Africa, and the Swazi tribes show ambivalent attitudes toward their elders. Generational conflicts over inheritance and use of farmland sometimes lead to fratricide and clan warfare—as indeed was the case with the Old Testament stories of Cain and Abel, Joseph and his brothers, and Isaac and Ishmael, the longest-running family feud in the history of the world. How to care for the infirm elderly is not an equation easily solved by any culture.

The Death of an Illusion

In 1946, the year after the war ended and the exodus of the young to the cities began, Edwin Muir, the Scottish poet and critic, used Shakespeare's tragedy *King Lear* as the lens through which to focus on how "the old generation and the new are set face to face, each assured of its own right to power." Lear's daughters, Goneril and Regan, Muir points out, consider themselves blameless. In fact, they see their father as "merely an old man who thinks and feels in a way they cannot understand, and [who] is a burden to them."

How much our current culture has adopted this attitude is evident in the way Jane Smiley reversed Shakespeare's *King Lear* in her novel *A Thousand Acres*. Here, the daughters are the victims of an autocratic and abusive patriarch. One daughter dies from the effects of her father's pesticides and the other two drift into urban isolation. They are freed from his power only by the loss of the land itself.

If industrialization isolated the elderly, where are they to find a foothold in today's electronic ether? In less than 20 years, from

1975 to 1993, the number of Americans over 65 who live with their adult children declined by half, dropping from 18 percent to less than 10 percent. There are doubtless many reasons for this decrease, from the improved health of older Americans to the number of two-or-more-job households. Nevertheless, a third of the over-65 population live entirely alone. One might expect the older that people get—and thus the more help they need—the more likely they are to live with one of their children. Just the reverse is true. If you make it to 85, the odds of your living alone jump to one in two.

I have noticed the tone of pride and satisfaction with which middle-aged children in America announce that their 80- or 90-year-old mother "still lives in her own house," as if voluntary isolation were the pinnacle of geriatric heroism. In other parts of the world, however, people would find this arrangement both strange and shameful. Most older people on this planet today live close to, if not in the household with, their children. At least until the last couple of decades, three-quarters of Japan's middle-aged children cared for their aging parents in their homes—almost eight times the rate in this country. In China, despite the deconstruction of traditional Confucian ethics by the half-century of communism, almost all old people still live with their sons' families. One researcher found only ten elderly people living apart from their families in a collective village of 40,000.

A bewildered delegate to a U.S.-China writers' conference once asked the American author Annie Dillard, "The old people in the United States—they *like* to live alone?"

No doubt some of them do. Or at least some of them prefer living alone to the changes and compromises that living with others entails. Independence is, after all, the chief and most honored virtue in this country. The ideal, ingrained in us early, persists even when we can, quite literally, no longer "stand on our own two feet." When our aging parents' need for help grows too obvious to ignore, we say they are beginning to "fail." Losing one's independence is, for Americans, a shameful thing. And needing help, we know, evokes in our potential benefactors pity, frustration, and fear—in roughly equal parts.

Independence. Autonomy. Isolation. On this unstable trinity the lives of older Americans are precariously balanced. But if you live long enough, independence inevitably becomes an illusion. Slowly the edges of your sovereign island start to erode. You can no longer keep up with the yard work, so you move to a condominium or even a retirement center. You can't see well enough to drive anymore. The checkbook gets tangled in knots, the Medicare maze impossible to negotiate. You call the pharmacy, and a computerized voice gives so many instructions about pushing phone buttons you hang up in despair.

Seeking help with these mundane chores of living means surrendering control as well. If you ask others to take you to the grocery store, you must fit your shopping to their schedule and preference for supermarkets. Rely on Meals on Wheels to deliver your dinner and you have to accept unfamiliar dishes. If your daughter volunteers to clean your house, you can't point out to her, the way you could when she was a teenager, the dust she missed. After a lifetime of doing and having things your own way, you may have to work at feeling—or even faking—gratitude.

Of course, the fear of losing control of one's own life afflicts middle-aged children—my generation—as well. We are as skittish about pledging an unknown number of years to the care of our increasingly needy parents as they are about surrendering their autonomy. No wonder it typically takes a crisis to break through the stolid denial both generations erect to shield themselves from the obvious. A parent has a heart attack or a wreck, falls ill or just down, often in a distant city or several states away. You rush there, shocked not only by the disaster, but by the deteriorated living situation. How could things have gotten so bad without your knowing about it?

You call your siblings, if they make reliable allies, and only then do you talk about what you're going to do about Mother or Dad. Despite the fact that this is one of the most predictable prospects you will have to face in your lifetime, no one has prepared for it. It comes as a complete surprise that Something Will Have to Be Done. Not next year, but next week. Or even tomorrow. You mentally inventory the entire family for the most flexible schedule, the most plentiful resources, the most compassionate or cooperative spouse. And no matter how much you love your parents and want to see them well cared for, you feel your own stomach clench as you try to imagine the future. Two sets of people, each with deep though unspoken fears and reservations, must now work out a way of dealing with a difficult situation. They will feel frightened, powerless, cornered, and overwhelmed. Their respective worlds are about to be turned upside down.

At this point, my parents live in their own home, but only because my father can still fix their breakfast, help my mother to the bathroom, and call for help if she falls. And also because I am nearby for emergencies—and to schedule and take them to their doctors' appointments, supervise their many medications, monitor their nutrition, and find suitable and reliable household help for them. During my daily visits I place their catalogue orders, pay their bills, deal with Medicare and their private insurance companies.

At night I lie in bed wondering how much longer my father's own precarious health—and strength—will hold out. What will I do if it doesn't? My parents' resources are not sufficient to hire round-the-clock nursing. I picture past scenes of my aunts and my own mother caring for their parents in their last days. And I remember that no one in our family has ever died—or lived—in a nursing home.

I still have many questions and quandaries about the future—my parents' and my own. But since coming back to Texas to help with my mother's care, I have at least learned not to repeat that oft-repeated cliché that undergirds and perpetuates our idolatry of independence: *I don't want to be a burden to my children.*

We are all, throughout our lives, a burden to others. From the moment of conception, we are nourished and nurtured by others. As adults we learn to pay for or negotiate our mutual needs, but the fact remains that it takes an invisible army of other people to grow our food, clean our clothes, maintain our roads, fuel our furnaces. When we marry, we accept another's pledge to stick with us in sickness and health, prosperity and poverty. The load we lay on others only becomes more visible, less deniable, as we age. Even though nothing is more predictable, Americans simply aren't much good at—and consistently fail to prepare themselves for—either bearing or being burdens. (As for wishing for a quick and trouble-free death that will cause our families no fuss or bother, only one in four of us can expect such an easy exit.)

Our still relatively new culture, which makes both living anywhere and living longer possible, will no doubt devote a good deal of public resources and private energy in the near future to figuring out how best to care for its older members. In the meantime, I will be moving into that category myself. Yet nothing in our culture to date encourages us to accept the reality of our future liability. Instead, we are enticed to believe in the Centrum Silver myth—that our latter days will be spent on cruise ships or jogging into the sunset, not alone but with our spouses. The truth is, though, should I live another 20 years, I *will* be a burden—to my spouse or my children or the state, if not all three. What I most want to learn during those decades, therefore, is not how to live longer, not necessarily even how to live a healthier or more productive life, but how best to be a burden. One that might also be a blessing.

I WANT TO BE A MOM
(From boundless.org)

"How many of you want to be at-home moms?"

The question, from my tenth grade English teacher, was directed at the females in the room. We made up over half of the class of 25 sophomores. I proudly raised my hand, then waited for at least a few others to join me. The room was completely still. Everyone stared at me.

Four years later not much has changed. Marriage is closer than ever for my peers, yet only a few of the young women I come into contact with admit they would postpone a career for children. Those who do confide in me only after I've told them of my own feelings. They seem relieved to find a contemporary who doesn't mock their desire.

When I finally got the nerve up to tell my adviser that I want to get married and be a mom after I graduate, I watched his expression go from surprise, to dismay, to disapproval. "I wouldn't have expected you to be that type," he said, shaking his head and looking at me with great disappointment. "You just seem so—involved."

He paused, then asked in a hushed, sad voice, "Is it pressure from your boyfriend?"

A laugh escaped me before I could stop it—his tone was the same as if he had asked me if my boyfriend was abusive.

"No," I informed him, "I don't have a boyfriend." Despite my desire to get married, I'm not at college to hunt down a husband. Marriage and raising a family will not be the epitome of my existence—I enjoy looking forward to them, but I'm not living in the future.

I do hope to someday serve as a wife and mother, and when God determines it is time for me to take on those roles, I will so do with a willing heart.

"Just" a Mom

Most people wonder why I am bothering to get a degree if all I want is to be a wife and mom. That question irks me.

I love to learn and want to have a wealth of knowledge to impart to my children. Why shouldn't a housewife be educated? I want to equip myself and hone my skills to the point of craft.

My mother earned her degree in elementary education 20 years ago, and promptly became a housemom after graduating. Since then my brother, sisters and I have been her highest priority, but during the tight times she helped out by using her degree for substitute teaching. Though we didn't like having her gone, she was able to carry some of the burden my father carried. I want to be able to do this for my own husband if the need ever arises.

I am at college because I realize there are seasons to life, and mothering will only be my summer. My mom, now 40, is the co-owner of my dad's window dealership. In the last five years, as my siblings and I have grown up and her mothering duties have lightened, she has become intricately involved in every aspect of the company, though very few people are aware of it. Depending on God's plan for me, I could be done rearing my children in 20 years like her. By age 30 I might even have enough time to do part-time illustration and writing during the day. I am thankful that technology has opened up even more avenues than my mother had available to her to accommodate home-based work.

"Unless the Lord builds the house, they labor in vain that try to build it." If God gives you children, rear them with your whole mind, soul and strength. If He has given you the talents to be an engineer, the same thing applies. But I am dubious that He would ever ask us to be fully both at one time. There seems to be a perception among women my age that we will have enough time and energy to do and be everything—full-time wife, mother and career woman all rolled into one. I agree that God wants us to use and enjoy the talents He's given us, but He never promised us inexhaustible resources. He created us with limitations and only placed 24 hours in a day. We cannot expect to juggle all the hats and be the best we can be at all of them. The reality is that if I choose to be full-time in a career, my husband and kids will only have me part-time.

Danielle Crittenden makes an excellent observation in *What Our Mothers Didn't Tell Us*—that quality time with kids can't be scheduled into a day. Children want a mother's presence, the knowledge that she will be there when they have a question or a story to tell—but quite often they simply want her to do her own work while they color and play with pals. And those memorable times—their first steps and words, their profound utterances of child wisdom, the moments of belly laughing together—happen at the most unexpected times during day-in, day-out living. The chances are much higher that a mother will miss out on them if she is working outside the home.

Money Can't Buy Me Love

I can guess what most people think when they find out about my lack of career aspirations. They picture me in 10 years: dressed in sweats doing laundry for my four kids; my degree collecting dust somewhere on a bookshelf; living in a one-income-sized home; driving a used minivan.

They imagine my peers, however, utilizing their education to the fullest. They will maintain a measure of independence unfettered by familial life, thanks to daycare, public schools and extracurricular activities. They will naturally be rewarded with great financial and material gain—but at what cost to their spouses and children?

The Christian life is about sacrifices, giving up certain things for the sake of greater long-term benefits. I know there could be times of financial strain in my marriage. I know I might encounter tension with the majority of my married female peers because of my choice to stay at home. I know I will have to give up a lot of personal time—there will be nights that I am itching to read a big fat novel in one sitting instead of reciting *Hop on Pop* for the fiftieth time to the kids. I'm not saying that I'm going to derive pleasure from changing diapers and cleaning up burpy blankets. But it's only by sacrifice that we understand what true love, commitment and maturity really mean. Jesus was the embodiment of this. Being a husband and father, or wife and mother, forces you to look outside yourself to the needs of others. As soon as I become a mother my children will become my career. What better way to utilize my time and talents?

I want my children to know that they are as important to me as a career. Because of the choices my mom made when she was little older than I, my three younger siblings are reaping the benefits of having a full-time mom, one who is available for conversation, hugs and laughs (and a healthy amount of arguments about chores) any time of day.

I want to give that gift to my own children. If it means I drive a beater car and shop at thrift stores for the rest of my life, so be it. Children don't know the difference between Goodwill and GAP. I certainly didn't. And if I have daughters, I will raise them with the knowledge that they have full abilities to be and do all that God wants, in their wholeness in Christ, in their education—and in the roles that may come with being a woman.

Worthwhile Wrinkles

There will always be women who scoff at me, who are disappointed because they think I let down our gender. There will always be the professors who sigh because I am not living up to their idea of potential. But I know what makes me happy and I'm slowly learning not to feel guilty about sharing it with people. I look forward to giving up my independence. The word *dependency* has come to carry negative connotations: "an unhealthy need for a person or substance, an addiction." But I see it as a positive reliance on others for companionship and love.

Mothering is a career choice that is rarely respected. We should recognize and affirm women who opt to invest time in their children. The Bible is clear that sons and daughters are among the greatest blessings we will ever receive.

A friend of mine once said his greatest desire is to create something beautiful and lasting. That stuck with me. I want to create a beautiful and lasting marriage with a man, and with that man I want to bear and rear children, which are the most exquisite and eternal creations we humans can take part in fashioning. Architects design buildings that will someday fall, programmers construct computer software that will eventually be obsolete—but fathers and mothers cultivate souls that will never die. How wonderful to experience just an inkling of what God feels as our Father.

When I am old and I look at my wrinkled hands, I want to know that the creases came from—among many things—years of playing music, reading books, drawing pictures and writing stories. But my greatest hope is that those lines will remind me most of hours spent washing my babies' and grandbabies' tummies, tucking them into bed and teaching them what I have learned.

BEN PATTERSON

HOLY WAR

(From *Leadership*)

Cast yourself into his arms not to be caressed but to wrestle with him. He loves that holy war. He may . . . lift you from your feet. But it will be to lift you from earth, and set you in the heavenly places which are theirs who fight the good fight and lay hold of God as their eternal life.

—P. T. Forsyth, *The Soul of Prayer*

"Why is it, when we talk to God, we call it prayer, but when God talks to us, we call it schizophrenia?" That quip by Lily Tomlin has taken on many layers of meaning for me since 1986, the year we learned that my seven-year-old son Joel had Tourette's syndrome.

We noticed it first when he started playing soccer. At practice and during games, if the action was elsewhere on the field, he would stand at his position and look directly at the sun. It was painful to his eyes, and we had warned him repeatedly that it could damage them permanently, but he couldn't seem to stop.

Then came other things he didn't seem to be able to control: blinking of the eyes, facial and body tics, contortions, jerks, ritual movements, random vocalizations, barking sounds, repeated clearing of the throat; and for awhile the barely suppressed urge to touch the burner on the stove when it was hot.

What Have I Done to My Son?

Having no name for what we were witnessing, we were scared. And as I watched Joel struggle, I struggled with guilt. I wondered: Was it something I had done to him?

Of all our kids, Joel was the one I had most often lost my temper with. Like his dad, he could be maddeningly bullheaded and combative. He was articulate beyond his years, and his words were often piercing and inflammatory. Words have great power in our household. I had frequently reacted to his words with words of my own. Over and over, in minute detail, I replayed mentally every confrontation we had ever had. Guilt and remorse pounded me like heavy surf.

Joel was scared, too. One night as Lauretta was tucking him into his bed, saying evening prayers, he spoke in the darkness, haltingly: "Mom, you know the things I do? . . . I know I'm not doing them. . . . I know Jesus wouldn't make me do them. . . . " The sentence trailed off before he spoke the alternative to Jesus and himself.

When she told me what he said, we held each other in quiet terror and slipped to our knees in the living room to pray. The moment I closed my eyes I saw, as in a vision, a large coiled python, its head resting on its giant body, its cold remorseless eyes staring. It seemed to me to be wrapped around my throat and my little boy's soul.

The worst came when I was away on a three-day prayer retreat at a desert monastery near Los Angeles. I telephoned home one evening and listened as Lauretta recounted an episode Joel had that day with what we were later to learn was coprolalia, the obsessive repetition of obscenities. The obscenity in question was the "f" word. Joe was a very moralistic child, and was stricken as he whispered involuntarily, over and over, a word he loathed.

She had handled it marvelously. Taking him into the back yard she sat with him in a swing and said, "Okay, let's say it out loud."

Joel was incredulous: "I can't say that awful word out loud."

"Well, can you quack it like a duck?"

Joel has been blessed with an impish, zany sense of humor. Her suggestion was all he needed. So mother and child sat in the swing quacking the "f" word—but not so loud that the neighbors or his siblings could hear. Then they mooed it like a cow. Then they clucked it like a chicken and crowed it like a rooster and whinnied it like a horse. Their laughter was tentative at first, then explosive. The obsession dissolved into hilarity. What a woman I married!

But as we talked that night in the darkness, she alone at home with the kids, I in a phone booth in the desert, the weight of the day's fear was heavy on us. Normally nothing keeps me from sleep but the lack of opportunity. I lay awake for a long time that night, and awakened often after I finally fell asleep.

The questions and accusations coiled tightly around my heart: What have I done to my boy? A prayer for God's mercy could barely be formed in my mind, much less pass through my lips.

Wrestling an Omnipotent Foe

I got up early the next day, dressed, and walked the stations of the cross at the monastery. At each station, through tears, I thanked God that the blood of his Son, the blood of the atonement, had paid for all my sins, including what I may have done to my son.

I got back to my room 20 minutes before breakfast and sat down to read Scripture before I went to the dining hall. When I had left home, I had impulsively grabbed a devotional book off my library shelf and put it in my bag. I picked it up and opened it to the readings for that particular day. The Scripture for the day was John 9: "As he went along, he saw a man blind from birth. His disciples asked him, 'Rabbi, who sinned, this man or his parents, that he was born blind?'"

I knew that kind of question well. I had been asking it daily, with the tentative answer, "his parent." What I had not yet considered was Jesus' answer.

"Neither this man nor his parents sinned," said Jesus, "but this happened so that the work of God might be displayed in his life."

An extraordinary coincidence? That on the day I was struggling as I was, the day's reading should be that? You'll never convince me that it was.

The tears came again, but now freely, joyfully. It was neither my sin nor his, but God, in his mysterious providence, doing a greater work. The coils disappeared; no more cold, remorseless eyes, but the face of the Father. God spoke, and everything that has followed with Joel has confirmed what he said. It wasn't about my sin but the work of God, his glory, and our growth in holiness.

"God whispers to us in our pleasures, speaks to us in our consciences, but shouts to us in our pain: it is his megaphone to rouse a deaf world." I have often wondered about those words of C. S. Lewis. Whatever else they may mean, they have come to mean this to me: that when he speaks thus, it is to rouse us to wrestle with him, the living God.

Holy Chutzpah

It's like the thing God does with Abraham when he announces to him what he plans to do to Sodom and Gomorrah. Knowing that Abraham had family in those cities, he throws down the gauntlet and says, in effect, "I'm going to destroy those cities and everyone in them, your nephew Lot and his family included. Now, what do you think of that, Abraham?"

And Abraham lets him know what he thinks. He says, "How could you do such a thing? Shame on you, God!"

"Will you sweep away the righteous with the wicked? . . . Far be it from you to do such a thing—to kill the righteous with the wicked, treating the righteous and the wicked alike. Far be it from you! Will not the Judge of the earth do right?"

Abraham is perplexed and bewildered at what he hears; so he expostulates and attacks. Then he bargains:

"What if there are 50 righteous people in the city? Will you really sweep it away and not spare the place for the sake of the 50 righteous people in it?"

The Lord says, "If I find 50 good people there, I'll spare the city."

Abraham tests God's love and justice with more questions: how about 40? Or 30? Or 20? Or 10? Each time God answers no, he will not destroy the city if that many righteous people can be found in it (Gen. 18:16–33).

If Abraham's prayer is nothing else, it is candid. Actually, it's more like chutzpah than candor. Once the dialogue begins, it can, and should, get that way. It took me a while. At first I was so devastated by what I saw in Joel, and so comforted that it wasn't my fault, that I could only whimper my gratitude. Lauretta and I adjusted. It's amazing how one can get used to what once seemed unbearable.

Then one night God kicked it up a notch for me. Lauretta and I were having dinner with some members of our church. The husband was a nurse working in a penitentiary. He was a good man whose skill as a chef almost offset his people skills. When, over dessert, we told him about our son's disorder, he gaped at us and launched into a speech the substance of which was: "Oh, no, not that! Anything but that! You don't want a son with Tourette's. That's horrible. No, it can't be that. Let's pray it isn't Tourette's." Apparently he had seen some shocking cases in the penitentiary. We gaped too. His wife glared at her husband.

On the way home that night the food sat heavily in my stomach as we contemplated the possibility that our son's disorder could get really nasty. I was mad. My prayers went from "What have I done?" to "What do you think you're doing?" Enough was enough. I had learned a good lesson about faith; I didn't need a Ph.D. I let God know how I felt. Of course he already knew before I spoke, so he wasn't surprised or shocked at what I said.

My estimation of his abilities and sensitivities didn't seem to upset him, either. He knows I have flawed standards and a limited perspective. He doesn't sweat the small stuff.

I read somewhere that the ability of a couple to express anger well can do wonders for their sex life. It's true, it's true. It seems there can be no warm fuzzies without their opposite (cold pricklies?). Both anger and tenderness are forms of passion. As is prayer. God doesn't mind our anger. He even relishes it, if it drives us to him instead of away from him. Better an outburst than a theologically correct and spiritually pallid rationale, and a dangling conversation.

No wonder we can get so bored with prayer. God is bored too. He wants to engage our hearts, not just our brains.

God Invites Candor, Really!

It was that way with Jeremiah. He got so exasperated with God and the terrible treatment God allowed him to suffer that he virtually accused him of rape. "You have seduced me, Lord, and I have let myself be seduced; you have overpowered me: you were the stronger" (20:7). Jeremiah was wrong, of course. God had done nothing of the sort. But that is how Jeremiah feels about what is happening in his life. And God gives no rebuke for him feeling the way he feels.

Ron Davis, a pitcher for the Minnesota Twins years ago, objected to a newspaper story about him criticizing the team's management for trading away some of their best players. He told reporters, "All I said was that the trades were stupid and dumb, and they took that and blew it way out of proportion." You can speak your mind with God and not be afraid that he will blow things out of proportion. He already knows what's inside. But we need to let it out for the dialogue to proceed.

If our faith in God cannot be bewildered and perplexed, then we have domesticated him, and our faith is no longer in him but in our religious systems. Beware: when you handle holy things often, your hands and heart can become cauterized and you are no longer burned and jolted by what you hear.

President Franklin Roosevelt was weary of the mindless small talk of White House receptions. Wondering if anyone was engaging in any real conversation, he conducted an experiment at a White House gathering. As he shook a hand and flashed that big smile he would say, "I murdered my grandmother this morning." With but one exception, the people would smile back and say something like, "You're doing a great job," or "How lovely." The exception was a foreign diplomat who responded quietly, "I'm sure she had it coming to her." If we are not shocked from time to time by the things God says and does, we have not been listening. How many of our prayers are like White House receptions? Does God feel about them as President Roosevelt did?

Benefits of Angry Prayer

Ah, perplexity! Bitter, sweet perplexity. G. Campbell Morgan said, "Faith is the answer to a question; and, therefore, is out of work when there is no question to ask." Questions are critical to faith. How else could it be with a finite human being coming to understand and trust an infinite God? No perplexity, no questions. No questions, no faith. So the God who cannot be pleased unless there is faith (Heb. 11:6) puts questions to us. To use Lewis's categories, sometimes he whispers them, sometimes he speaks them, and sometimes he shouts them.

Through circumstances he nudges us or draws us or jolts us into prayer. Suddenly we are faced with something that challenges our deepest securities, knocks away all of our props or violates everything we ever believed to be true about God and his ways.

When these things happen, we can be sure of this: that whatever else we do not know, we can know that God has taken the initiative with us to pray. Seen from this perspective, the Book of Job is a book about prayer.

Where do the questions of faith lead us? To greater faith. Abraham's and Ben Patterson's wrestling with God take them to the place where they discover God to be better than they had ever before imagined.

Jacob wrestles and becomes Israel, a new man. And when Job wrestles, though he has not one of his questions answered, he says in the end that it is more than enough, that he is satisfied and fulfilled. For while before he had only heard about God, now he has seen him. To gain even a glimpse of the glory and goodness of God is reason enough to wrestle.

It's true, you know. God's glory is enough. I'll never forget sitting in an evening service in my church and knowing this was true. It had been a tough year. I didn't like being a pastor anymore, but couldn't think of anything else I could do. The choir was performing a beautiful piece. This is hard to explain, and may sound a little weird to someone who has never had the experience, but in the beauty of the music I got a glimpse of God's transcendent beauty and goodness, just for a moment. It was like a spear of longing and delight had pierced my heart. The ache was exquisite. And my first thought was, "Lord, you are enough. I'll do this lousy job forever if you let me walk with you and get just a peek at you once in awhile."

There is no pain or perplexity so heavy that they outweigh his glory. And it would seem that both are necessary for us to see it.

God Loves a "Good Fight"

God "loves that holy war," writes P. T. Forsyth, using the image of two Greco-Roman wrestlers. "Cast yourself into his arms not to

be caressed but to wrestle with him. . . . He may be too many for
you, and lift you from your feet. But it will be to lift you from
earth, and set you in the heavenly places which are theirs who
fight the good fight and lay hold of God as their eternal life."

Did my wrestling end that morning in the monastery? No. Or
after I recovered from the nurse's speech? No. Has God become
grander? Yes.

Joel, who is now a freshman in college, agrees. I asked him if I
could write about him and our struggle. He looked at me with
level gaze and said quietly, but emphatically, "Absolutely, Dad."
He is growing into an extraordinary young man. He has both a
physical condition and an intuitive sense of things spiritual that
set him apart, not in spite of his struggle but because of it.

I don't just love him, I admire him. I want to be like him when
I grow up.

And whenever I am tempted to say that he has a mild case of
the syndrome, I am reminded of the fact that he has been much
prayed for. I also know that Tourette's syndrome is often unpre-
dictable, that it can wax and wane over time and that there is no
absolute "trajectory" for the disorder. It can get worse or better,
or worse and better over the years. Joel knows that, too. But
God's grace will also be sufficient over time.

At the Risk of Sounding Crazy . . .

The best has been the laughter. When we were first confronted
with Tourette's, we never dreamed laughter would come, but it
has. We have sat around the dinner table and laughed with Joel
about the weird and often funny things that can happen to someone with Tourette's. The episode with the "f" word was the
antecedent. Like many with the disorder, Joel is extremely creative and blessed with a zany, rapid-fire Robin Williams kind of
wit. He has said, only half-jokingly, that he thinks those with
Tourette's are one step above, on the evolutionary ladder, those

who are normal. I'm not willing to go that far. But hey, gratitude for God's grace should make us a little excessive in our judgments.

Are we crazy? Lily Tomlin's crack about prayer and schizophrenia is probably accurate as it applies to the way many in our culture and in the church think about such things. And I admit that I have even wondered out loud, "Is that really you, God? Or just my wishful thinking?" Unlike some theological points, questions like this rarely have a neat answer. But I've come to believe that God is not nearly as fastidious in matters of faith as we may like him to be, and that when faith moves mountains, there is bound to be rubble.

Earlier in my Christian experience, I was afraid to name something as the voice of God for fear I might be wrong and look dumb. Then it occurred to me that I was probably missing a lot because of my fear of how I might look. Which was worse, to always look cool and rational but risk missing the voice of God? Or to risk looking a little credulous and crazy once in a while, but hear God, at least more often than I had been? I've opted for the latter.

Call it prayer and schizophrenia if you will, but I think trying to look cool was something we were supposed to have given up in junior high.

WISE TEACHERS, SOUND TEACHING

(From *Christian Century*)

In Ephesus, Timothy walked into a congregational mess with the mandate to straighten it out. He inherited both the legacy (left by Paul) and the problems for which others (among whom were Hymanaeus and Alexander) were responsible. Like the *tohu wabohu* of Genesis 1:2, pastoral vocation doesn't begin with a clean slate.

A congregational mess provides a particularly perilous condition for leaders, for it convinces us that our pastoral presence is vital and necessary. Others have messed up, done badly, behaved irresponsibly, and we are called in to make a difference. The very fact that we are called in must mean that we are competent, that we are capable.

We are flattered, of course. We've been noticed. "We need you," they say. "Get us out of this. We've read your résumé, called your references, heard you preach—rescue us."

We respond to their plea, and become involved in a rescue mission. But eventually we become chained to the agenda set before us, slaves to the conditions we've entered. The dimensions of our world shift from God's large and free salvation to the cramped conditions of what others need.

There's a neurotic aspect to this. It's like a person who gets caught up in a flood and, while being swept along by a torrent, grabs on to a branch and holds on for dear life. It takes days for the flood to recede. Meanwhile, the person holds on to the branch—saved, rescued, alive. Eventually, the flood waters are gone and the poor soul is still holding on to the branch. People come by and say, "Come on down." But the person replies, "No way. I'm saved. This is where I found salvation; this is what saved me. I'm not going to leave this saved place."

This way of life accepts the conditions of sin as the conditions in which we work. Of course, we always work in those conditions, but they don't define our world. They just provide the material for our world, for our gospel. We do not have to become constricted by those conditions. Timothy wasn't.

Ephesus might seem to be the showcase church of the New Testament. It was a missionary church established by the eloquent and learned Jewish preacher Apollos (Acts 18:24). Paul stopped to visit this fledgling Christian community on his second missionary journey. He met with the tiny congregation (it had only 12 members), and guided them into receiving the Holy Spirit. He then stayed on for three months, using the synagogue as his center for preaching and teaching on "the kingdom of God." That visit, following the dramatic encounters with the seven sons of Sceva and the mob scene incited by Demetrius over the goddess Artemis, extended to three years.

The other Pauline letters were provoked by something that went wrong—wrong thinking or bad behavior. But the dominant concern of the Letter to the Ephesians isn't human problems. It's God's glory. The Letter to the Ephesians represents the best of what we are capable of in the Christian life, calling us to a mature wholeness.

But by the time Timothy was sent to Ephesus, it was a mess. Good churches can go bad. Surprisingly, sinners show up. Wonderful beginnings end up in terrible catastrophes.

We don't know exactly what went wrong with the Ephesian church; nothing is spelled out. What is clear is that the religion of the culture had overturned the gospel. Paul's two letters to Timothy give us glimpses of what was happening.

Paul tells Timothy to deal with "certain persons" who are obsessed with "religion" but apparently want nothing to do with God. Here is a sampling of phrases that describe the "religious" activities of these people:

- Putting high value on myths and endless genealogies which promote speculations
- Giving heed to deceitful spirits and doctrines of demons
- Being guided by the hypocrisy of liars
- Forbidding marriage and enjoining abstinence from certain foods
- Imagining that godliness is a means of gain
- Participating in godless chatter
- Starting stupid, senseless controversies

We don't know what the "godless chatter" was in Ephesus. It was no doubt a form of gnosticism, which creates an elite body of insiders who cultivate a higher form of religion that despises common people, common things and anything that has to do with a commitment to a moral life. Jesus would be far too common for people like this. The "godless chatter," whatever its actual content, would be shaped by the culture and not by the cross of Jesus.

What is most apparent about these phrases is that they refer to a lot of talk—speculations, controversies, and chatter. There is some reference to behavior (about marriage and diet) and to an item of doctrine (resurrection), but mostly we are dealing with religious talk. These people loved to talk about religion. T. H. White's description of the older Guinevere, who became a nun after the death of Arthur, could easily describe these Ephesian teachers: "She became a wonderful theologian, but cared nothing about God."

Churches are faced with this problem continuously. The culture seeps into the church, bringing with it a religion without commitment; spirituality without content; aspiration and talk and longing, fulfillment and needs, but not much concern about God.

In 1997 we had a remarkable encounter with this old Ephesian stuff. For weeks the attention of the world was captured by the death of Princess Diana. I knew next to nothing about Diana at the time. But in three weeks I got a crash course in Diana religion—for this was a religious event. Diana was treated with the veneration and adoration of a goddess. At her death, the world fell down and worshiped.

Diana was the perfect goddess for a religion that didn't want anything to do with the God and Father of our Lord Jesus Christ, but was desperate to worship someone or something that would provide a sense of beauty and transcendence.

I noticed the parallels to the ancient Canaanite sex/fertility goddesses Astarte and Asherah. Diana was a perfect fit for the role: the fragile beauty, tinged with sadness; the poignant innocence, with suggestive hints of slightly corrupt sexuality. Her identification with the poor and the oppressed, her compassion for people with AIDS, her campaign against landmines, and the rejection by her husband made her sympathetic to us. She summed up the spiritual aspirations of a sexually indulgent culture that was also filled with misunderstanding and loss and hurt and rejection.

In Edinburgh I watched long lines of men and women and children carrying bouquets of flowers to place on appointed shrines throughout the city. They were silent and weeping, unutterably moved by the death of their goddess. I read the meditations on Diana in the daily newspapers. I remembered that the Roman name for Artemis was Diana, Diana of the Ephesians. Diana, the sex goddess who provided mythology and set the moral tone to the city, was back—the fertility goddess of the ancient world had seized the imagination of the modern world.

I'm not suggesting that the Diana cult of Ephesus and the Diana cult of 1997 have the same content, but the effect is the same. The Ephesian Diana cult, a pastiche of stories, superstitions, and systems of thought endemic to the ancient East, served the city's religious needs. The recent Diana cult is also a pastiche of stories and longings and public relations efforts that serves the religious needs of an astounding number of people. Her death brought into the open just how wide her influence extended. Diana evoked the best of people—but only the best of what they want for themselves, not of what God wants. She offered "good" without morality, transcendence without God.

Timothy was sent to Ephesus to counter the effects of the Artemis/Diana religious culture. The gospel that Jesus brought and that Paul and Timothy preached is not first of all about us; it is about God, the God who created us and wills to save us; the Jesus who gave himself for us and wants us to deny ourselves and follow him wherever he leads us, including the cross; and the Holy Spirit who descends upon us in order to reproduce the resurrection in our ordinary lives. None of this involves fulfilling our needs as we define them. Our needs are sin needs—the need to get our own way, to be self-important, to be in control of our own lives.

The wonderful Ephesian church that had begun so robustly, with such a sense of new life—this Christ-centered church was dissipating in a religious stewpot of hyped-up feelings, discussion groups, and interest gatherings.

When the church finds itself overwhelmed by the culture, what is it to do? What is Timothy to do? Conventional wisdom tells us that when the problem is large, the strategy must be large. We need to acquire a vision that is adequate to the dimensions of the trouble. But that isn't what happens here. If we look for it, we're disappointed. Timothy isn't charged to refute or expose the Diana spirituality of Ephesus. Paul simply tells him to avoid it. He has bigger fish to fry: he is to teach and to pray.

The overriding concern in the pastoral epistles is for "healthy" or "sound" teaching. Eight times in these three letters to Timothy and Titus we find concern for the "health" of teaching or words.

Sometimes "teaching" is translated as "doctrine" and so we get the impression that orthodoxy is at issue. But this isn't quite right, for Timothy is given the mandate to teach in a way that brings *health* to people. Words in Ephesus have gotten sick; the "godless chatter" in Ephesus is infecting souls. It is important not to see Timothy as a defender of orthodoxy, as someone who argues for the truth of the gospel. He is a teacher.

The vocation of pastor is the best of all contexts in which to teach. But it is a particular kind of teaching, the kind referred to here as "sound teaching." Frances Young translates the phrase as "healthy teaching" or "healthy words." In Timothy, "sound" and "healthy" define the kind of teaching and speaking that is going to be at the center of the work of reforming the Ephesian church.

Paul's phrase "sound words" or "sound doctrine," as J.N.D. Kelly puts it, "expresses his conviction that a morally disordered life is, as it were, diseased and stands in need of treatment . . . whereas a life based on the teaching of the gospel is clean and healthy."

The Greek word for "sound" is *hygien*, from which we get *hygiene*. The main thing that Timothy is to do in Ephesus in order to clean up the mess is to teach sound words, sound truth, healthy thinking and believing. Verbal hygiene. Healthy gospel. Words matter. The way we speak and use words matters. Nothing a pastor does is more important than the way she or he uses words.

In *The Cloister Walk*, Kathleen Norris tells the story of the time she heard the poet Diane Glancy astound a group of pastors, mostly Protestant:

She began her poetry reading by saying that she loved Christianity because it was a blood religion. People gasped in shock; I was overjoyed, thinking, *Hit 'em, Diane, hit 'em where they live.* One man later told me that Diane's language had led him to believe that she was some kind of fundamentalist, an impression that was rudely shattered when she read a marvelous poem about angels speaking to her through the carburetor of an old car as she drove down a rural highway at night. Diane told the clergy that she appreciated the relationship of the Christian religion to words. "The creation came into being when God spoke," she said, reminding us of Paul's belief that "faith comes through hearing." Diane saw this regard for words as connected not only to writing but to living. "You build a world in what you say," she said. "Words—as I speak or write them—make a path on which I walk."

But not all people use words that way. There is a great chasm in our Western world in the way words are used. It is the split between words that *describe* the world and reality from as much distance as possible through generalities and abstractions, and words that *express* the world and reality by entering it, participating in it by metaphor and command. Describing words can be set under the Latin term *scientia*, expressing words under the term *sapientia*—or in English, science and wisdom. Science is information stored in the head that can be used impersonally; wisdom is intelligence that comes from the heart, which can only be lived personally in relationships.

If we don't discern the distinction between these two ways of knowing, we will treat matters of the gospel wrongly and therefore lead people wrongly. All knowledge has content to it. But science depersonalizes knowledge in order to make it more exact, precise, objective, manageable. Wisdom personalizes knowledge in order to live intensely, faithfully, healthily.

For science, an item of knowledge is the same in any place or time for any kind of person. For wisdom, an item of knowledge is custom-made. "Two plus two equals four" means exactly the same thing for a five-year-old kindergartner and a 55-year-old Nobel Prize–winning economist. "I love you" means something different every time it is said, depending on who says it, the tone in which it is used, the circumstances surrounding the statement, and the person to whom the statement is addressed.

Paul writes about *sapientia,* or wisdom-lived words, while the Ephesians were engaged in *scientia,* "godless chatter." This is an important distinction because we are taught in school to speak in *scientia* but not in *sapientia.*

I frequently have conversations with pastors who tell me that they would like to go into teaching. What they mean by that is they want to get a graduate degree and get a position as a professor in a school. Being a professor is honorable and can be Christ-honoring work. The work of research, separating error from truth, getting things straight, training minds to think accurately—all this is terribly important. But it also takes place in conditions that treat knowledge as information, as something to be constantly used. If you want to teach wisdom, you find yourself going against the stream. Educational organizations and bureaucracies have no interest in how you live, or even if you do live.

I am not putting down schools. But I know I was a much better teacher as a pastor in a congregation than I have been as a professor in a school. Virtually everything I have taught in the classroom I taught first and probably better to my congregation.

In preparing to teach a course, I looked through a folder of accumulated notes and realized that I first taught the course to an adult class consisting of three women: Jennifer, a widow of about 60 years of age with an eighth-grade schooling, whose primary occupations were keeping a brood of chickens and a goat and watching the soaps on television; Penny, 55, an army wife who treated her retired military husband and her teenage son and daughter as items of furniture in her antiseptic house, dusting them off and placing them in positions that would show them off to her best advantage, and then getting upset when they didn't stay where she put them—she was, as you can imagine, in a perpetual state of upset; and Brenda, married, mother of two teenage sons, a timid, shy, introverted hypochondriac who read her frequently updated diagnoses and prescriptions from about a dozen doctors as horoscopes—the scriptures by which she lived. (Ironically, she lived the longest of the three.)

Looking back, I could not have picked a more ideal student body for my teaching. As I taught my fledging course in spiritual formation, using Ephesians as my text, I learned the difference between information and wisdom, and that wisdom was all that mattered to these three women. It was slow work, but gospel words have power in them. These women learned with their lives. The three women are now dead. I sometimes wonder if they are amused as they see me teach bright and gifted students from all over the world who pay high fees to be in the class. They paid by putting a dollar or two in the Sunday offering.

All wisdom is acquired relationally, in the context of family and friends, work and neighborhood, under the conditions of sin and forgiveness, within the complex stories that the Holy Spirit has been writing and continues to write of our lives.

Paul tells Timothy: "Continue in what you have learned and have firmly believed, knowing from whom you learned it . . ." (2 Tim. 3:14). *From whom*—that is the only way to get wisdom—from whom, a person. And so what better place to teach persons personally than in a congregation where you have access to everything that makes up their personhood—their families, their work, the weather, their neighborhood, their sins, their stories—

and over a period of years, sometimes decades. In a church, you get people in the setting where their main business is living, up to their armpits in life.

I can't think of a better or more important place to be a teacher, a wisdom teacher, than in a church. As Paul put it: "If you put these instructions before the brethren, you will be a good minister of Christ Jesus, nourished on the words of the faith and the good doctrine which you have followed."

ROBERT ROYAL

COLUMBUS AND THE
BEGINNING OF THE WORLD

(From *First Things*)

As Orson Welles famously remarked, playing the unscrupulous Harry Lime in the film *The Third Man:* "In Italy for thirty years, under the Borgias, they had warfare, terror, murder, and bloodshed, but they produced Michelangelo, Leonardo da Vinci, and the Renaissance. In Switzerland they had brotherly love. They had five hundred years of democracy and peace, and what did they produce? The cuckoo clock." Lime's history was more than a little vague and self-serving. (Welles himself seems to have been titillated by this dangerous truth since he added it to Graham Greene's original script for the film.) Fifteenth-century Italy in particular, and Europe more generally, drew their vitality from a lot more than Borgias and Machiavellianism. But it is a paradox of history that social turmoil often offers rich soil for human achievement.

The world we know began in the fifteenth century. Not the world of course in the sense of human life or human civilizations, which had already existed for millennia, but the world as a concrete reality in which all parts of the globe had come into contact with one another and begun to recognize themselves as part of a single human race—a process still underway. The spherical globe we had known about since the classical world; in the Middle

Ages, readers of Dante took it for granted. Yet it was only because of a small expedition by a few men driven by a mishmash of personal ambition, religious motives, and the desire for profit that an old mathematical calculation was turned into a new human fact. Or as a historian sixty years later accurately characterized the discovery of the New World, it was "the greatest event since the creation of the world (excluding the incarnation and death of Him who created it)."

In our own confused way, we continue to pay homage to that achievement. In 1999, NASA will put a satellite into an orbit a little less than a million miles out into space at what is called L-1, the libration point where the gravity of the earth and the sun exactly balance one another. Equipped with a telescopic lens and video camera, it will provide a twenty-four-hour-a-day image of the surface of the earth. Not surprisingly, one of the enthusiasts behind the project is Al Gore, probably the most environmentally agitated public figure alive. But in spite of the damage that Gore and many others believe we humans have inflicted on the planet since our first large steps in exploring it, and despite the laments of multiculturalists about Europe's rise to world dominance, the new satellite will be called Triana, after Rodrigo de Triana, who first spotted lights on land from the deck of the Pinta during the first voyage of Columbus.

Perhaps the name is only a bow to growing Hispanic influence in the United States; perhaps it hints that we would like to think of ourselves as equally on the verge of another great age of discovery. But whatever our sense of the future, the Columbus discoveries and the European intellectual and religious developments that lay behind them are today at best taken for granted, at worst viewed as the beginning of a sinister Western hegemony over man and nature. The last five centuries, of course, offer the usual human spectacle of great glories mixed with grim atrocities. But we cannot evaluate the voyages of discovery properly—

much less the fifteenth-century culture from which they sprang—
without gratitude for what they achieved or understanding of their
human dimensions. In the fifteenth century, the discoveries were
rightly regarded as close to a miracle, especially given the way
the century had begun.

The early 1400s were marked by profound religious, political,
economic, and even environmental turmoil. At one point in the
first decade of the century, there were simultaneously three
claimants to the papal throne and three to the crown of the Holy
Roman Empire. And the large-scale institutional crises were only
a small part of the story. Europe was still suffering from the dev-
astation wrought at the height of the Black Death over half a
century earlier and in smaller waves thereafter. Overall, something like 40 percent of the population disappeared in the
mid—fourteenth century, in some regions even more. Land lay
fallow for lack of workers, villages were deserted, poverty spread.
As many modern environmentalists have devoutly wished, nature
took its vengeance as human population decreased. Wolves multiplied and returned, even appearing in capital cities. Human
predators—in the form of brigands—made travel unsafe over
wide areas. The consequences of the retreat of civilization
spurred Henry V, fabled victor of Agincourt, to offer rewards for
the elimination of both types of pests. Though the beauty of
landscapes emerged as never before in contemporary painting
and literature, it was not a century that indulged itself in easy
sentimentality about the goodness of unimproved nature, human
or otherwise. On the contrary, natural hardships spurred the fifteenth century to nearly unparalleled achievements.

But if the internal situation were not enough, Europe was also
being squeezed by forces from outside. In 1453, the Ottoman
Turks finally succeeded in taking Byzantium. Turkish troops had
already been fighting as far into the Balkans as Belgrade a few
years earlier. Otranto, in the heel of Italy, fell to them in 1480 for

a time. We might have expected the Christian powers to lay aside rivalries momentarily and defend themselves from an alien culture and religion. But the main Atlantic nation-states—England, France, and Spain—were still only beginning to take shape. The rest of Western Europe was broken, despite the theoretical claims of the emperor, into a crazy quilt of competing small powers. So no coordinated effort occurred, though Pius II and other popes called for a crusade. Pius even wrote to Sultan Muhammad II, conqueror of Constantinople, inviting him to convert to Christianity. Whether this letter was intended seriously or as a mere pretext for further action, it failed. Neither "European" nor "Christian" interests were sufficiently united to galvanize the effort. The Pope died in 1464 at the eastern Italian port of Ancona waiting for his people to rally behind him.

A crusade to retake the Holy Land was sometimes a mere pipe dream, sometimes a serious proposal during the course of the century. Ferdinand of Spain listened frequently to such plans, but refrained from doing much. (Machiavelli praises him in *The Prince* as one of those rulers who shrewdly take pains to appear good without necessarily being so.) Charles VIII of France invaded Italy in 1494 but also had in mind an attempt to retake Constantinople and restore the Eastern Christian Empire. Earlier, Henry V, on his way to Agincourt, had proclaimed his intentions not only to assume the French throne but to "build again the walls of Jerusalem." Western Europe had a persistent if vague sense of responsibility to defend Christianity from Islamic military threats and a deeper need to recover the parts of Christendom lost to Muslim conquest, even if the good intentions were thwarted by intra-European distractions.

Had Islam continued its advance, much of Europe might have then resembled the cultures we now associate with the Middle East. The Americas might have been largely Muslim countries as opposed to largely Christian ones. Islam was more advanced than Europe in 1492, but in the paradoxical ways of culture, its very superiority contributed to its being surpassed. Muslims do not seem to have taken much interest in Western technical developments in navigation, and even well-placed countries like Morocco were never moved to brave the high seas in search of new lands. European technological innovation and military advance may have been born of necessity, given the superiority of outside cultures and the conflicts and rivalries among European nations.

This reminds us of something often overlooked in most contemporary historical surveys. The "Eurocentric" forces, of which we now hear so much criticism, were actually something quite different in the fifteenth century. What we today call "Europeans" thought of themselves as part of Christendom, and a Christendom, as we shall see, that desperately needed to return to some of its founding truths. Similarly, they did not regard themselves as the bearers of the highest culture. Ancient Greece and Rome, they knew, had lived at a higher level, which is why the Renaissance felt the need to recover and imitate classical models. The fabled wealth of the distant Orient and the clearly superior civilization of nearby Islam did not allow Christendom to think itself culturally advanced or, more significantly, to turn in on itself, as self-satisfied empires of the time such as China did. Contemporary European maps—the ones all the early mariners consulted in the Age of Discovery—bear witness to their central belief: Jerusalem, not Europe, was the center of the world.

But this very sense of threat and inferiority, combined with the unsettled social diversity of Europe at the time, gave Europeans a rich and dynamic restlessness. Not surprisingly, the rise towards a renewed Europe began in the places least affected by the population implosion and, therefore, more prosperous: what we today call the Low Countries and, above all, Northern Italy.

Renascences, as Erwin Panofsky demonstrated a few decades ago, had been occurring in Europe since the twelfth century. But the one that took place in Northern Italy in the fifteenth century— the one we call *the* Renaissance—produced multiple and wide-ranging consequences.

Pius II was in many ways emblematic of the midcentury. A cultivated humanist born in Siena in 1405 with the imposing name Aeneas Sylvius Piccolomini, he initially came under the spell of St. Bernardino, who preached a strictly observant reformed Franciscan life (of which more anon). But he shortly became attracted to the exciting life of the Renaissance Italian humanists, which is to say libertinism and literary pursuits. He shifted parties among papal contenders, pursuing his own ambitions for many years, wrote a popular history (*Historia rerum ubique gestarum*) that gathered together wide-ranging facts and fictions about foreign lands, and even became imperial poet and secretary to the Holy Roman Emperor Frederick III. But compared with the squabbling popes and anti-popes who preceded him and the colorful escapades of the Borgias, Pius had his virtues. He was learned and hard-working, enjoyed nature, sought reform, and could have made a difference in Europe had his office enjoyed the respect it once had and was to have again later. The religious renaissance, however, like the cultural, scientific, and artistic one with which we are more familiar, had to come from other sources.

Renaissance achievements found multiple and overlapping uses in a Europe in ferment. The geometry developed by the Florentine Paolo Toscanelli allowed Fillippo Brunelleschi, over the objections of a commission of Florentine experts, to dare construction of the unsupported dome that crowns the magnificent Florentine Duomo. Just a few decades later, an intellectually curious Genoese mariner corresponded with Toscanelli in preparation for his attempts to convince another panel of experts in

Spain that it was possible to sail west to the Indies (no serious thinker at the time, by the way, believed the earth was flat). His figures were wrong; the distance was greater than he claimed. The experts—and perhaps Columbus himself—knew it. But it was an age when for various reasons people had the faith to attempt things beyond what was previously thought possible. It is worth looking closely at some of those reasons.

Much has recently been written, for example, claiming that the Christian dimension of Columbus' personality was merely a cover for greed and ambition. These alleged traits are then read as a metaphor for a hypocritical European expansion under the cover of religion. Hypocrites certainly existed in the fifteenth century, as they do today. But real history—as opposed to anachronistic morality tales—is always more complex than the simple motives we project back onto figures quite different from ourselves. Like the Italian humanists, who are often wrongly portrayed as modern unbelieving intellectuals, Columbus combined his faith with new knowledge and new interests. But that did not make his faith any less real. He wanted that Renaissance ideal, glory: in this case, that of an unprecedented voyage. He drove hard bargains with Ferdinand and Isabella to secure the financial benefits of his discoveries for himself and his descendants. (The Muslim conquests and consequent monopolies over Eastern trade routes made the European search for alternate routes all the more necessary and profitable.) Yet when all the mundane reasons have been listed, the spiritual dimension of the project remains in ways that are quite unexpected.

In the preface to his *Libro de las profecias* (Book of Prophecies), an anthology of prophetic texts that he compiled near the end of his life, Columbus relates to Ferdinand and Isabella how, long before he ever approached them, he had become convinced that the westward voyage was not merely possible but his own personal vocation:

During this time, I searched out and studied all kinds of texts: geographies, histories, chronologies, philosoph[ies], and other subjects. With a hand that could be felt, the Lord opened my mind to the fact that it would be possible to sail from here to the Indies, and He opened my will to desire to accomplish this project. This was the fire that burned within me when I came to visit your Highnesses.

Of course, the reading alone suggests we are dealing with an unusual kind of sailor, one who, like the humanists of his day, has engaged in sifting and comparing ancient and modern knowledge for new purposes. There is some irony, then, in the fact that he claims that God intended to produce a *milagro ebidentisimo* ("highly visible miracle") in this enterprise by using an uneducated man: "For the execution of the journey to the Indies, I was not aided by intelligence, by mathematics, or by maps. It was simply the fulfillment of what Isaiah had prophesied."

Columbus clearly employed considerable intelligence, mathematical skill, and geographical knowledge in planning his route. He also knew from much experience at sea that winds in the Atlantic nearer the equator would carry him west, those to be found more to the north would take him east, back to Europe. And he was alert to other environmental signs. Late in the first voyage he turned south to follow a flock of birds that he rightly assumed were headed towards land. Without this chance or providential fact, he probably would have come ashore somewhere between Virginia and Florida instead of the Caribbean, with doubtless immensely different effects on subsequent world history.

Despite all the knowledge, abstract and practical, that Columbus brought to bear on his task, the religious intuitions he describes may strike us as bordering on delusion, on a par with the equally unexpected mystical speculations of the mathematician Pascal, or

Newton's commentaries on the prophecies in the Book of Daniel. But anyone familiar with how prophecies have functioned throughout history knows they often work themselves out in ways their authors never envisioned. In Columbus' case, we may wish to avoid judging too quickly the "hand that could be felt" and other evidence that at times he seems to have heard something like divine locutions. They may have been delusions, intuitions, or something else moving in the depths of human history.

Far from being a later and idealized reinterpretation of his own past, Columbus' remarks are confirmed by a curious source. Recent scholars have discovered notes in Columbus' own hand dated 1481, over a decade before his first voyage, in the back of a copy of Aeneas Sylvius Piccolomini's (the later Pius II) *Historia rerum ubique gestarum*. There Columbus compiles a shorter list of prophecies from various sources which, it now seems perfectly clear, guided his whole life project.

Columbus' religious side seems to have grown out of a religious renaissance that occurred in fifteenth-century Europe. The *devotio moderna*, beginning with Gerard Groote and the Brethren of the Common Life, spread among both religious and lay people, calling for a return to a more personal religion modeled on the evangelical virtues of the early Church. Its best-known writer was Thomas à Kempis, whose *Imitation of Christ* (ca. 1427) has influenced numerous individuals and movements, Catholic and Protestant, over the centuries. As late as the middle of the sixteenth century, Ignatius of Loyola, for example, the founder of the Jesuits, made it the first book he read when he decided to begin a serious religious life. The *devotio moderna* shaped figures as diverse as Nicholas of Cusa and Erasmus. In many ways, it paralleled the impulses behind the secular Renaissance in its living reappropriation of the religious past as the basis for the future.

Less known, however, is the Observant or Observantine current within the fifteenth century, first among the Franciscans, but later among other orders and lay groups. In fact, one of the major religious disputes for monasteries at the time was the need to choose between strict Observant and non-reformed Conventual rules. (Martin Luther began his religious life in an Observant Augustinian community.) The Franciscans numbered among their members figures like Saint Bernardino of Siena, Saint James of the Marches, and Saint John Capistrano. Their efforts, too, looked to a religious renaissance by way of return to the more austere and humble ways of early Christianity. For our present purposes, it is also necessary to note that, mixed in with that more austere life, there were occasionally garbled versions of the millennial speculations of Joachim of Fiore, a twelfth-century Cistercian abbot, for whom a new age of the Holy Spirit and the final age of the world seemed not far distant.

We have no indisputable evidence that Columbus was a third-order Franciscan Observantine, but his way of dress in his final years in Spain appears to have been similar to theirs. When he traveled through Spain, he stayed at Franciscan monasteries rather than the homes of noblemen. Uncertainties about Columbus' early history and the history of the Observants in Spain prevent any greater precision, but it is clear that, mixed in with his other motives, he early on had absorbed some of the millennial currents of his time. Specifically, he seems to have believed that one reason to open the Western route to the Orient was to enable the gospel finally to be preached to all nations, a prerequisite to the end of the world and the triumphal second coming of Christ that some Joachimites predicted would occur in the middle of the sixteenth century.

Significantly, Columbus also seems to have believed something not found in any of Joachim's writings: that Joachim had predicted that a king of Spain would liberate the Holy Land. Though Columbus had a personal reason to keep Ferdinand and Isabella interested in the enterprise of the Indies, he also often

urged them to undertake a crusade. The fact that Spain recon-
quered the kingdom of Granada only at the beginning of 1492
gave Spaniards a sense greater than that of most other Europeans
of the need to resist Muslim incursions. In less savory forms, this
sense contributed to the Inquisition's injustices to Spanish Muslims and Jews, who were expelled from Spain on the very day
Columbus set sail. Columbus' urgings went unheeded, but we
have good evidence of his sincerity. For the last decade of his life
the various wills he made altered different clauses, but one
remained constant: he directed the executors of his estate to set
up a fund in Genoa's Bank of Saint George to help pay for the liberation of Jerusalem. Whatever other motives we may attribute to
him, there is no question that on spiritual matters he put his
money where his mouth was.

Much of this real history has been obscured for a long time by
persons who found it expedient to use Columbus as a symbolic
figure. For most older Americans, he was presented as a heroic
proto-American, combating the obscurantism of reactionary
Spanish Catholics who thought he would sail off the end of the
flat earth. (As we have seen, neither Columbus nor his intellectual
critics believed in such absurdities.) In that reading, he became a
forerunner of American Protestantism, modern science, and capi-
talist enterprise. It is no great loss that we have discarded that
historical illusion.

Columbus also did service as an ethnic hero for Catholics,
mostly Irish and Italian, during the large waves of immigration at
the end of the nineteenth and beginning of the twentieth century. There was less harm here, because he was a true hero.
Enthusiasm grew so heated that on the four hundredth anniver-
sary of his voyage in 1892 efforts were made to have him canon-
ized. But Leo XIII, fully aware of Columbus' irregular marital
situation (for reasons of inheritance he never married the woman

he lived with after his wife died), contented himself with praising his human virtues: "For the exploit is in itself the highest and grandest which any age has ever seen accomplished by man; and he who achieved it, for the greatness of mind and heart, can be compared to but few in the history of humanity."

In recent years, of course, Columbus' standing as hero has come under severe assault. He and the culture he represented have been castigated for initiating the modern cultural dominance of Europe and every subsequent world evil: colonialism, slavery, cultural imperialism, environmental damage, and religious bigotry. There is a kernel of truth in these charges, but obviously to equate a single individual or a complex entity like a culture with what are currently judged to be the negative dimensions of the emergence of an interconnected human world is to do great historical injustice to both individuals and ideas.

Europeans, for example, had an ambivalent stance toward the new peoples they encountered. On the one hand, there arose almost instantaneously the beginnings of the "noble savage" myth, which had a varied career in the hands of writers like Thomas More, Montaigne, and Rousseau. On the other hand, actual experience of the new cultures revealed peoples who displayed much savagery and sometimes little nobility.

Columbus himself adhered to one side or the other in this culture war at different times in his life. In one of his first communications with the Spanish monarchs after the discovery, he described the Taínos of the Caribbean in glowing terms:

> I see and know that these people have no religion whatever, nor are they idolaters, but rather they are very meek and know no evil. They do not kill or capture others and are without weapons. They are so timid that a hundred of them flee from one of us, even if we are teasing. They are very trusting; they believe there is a God in Heaven, and they

firmly believe that we come from Heaven. They learn very quickly any prayer we tell them to say, and they make the sign of the cross. Therefore Your Highnesses must resolve to make them Christians.

As the self-contradictions of this passage suggest, Columbus was under the spell of one current in European mythology that believed such "uncivilized" peoples to be somehow closer to the conditions of the Garden of Eden than those enmeshed in the conflicts of "civilization."

In fact, the Taínos themselves were enmeshed in the tribal raiding, slavery, and cannibalism that existed in the Caribbean long before any European arrived (the word "cannibal" is a corruption of the native term for the fierce Caribs who eventually gave their name to the whole region). Columbus was for a while on surprisingly good terms with his Taínos, who in turn used the Spaniards to their advantage against their enemies. But the distance between the cultures was great, and, with the arrival of less-than-ideal explorers in subsequent voyages, the situation took a bad turn. Toward the end of his third voyage, Columbus wrote to complain about criticism of his governorship over both natives and Spaniards:

At home they judge me as a governor sent to Sicily or to a city or two under settled government and where the laws can be fully maintained, without fear of all being lost. . . . I ought to be judged as a captain who went from Spain to the Indies to conquer a people, warlike and numerous, and with customs and beliefs very different from ours.

Columbus had discovered that the Indians were real flesh-and-blood human beings, with the same mix of good and evil that everywhere constitutes the human condition.

Today, the usual way of characterizing the behavior of the Europeans at this early stage is to fault them for not having the kind of sensitivity to the Other that a modern anthropologist or ethnologist would bring to such situations. Overlooked in this condemnation is the fact that it was precisely out of these tumultuous conflicts that the West began to learn how to understand different cultures as objectively as possible in their own terms. Columbus himself astutely noted differences between the various subgroupings of Taínos as well as their distinctiveness from other tribes. And even when he was driven to harsh action—against both Indians and Spaniards—it was not out of mere desire for power. Bartolomé de las Casas, the well-known defender of the Indians, notes the "sweetness and benignity" of the admiral's character and, even while condemning what actually occurred, remarks, "Truly I would not dare blame the admiral's intentions, for I knew him well and I know his intentions were good." Las Casas attributes Columbus' shortcomings not to malign intent but to ignorance concerning how to handle an unprecedented situation.

This raises the question of larger intentions and the world impact of fifteenth-century European culture. The atrocities committed by Spain, England, Holland, and other European powers as they spread out over the globe in ensuing centuries are clear enough. No one today defends them. Less known, however, are the currents within that culture that have led to the very universal principles by which, in retrospect, we criticize that behavior today. For instance, not only Las Casas, but a weighty array of other religious thinkers, began trying to specify what European moral obligations were to the new peoples.

Las Casas, who was the bishop of Chiapas, Mexico, where relations between mostly native populations and the central government remain dicey even today, bent over backwards to understand local practices. He once even described human sacrifices as reflecting an authentic piety and said that "even if cruel [they] were meticulous, delicate, and exquisite," a view that some of his critics have remarked exhibits a certain coldness toward the victims. Other missionaries learned native languages and recorded native beliefs. The information coming from the New World stimulated Francisco de la Vitoria, a Dominican theologian at the University of Salamanca in Spain, to develop principles of natural law that, in standard histories, are rightly given credit as the origin of modern international law. To read Vitoria on the Indies is to encounter an atmosphere closer to the UN Universal Declaration of Human Rights than to sinister Eurocentrism.

Las Casas and Vitoria influenced Pope Paul III to make a remarkable statement in his 1536 encyclical *Sublimis Deus*:

> Indians and all other people who may later be discovered by the Christians are by no means to be deprived of their liberty or the possession of their property, even though they be outside the faith of Jesus Christ. . . . Should the contrary happen it shall be null and of no effect. . . . By virtue of our apostolic authority we declare . . . that the said Indians and other peoples should be converted to the faith of Jesus Christ by preaching the word of God and by the example of good and holy living.

The Spanish crown itself had moral qualms about the conquest. Besides passing various laws trying to eliminate atrocities, it took a step unmatched before or since by any expanding empire: it called a halt to the process while theologians examined the question. In the middle of the sixteenth century, Charles V ordered a theological commission to debate the issue at the monastery of Valladolid. Las Casas defended the Indians. Juan Ginés de Sepúlveda, the greatest authority on Aristotle at the time, argued that Indians were slaves by nature and thus rightly subject to Spanish conquest. Though the commission never arrived at a clear vote and the Spanish settlers were soon back to their old ways, Las Casas' views were clearly superior and eventually prevailed.

Conquest aside, the question of even peaceful evangelizing remains very much with us. Today, most people, even Christians, believe it somehow improper to evangelize. The injunction to preach the gospel to all nations, so dear to Columbus' heart, seems an embarrassment, not least because of the ways the command has been misused. But some of the earlier missionaries tried a kind of inculturation that recognized what was good in the native practices and tried to build a symbolic bridge between them and the Christian faith. The Franciscans in New Spain and the Jesuits in Canada, for example, tried this approach. Not a few of them found martyrdom.

Many contemporary believers do not think that there was much need to evangelize. This usually arises out of the assumption that native religions are valid in their own way. It will not do, however, given the anthropological evidence, to make facile assumptions that all spiritual practices are on an equal plane. The early explorers who encountered them did not think so, and neither should we. For example, the Mexican novelist Carlos Fuentes, no special friend of Christianity or the Spanish conquest, in the very act of admiring the richness of Aztec culture characterizes the Aztec gods as "a whole pantheon of fear." Fuentes deplores the way that missionaries often collaborated with unjust appropriation of native land, but on a theological level notes the epochal shift in native cultures thanks to Christian influence: "One can only imagine the astonishment of the hundreds and thousands of Indians who asked for baptism as they came to realize that they were being asked to adore a god who sacrificed himself for men instead of asking men to sacrifice themselves to gods, as the Aztec religion demanded."

This Copernican Revolution in religious thought has changed religious practice around the world since it was first proclaimed in Palestine two millennia ago, yet it is all but invisible to modern critics of evangelization. Any of us, transported to the Aztec capital Tenochtitlàn or to many other places around the world before the influence of Christianity and Europe, would react the way the conquistadors did—with rage and horror. We might not feel much different about some of the ways that Europeans, imitating Islamic practice, evangelized at times by the sword and perpetrated grave injustices around the world. But it is reductionist in the extreme to regard evangelization simply as imperialism. The usual uncritical way in which we are urged to respect the values of other cultures has only the merest grain of truth buried beneath what is otherwise religious indifferentism.

For all our sense of superiority to this now half-millennium-old story, we still face some of the same questions that emerged in the fifteenth century. We still have not found an adequate way to do justice to the claims of both universal principle and particular communities. We have what Václav Havel has called a "thin veneer of global civilization" mostly consisting of CNN, Coca-Cola, blue jeans, rock music, and perhaps the beginning glimmer of something approaching a global agreement on how we should treat one another and the planet.

But that minimal unity conceals deeper conflicts involving not only resistance to superficiality but the survival of particular communities of meaning. We say, for example, that we have an equal respect for all cultures—until we come up against religious castes and sexism, clitorectomies and deliberate persecution. Then we believe that universal principles may take precedence. But whose universal principles? A Malaysian prime minister has lately instructed us that, contrary to international assumptions, "Western values are Western values: Asian values are universal values." It may take another five hundred years to decide whether that is so, or whether the opposition it assumes between East and West will persist.

All of this may seem a long way from the fifteenth century. But it is not mere historical fantasy to see in that beginning some of the global issues that are now inescapably on the agenda for the new millennium. Christianity and Islam, the two major prose-lytizing faiths in the world, are still seeking a modus vivendi. The global culture initiated by Columbus will always be inescapably European in origin and, probably, in basic shape. We chose long ago not to stay quietly at home and build the otherwise quite wonderful contraptions called cuckoo clocks. That decision brought (and brings) many challenges, but the very struggle should remind us of the glorious and ultimately providential destiny of the ongoing global journey that began in the fifteenth century.

KRISTER STENDAHL

COME HOLY SPIRIT—
RENEW THE WHOLE CREATION

(From *Cross Point*)

The life and ministry of Jesus are seen by all the evangelists as permeated by the Spirit. This is expressed in many ways and at different points in the ongoing story, and the Spirit is the energy by which his mighty deeds are wrought.

All four Gospels begin the ministry of Jesus with the same story: the baptism in the Jordan where the Holy Spirit descends on Jesus in the likeness of a dove (Mark 1:8–11; Matt. 3:13–17; Luke 3:21–22; John 1:29–34). The endearing symbol of the dove with its proverbial gentleness (Matt. 10:16) makes a Jewish *Targum* (the Aramaic translation of the Hebrew) render "the voice of the turtle-dove" in the Song of Songs (2:12) as "the voice of the Holy Spirit of redemption." In more recent times the dove has become the powerfully powerless symbol of peace, especially when the dove has the olive branch in her beak. That reminds us of the story of Noah, where the dove brings the good tidings of having found dry land after the flood—which the more warlike raven did not. So the world has new hope for life, the catastrophe was not final, and God enters into covenant with the creation not to destroy it. And the rainbow is the sign for that unconditional promise (Gen. 8 to 9).

When we read that story in a nuclear age, we are haunted by the afterthought: God has promised it all right and that unconditionally—but did the writer of the holy text ever fathom that human beings could themselves trigger global destruction?

For the evangelists the gentle dove represents the Spirit as "descending and remaining" over Jesus as the Spirit had hovered over the waters at creation (Gen. 1), and as the Presence of God rests on whatever is holy. Thus Jesus is empowered to baptize with the Holy Spirit as he is authorized and proclaimed as the Son of God. The Gospel of John brings it all together:

> And John [the Baptist] bore witness, "I saw the Spirit descend as a dove from heaven, and it remained on him. I myself did not know him, but he who sent me to baptize with water said to me, 'He on whom you see the Spirit descend and remain, this is he who baptizes with the Holy Spirit.' And I have seen and have borne witness that this is the Son of God." (John 1:32–34)

And Luke has a surprising and beautiful way of taking the ancestry of Jesus beyond Abraham (where Matthew stops) all the way back to God, not only to Adam: ". . . Seth (son) of Adam (son) of God." He links the genealogy to the descent of the Spirit at the baptism of Jesus (Luke 3:23–38)—not to the Christmas story as does Matthew—thus affirming that Jesus is "the Son of God."

In Matthew's and Luke's Gospels the story begins at the birth of Jesus as a miracle of the Holy Spirit. It is especially in Luke's tender image of the Virgin Mary that divinity and humanity are brought together by a mystery in which the *imago Dei* is restored: human existence in the image of God. Or with thee words from the Epistle to the Colossians: "For in Christ the whole fullness of divinity dwells bodily . . ." (2:9).

"In the beginning was the Word" (the Logos, with the further connotation of structuring power, and reason) . . ."and the Word became flesh . . . is how John says it. Just as the spirit was with God at creation, so also was the mighty and clear Word—and Wisdom/Sophia, the sister of the Word. Such thoughts of loving reflection among interpreters of the holy texts intensify the link between the beginning in creation and the recreative break-through in Jesus Christ as the Son of God, made known as such when the Holy Spirit descends and rests on him.

The three synoptic Gospels (i.e., Matthew, Mark and Luke) want us to remember that the first event in the life of Jesus once he was under the sway of the Spirit was his time of testing by the temptations in the wilderness.

Actually they all say that it was by that very Spirit of God that he was placed in that arid and devastated place among the wild and unfriendly beasts. This is the reverse image of paradise. The writers and readers of the Gospels no doubt saw Jesus pass-ing the test as a sign that it was now possible in the power of the Holy Spirit to stand up against the assault of Satan and be minis-tered to by God's good angels. The reversal of the expulsion from paradise is in the making. One comes to think of Jesus' words to the criminal at his side at Golgotha: "Today you shall be with me in paradise" (Luke 23:43).

And so Jesus returned to Galilee, as Luke puts it, "in the power of the spirit," and then Luke sees the whole ministry of Jesus through the prism of the words of the prophet Isaiah read that day in his home synagogue:

The Spirit of the Lord is upon me because he has anointed me to preach the good news to the poor. He has sent me to proclaim release to the captives and recovering of sight to the blind, to set at liberty those who are oppressed, to proclaim the welcome year of the Lord (Luke 4:18–19/Isaiah 61:1–2a).

Energized and authenticated by the Spirit, Jesus' ministry will be one of liberation, healing and justice. It will be a ministry where words and actions are woven into one. By the power of the

Spirit persons are healed and relationships mended. We often feel that his words are mainly commentaries on and illustrations of his acts of healing and restoring life. It is surprising—and striking—that not a single passage in the synoptic Gospels refers to the Holy Spirit as the source or authenticator of the *words* of Jesus. The spirit engenders *action.* The Spirit of the Lord rests upon him and works through him nothing less than a renewal of creation.

In the language of the Gospels, the term for that renewal os the kingdom of God/of heaven. (In spite of all its difficult associations with kings and other male potentates of this world, I prefer the word "kingdom" to "realm" or "reign" or "dominion," for it does have a concrete and social dimension, with people and communities restored. To me that rescues the word "kingdom" for our use, redeeming it from being just an expression of power.) And, as we have seen already, this deliberate choice is the clearest sign that his ministry is to be seen as the crucial act in the great biblical drama of God's ever ongoing struggle for the mending of the creation by the work of the Spirit.

The Gospel of John enriches our faith by giving us its own quite distinct understanding of Jesus' life and ministry. The other Gospels write and think in metaphors drawn from the social and political life (kingdom, justice, servants, masters, etc.); the Gospel of John uses a language of the life sciences, speaking much of birth and life and growth, and of branches remaining, abiding in the tree to be enlivened by the sap. Thus Jesus came that we should have life, and that abundantly (10:10). In John it is all about life, the processes of life. From the beginning was the Word, the Logos . . . and it was life, and the life was the light of humanity (1:1 and 4). And so John speaks of the Spirit giving birth to a new life of divine quality (the Greek word *anothen* in John 3:3 can mean both born "anew" and born "from above"). For John faith is really to live by this stream of life. "Those who believe in me . . . out of their hearts shall flow rivers of living water. Now this he said about the Spirit which those who believed in him were about to receive . . . " (7:38–39). The life of faith is the eternal life; it is a life called eternal since it is in communion and continuity with the Eternal One. TO John "eternal" does not refer to quantity of time, but to quality of life. "Truly, truly I say to you, those who hear my word and believe God who sent me, have eternal life and do not come into judgement, but have passed from death to life" (5:24, cf. 11.25–26).

Thus it is all about life, the life born by the Spirit. I belong to a church that believes it right to baptize infants, and part of the liturgy stresses the need for a new birth. It seems odd, considering that the baby has just been born a few days or weeks before. Precisely for that reason I have had to reflect on the Johannine birth–language by which a new birth is seen as reinforcing and revitalizing life on the model of the creation itself, that is when God breathed breath/spirit into earthly matter. "That which is born of the flesh is flesh, and that which is born of the Spirit, spirit" (John 3:6). In the culture in which I live, I have come to feel strongly that when a little child is baptized, it is set free from all the social shackles of class and race and gender and even, somehow, the genetic chains of causality. Born anew in the Spirit in holy baptism, the child is restored into the freshness of the day of creation, now pulsating with a life of divine quality. And if this liberation from all that binds and hampers the fullness of life is true about a baby, imagine the grace of baptism in later years when life has become so much more entangled in circumstances both of our own making and of our surroundings.

It is all about life, a life mirrored in the divine life of the Holy Trinity, of which the Gospel of John writes with such insight. Especially when the Gospel grounds the oneness of the church, not in divine or authoritarian principles that rule the world, but using that "biological" language of being interwoven in an abiding manner: ". . . that they may all be one, even as thou, Father, art in me, and I in thee, that also they may be in us . . . " (17:21). As I read and mediate on such words I almost see the flow of the life giving spirit through the arteries and veins of God's creation. And the flow of that energy is perfectly unobstructed. And what we call sin and disobedience becomes the obstruction and the hardening of the arteries—impeding the flow of the Holy Spirit, the life-blood of abundant life.

Before we leave the rich and deeply beneficial insights of the Johannine perspective and its language of life, we must also remember that John does not use words that refer to death and dying when he speaks of the crucifixion. It is as if his sharp focus on LIFE makes him shy away from such words. Rather, Jesus is "lifted up," both in analogy to how Moses lifted up the serpent in the wilderness for the healing of the people (3:14), and in cosmic exaltation: "[W]hen I am lifted up from the earth, I shall draw all things unto myself" (12:32). To John the death of Jesus is his glory: ". . . the time has come for the Son of Man to be glorified" (12:23). And so, to John's memory and understanding, the final word of Jesus as he is lifted up on the cross is one of victory, even triumph: "It is accomplished" (19:30). Then the sentence by which John concludes this part of the story can be translated: "And bowing his head he *handed over* the Spirit" . . . back to God or on to the church. For John, Jesus does not breathe his last; he does not just yield up his spirit. He actively hands over the Spirit, the Spirit that he had promised would guide the disciples in days to come, the Spirit that had descended and remained over him as his ministry began. Had he not said: ". . . It is to your advantage that I go away, for if I do not go away, the Counselor [the Spirit] will not come to you . . ." (16:7)?

The Defense Attorney

There is another lesson about the work of the Spirit to be learned from the Gospels. Recorded by the synoptic evangelists is only one situation in which the disciples are assured of the special assistance of the Holy Spirit, and that is when they are dragged before the authorities, be they religious or secular. Then they need not worry in advance about what to say, for it will be given to them by the Spirit, "for it is not you who speak but the Holy Spirit" (Mark 13:11; cf. Luke 12:11–12; Matt. 10:18–20).

In the Gospel of John the Holy Spirit is called by a title that can have many meanings and connotations: *Parakletos* (John 14:16, 26; 15:26; 16:7; cf. about Jesus in 1 John 2:1). The translators choose different words: Comforter (AV/KJV, The Living Bible, so also Luther); Counselor (NIV, RSV); "the one who is coming to stand by you" (Phillips); advocate (NEB); Advocate (NRSV); Helper (New American Standard and as an alternative in NRSV). Even when the word is given the more general sense of Comforter or even Helper, the connotation of Advocate, counsel for the defense, should not be lost, especially in the light of the assurance of the Spirit's assistance when a disciple of Jesus is taken to law courts or faces other authorities.

Which all goes a long way to warn us against thinking of the Spirit primarily as comfort for the already comfortable, or as belonging primarily to the realm of warm religious experiences of grace and forgiveness.

It seems that one indispensable function of the Spirit is to make our witness for Christ and the kingdom of justice and peace on earth bold enough to confront and rattle the powers that be. Then it feels good to have an able defense lawyer with you, especially for those who cannot afford the services of the legal profession.

In Fellowship with the Holy Spirit

Most Bible readers would have noticed that the frequent references to the kingdom that characterize the Gospels of Matthew, Mark, and Luke are not found in the Epistles or in the Acts of the

Apostles. This is the more striking when we read the Acts of the Apostles, for here it is the same writer who holds the pen—or dictates the words. Luke seems to be aware of this difference between Jesus' language and the language of the church. He actually makes of it a programmatic point.

Because the kingdom was the central theme in the teaching and preaching of Jesus, the Book of Acts begins at that point. Also, the risen Lord was "speaking of the kingdom of God" during those forty days before the Ascension (1:3). Thus it is only natural that the disciples should ask if the time has come for "restoring the kingdom." Jesus answers that God's timing is not for human knowing or calculation: "BUT you shall receive power when the Holy Spirit has come upon you, and you shall be my witnesses in Jerusalem and Judea and Samaria and to the end of the earth" (1:8).

The Acts of the Holy Spirit

Luke has a great sense of symmetry, and his traditions are organized in orderly patterns of time and space. The ministry of Jesus began with the descending of the Spirit, and so Jesus progresses from the provinces to the city of Jerusalem. Now the life of the church begins in Jerusalem, in the Temple, with the descending of the Spirit on the disciples, and in the power of that Spirit they will bear witness in words and actions and through martyrdom (the Greek word for "witness") far beyond the lands traversed by Jesus. The Book of Acts itself brings the witness all the way to Rome, the capital of the world that Luke knew.

Now the Spirit is the energy and the guide engineering the life and expansion of the church in the world of the Jewish diaspora and through it to the Gentile world. The ecstatic speech, the speaking in tongues, of which we also know from Paul (Romans 8:26; 1 Cor. 12–14), is seen by Luke as a symbol of the global outreach across all barriers of language and culture (Acts 2:5–13).

The Acts of the Apostles could just as well, or even better, be called "the Acts of the Holy Spirit," and there are indeed few chapters in the book without specific references to such acts. Here are a few examples. Beyond the breakthrough experiences of Pentecost in chapter 2 there is the power of healing in chapter 3. We see a community with its boldness of speech and willingness to share with one another all their belongings (chapter 4). Hence the gruesome story about Ananias and Sapphira. When they lied to the church about their wealth, they actually lied to the Holy Spirit (5:3) and to God. "You have not lied to people but to God" (5:4).

Peter's decisive move to full acceptance of Gentiles comes not until the Holy Spirit descends on Cornelius and his people (10:44–47). When the ensuing theological controversies are settled in the so-called Apostolic Council in Jerusalem, a letter is sent out to the churches in which the decision is presented with the words: "For it has seemed good to the Holy Spirit and to us . . ." (15:28). Also Paul's itinerary is led by the Spirit, as it tells him what he can expect (20:23), or as it hinders him from following his own plans (16:6; cf. Paul's own, less benign understanding of the same event in 1 Thess. 2:18, ". . . but Satan hindered us"). And at the very end of the book it is the Holy Spirit that had foreseen that the expansion of the church would be in the Gentile world to which the apostles bear witness (28:25–28).

No Nostalgia

So the stage is set for the first decades, and for all times in the community of those devoted to Jesus Christ. It is striking that the followers of Jesus did not dream themselves back to the time when he had walked with them and talked with them. It is astonishing how small a role the words of Jesus, which were later made part of our Gospels, play in the early Christian writings, the letters of Paul and of others, and even in Luke's account of the first decades of the church. In Luke's case we know that he knew that material since he had written his "first book," his Gospel, after careful research (Luke 1:1–4).

So they did not look back in nostalgia. They looked forward and they lived powerfully in the *now* of the Holy Spirit. One really feels the truth of Jesus' words of farewell in the Gospel of John: "I tell you the truth: It is to your advantage that I go away, for if I do not go away, the Counselor will not come to you, but if I go, I will send him to you. . . . I have yet many things to say to you, but you cannot bear them now. When the Spirit of truth comes, it will guide you into all the truth . . ." (16:7ff.).

Thus, when we pray: *Come, Holy Spirit*, our prayer is well in keeping with the mode and mood of faith which was tried and tested as the church began to understand itself, its promises, and its identity.

GLENN TINDER

FROM THE ENDS OF THE EARTH

(From *Christianity Today*)

Karl Barth speaks of the Incarnation in terms of a journey by Christ into "a far country." My own encounter with Christ began in a far country.

I was raised, very intensively, in Christian Science. I say "very intensively" because I was an only child, and my mother was a highly intelligent and conscientious Christian Scientist. Understandably, she saw one of her main responsibilities as a mother to be that of instilling Christian Science as deeply as possible in her one and only child. (My father, although a gentle and sensitive man, was rather detached as a parent.) Every day began with readings from Mary Baker Eddy's *Science and Health* as well as from the Bible. The world and daily life were construed for me according to the standards of Christian Science. I do not mean to make this sound like indoctrination in the pejorative sense of that term. It was a conscientious mother's effort to raise up her son in the truth.

Christian Science is not a form of Christianity. It is not even near enough to Christianity in the traditional sense of the term to be called a heresy. It is often thought of as centered on faith healing, and it is true, as the very title of Mary Baker Eddy's book suggests, that it is centered on the achievement of health. This is not, strictly speaking, a matter of healing, however, for the very reality of sickness is denied. Sickness is an illusion. Faith, therefore, does not bring healing but rather a realization that one was never sick to begin with.

No phrase is more common among Christian Scientists than "knowing the truth." This means that when the illusion of sickness arises, you continually tell yourself that in actuality you are perfectly healthy. This is apt to bring peace of mind, which may be physically beneficial. Hence, in many instances, "knowing the truth" unquestionably plays a part in the restoration of health.

When that happens, however, it is not a healing that has occurred, in the view of Christian Scientists, but rather a realization of what has been true all along. In fact, Christian Scientists deny the reality not only of sickness but of all evil. This means that they deny the reality of sin, and in doing this they deny the very fallenness of the human race. The crucifixion becomes pointless (although the symbol of the cross is retained, a crucifix is never seen, as far as I know, in Christian Science churches or publications). The core truth is not that we are saved. It is rather that we have never been lost.

To common sense, much of this may seem absurd. It is, however, a daring and quite logical response to what is often called "the problem of theodicy": How can there be evil in a world created by a good and omnipotent God? Mary Baker Eddy answered, simply, that there can't and therefore isn't. Christian Scientists are people with the nerve required for living according to this answer—the nerve, for example, to spurn all medical help in time of illness. My mother had this kind of nerve, and for the first seventeen years of my life (until I left for college) my mother did her best to instill it in me.

There have probably been worse doctrines in the twentieth century than Christian Science—communism, for example, and fascism. Nonetheless, it is radically in error and, in spite of its benign appearance, can be profoundly harmful. For one thing, in teaching you to avert your eyes from evil, it teaches you to ignore your own sinful impulses—your pride, callousness, and sensuality. The Christian Scientists I have known have been quite decent people. This is owing not to their principles, however, but in most cases to the kind of training they received before becoming Christian Scientists. I consider my mother to have been quite a good person, but in my view, this was because she had been raised as a Quaker and never succeeded in becoming an altogether logical Christian Scientist. A logical Christian Scientist does not deplore and try to eradicate sinful desires but tries simply not to notice them. Nor does a logical Christian Scientist who has committed a grave wrong suffer pangs of guilt and seek redemption; rather, the whole matter is as far as possible erased from one's mind. Christian penitence becomes impossible.

Equally dangerous is that Christian Scientists who learn to avert their eyes from evil learn to ignore the illnesses and other troubles being undergone by friends and relatives. As strange as it may seem, Christian Scientists who are rigorously practicing their creed do not ask someone ill, "How are you feeling this morning?" or "Are you feeling any better?" They resolutely deny the reality of the suffering. Such a habit is compatible with graciousness and cheerfulness—but not with deeply felt expressions of sympathy or concern. This does not mean that no attention is paid to others. It means rather that those who are ill, bereaved, depressed, or in any other way afflicted are subjected to a process of silent reconstruction. They are seen as not ill, not bereaved, not depressed. This of course means simply that they are not seen.

Though my mother was a very serious Christian Scientist, she did not rigorously work out or adhere to the implications of her creed. When I had the measles, she illogically saw to it that I was shielded from the light that would have damaged my eyes, and she illogically allowed me to be vaccinated against illnesses.

Above all, I want to say that she had little resemblance to the monument of self-righteousness and self-absorption that her creed implicitly encouraged her to be. I doubt that she ever more than half believed in the principles of Christian Science, even though she thought she believed in them wholeheartedly. After all, she had not been raised in those principles. I, of course, had been, and unfortunately, I unreservedly embraced them. As a result, although I was painfully conscientious, I was insensitive to my own sinful potentialities and not much attuned to the feelings and sufferings of others—conditions fateful for my life, as I will show. The principles of penitence and forgiveness were meaningless to me.

I give this background to show that I came to Christianity from a place very distant from Christianity. In Isaiah 41:8–9, God addresses "Israel, my servant, Jacob, whom I have chosen," as "you whom I took from the ends of the earth, and called from its farthest corners." I am conscious, in my Christian faith, of having been taken from the ends of the earth. I am of course speaking spiritually. But the spiritual fact is symbolized physically.

I was born on a cattle ranch near a small town in the far West. The scenery, with towering mountains a few miles away on both sides, standing forth in the crystalline desert air, was dramatic and testified daily to the Creator of the physical universe. But the nearest city was almost three hundred miles away and could be reached only by crossing a great desert. In that sense, I was at the ends of the earth physically as well as spiritually.

It was not only Christian Science, however, that placed me at the ends of the earth. After graduating from college and spending three years in the navy during World War II, I entered a spiritual environment very different from that of Christian Science—yet no less distant from real Christianity. This was the world of American social science. On my release from the navy, I undertook graduate work in political science, first at Claremont, then at Berkeley, where I finally received a Ph.D. No longer was I a Christian Scientist. But I was not a Christian either; indeed, I scarcely knew what Christianity was and did not really care.

I was interested mainly in political philosophy. I was attracted to certain thinkers who were in a broad sense religious (although not Christian), such as Plato and the English Hegelians. But I had little interest in the great Christian political philosophers such as Augustine and Aquinas. And my intellectual mentor among the major political philosophers was an outspoken atheist, John Stuart Mill. What needs emphasis, however, is not the canon of political philosophy, which includes figures of unquestionable spiritual stature, but rather the atmosphere of social science in most American universities.

There were Christians in the political science departments of secular colleges and universities. But they were very quiet about their faith. For the sake of professional survival and advancement, they had to be. The reigning assumption was that a respectable intellectual not only had no belief in God but had no interest even in the possibility of such a belief. Religion was not a live issue for anyone in pursuit of the kind of truth sought by political scientists. No one said this; the assumption was so dominant and unquestioned that no one had to. (The situation today is somewhat, although not entirely, different.)

In the time I spent as a graduate student and professor before becoming a Christian—a period of about twenty years—I never had a single professor, or a single friend or colleague, who expressed any definite interest in Christianity. Two or three friends were Christians, but, obedient to the reigning code, they were very quiet Christians. I knew of their faith only from chance remarks.

It was in this setting, and contrary to every reasonable expectation, that I became a Christian. It happened so gradually that I am embarrassed by my slowness of heart. Yet in looking back it seems to have happened inexorably, as though some irresistible force (like grace!) were behind it. When I was finally baptized, in my early forties, I had spent all of my life at the ends of the earth. In spite of this, I became a Christian—one for whom, as for any Christian, Christianity is not one among several activities and interests but is rather the center of the universe, the axis of history—in a word, life itself.

I dislike the casual way in which some Christians speak of miracles, as though we see them all around us, every day; the mystery and wonder of divine action tends thus to be obscured. But I am willing, soberly and tentatively, to think of my conversion as a miracle, for there was nothing in my childhood and youth, and nothing in the spiritual setting I inhabited as an adult, to explain it.

One circumstance that placed me at an even greater distance from God than did Christian Science or academic life consisted not in conditions to which I was subject but in acts for which I was responsible. It belongs to the time that separated my life as a Christian Scientist from my life as an academician—the three years I spent in the U.S. Navy.

The bulk of my time upon entering the navy in July 1943 was spent aboard a large landing ship in the Pacific, mainly in the Philippine Islands. I was an officer in charge of the deck force and responsible for the general maintenance of the ship. Later I became navigator and general manager of the ship under the captain. The crew was made up of about ten officers and a hundred men. We carried trucks and tanks, along with soldiers, and took part in most of the major landings in the Philippines—usually, however, coming in sometime after D-day, and usually in rather undramatic circumstances. There were occasional air raids, once a period of shelling from a large Japanese gun inland, and now and then sounds of combat in the distance. If I was "seeing action," however, I was doing so in almost the literal sense of the phrase—*seeing* it without being very much involved in it.

In March 1945 our ship put into Manila Harbor. Most of the fighting in Manila—some of the bloodiest combat of World War II—was over, and the American forces had taken the city. But there were isolated centers of Japanese resistance on the outskirts of the city, and Japanese bodies, often grotesquely bloated, were a common sight in the water and on the beaches.

A particularly fateful circumstance in my own destiny was this: scattered throughout the bay were dozens of Japanese cargo ships, sunk by American planes and resting on the bottom of the harbor, but with superstructures and upper decks still protruding above the surface of the water. They were oceangoing vessels, and most of them were largely intact. We were drawn by the prospect of seeing staterooms, bridges, and other operational areas so recently occupied by the Japanese, now for over three years a mysterious and fearsome antagonist. So a day or so after coming to anchor, a group of us, with me as the officer in charge, got together and set off in a small boat to look at some of the ships.

Only one thing kept the expedition from being an altogether carefree outing. There were rumors that Japanese soldiers, resisting capture to the last—perhaps with guns or hand grenades— had found their way out to some of the ships. We did not really expect to encounter any such soldiers, but as a precaution, we armed ourselves, many with automatic weapons, before embarking on our explorations.

We had gone through two or three ships and were tying up our boat at the side of another. Suddenly there was shattering gunfire right at my side. One of our sailors had seen a Japanese soldier on the ship, only 20 or 30 feet away. We were all so absurdly frightened that we were afraid to expose ourselves even to the extent of standing up to cast off the line secured to the ship. We severed it with gunfire and immediately went to the beach and found an American army officer, exhausted and unshaven, stretched out languidly in a folding chair near a large building in which we could hear occasional gunfire; inside were Japanese holdouts. We told him what had happened. He was courteous but completely uninterested. He gave us a hand grenade and left it to us to decide what to do next.

We returned to the ship and, trembling with fear, went aboard. We thought the Japanese soldier had been hit and probably killed, but we weren't sure; he might still be alive, and he might have companions. I crept up to a porthole and looked into a cabin where we thought the soldier might be. In the semidarkness, I seemed to see a figure on the deck, perhaps reclining against a bulkhead. Shielding myself as fully as possible, I reached through the porthole and fired several times. We found the soldier, indeed dead, in the cabin into which I had fired. He was unarmed.

At the time, I thought little about it. He had made no effort to surrender, and I assumed we could not have safely tried to capture him. I assumed also that a Japanese soldier would rather die than be captured. These were sound assumptions, but they rendered me insensitive to what had happened. When we returned to our ship, I was in an untroubled frame of mind.

During the next few days, as I recall, no one said much about the killing of the Japanese soldier. And probably no one thought much more about it than I did. But one afternoon some sailors asked if I would serve as officer in charge of another exploratory expedition; we had looked into only a few of the many hulks out in the bay. Unthinkingly, I agreed. Again we armed ourselves and set out. Again we crept, tense and frightened, yet feeling a sense of adventure, down passageways, around corners, into staterooms, able often to see only a few feet ahead, fearing that at any moment we would be faced with one or more armed and suicidal enemy soldiers.

Nothing eventful occurred, however, until I had gone out on the main deck of one of the ships while a group of sailors was prowling around inside. Then, from somewhere within the ship, came the sound of gunfire. I was told that another Japanese soldier had been killed. When I arrived at the scene the soldier, presumably dead, lay on the deck with his back to me. Assuming it would be unsafe to approach him, since conceivably he was armed and only feigning death, I fired into his body.

As strange as it may sound, this all happened rather casually. I saw no blood; I had seen no one fall under a hail of bullets. Movie violence today is far more horrifying and "realistic" than this was. I scarcely even looked at the body. Only later did someone tell me that this soldier, too, had been unarmed.

I was still untroubled, cushioned as before by the assumption that the shootings were unavoidable and that the dead soldiers preferred death to the disgrace of being captured. There was nothing in my motives to trouble me. We had not set out to kill Japanese soldiers and found no satisfaction or thrills in the fact that we had. If we had somehow found ourselves with a captured and unarmed Japanese soldier in our custody, I am quite sure that we would have done him no harm. Our aim had been to find relief from the boredom of shipboard life by exploring some great deserted oceangoing vessels. The killings seemed incidental, unavoidable, devoid of hatred or pleasure. And I, personally, had not faced and shot a living man. So again, some days passed during which I carried on my normal shipboard duties and thought little of what had happened.

I still don't know why this period of complacency ended as suddenly as it did. But I vividly remember, and will always remember, the moment it happened. I was stepping into my stateroom. Suddenly I was nearly felled with the realization that I was responsible for the needless loss of two human lives. I had been officer in charge of the two exploratory expeditions, and I had fired my gun into the bodies, probably dead but possibly living, of both of the soldiers we had killed. I was not simply conscience-stricken. I was incredulous that I, a rather conscientious and even straitlaced young man, had fallen into such a moral abyss. (In college I neither smoked nor drank; I cried in pity over the first fish I caught as a child; I could never bear the idea of hunting; on the ship I meticulously enforced all safety regulations, thinking how awful it would be were there a fatal shipboard accident.) The terrible word *murder* invaded my mind. It was as though I had been dreaming all during the preceding week, during the ship explorations and the killings, and suddenly the dream had turned into a terrible, and entirely unacceptable, reality. There is no exaggeration in saying that at the moment this happened my life changed forever.

The ensuing weeks are unclear in my memory. I do know that they were spent in a state of what might be called metaphysical panic. I realized that I had committed an offense against something holy and, as far as I knew, remorseless and unforgiving. I had never had anything like "a religious experience." God, for me, was merely the one who had created a good universe and then conveniently disappeared, leaving the human race to know the truth about it and enjoy it. Now, unexpectedly, an angry God—or at least a divine and implacable law, menacing and offended—towered over me. Christian Science gave me no help at all: denying evil, it had nothing to say about forgiveness. And it had made me a stranger to Christianity. It is a mark of this estrangement that there was a Christian chaplain on our ship and, although I was nearly drowning in anguish, it never occurred to me to talk with him. I talked with no one. I went through the motions required of me by my shipboard duties while despairingly casting about in my mind to discover how I could go on living.

This period abruptly ended after perhaps two or three weeks of moral agony. I had with me on the ship not only *Science and Health* but also a Bible, given to me by my mother on my ninth birthday. One afternoon I was leafing through the Bible in a mood of desperation. My eyes fell on the words of Psalm 118:24: "This is the day which the Lord hath made; we will rejoice and be glad in it."

I knew in an instant that in spite of what I had done, God's universe remained intact, that I inhabited a day that God had made, and that I could live. The inward experience immediately found an outward symbol. The sunlight on the waves of the blue Pacific Ocean took on a splendor and significance they had never before had but never lost during my remaining time at sea. In those sunlit waves about me I saw a sign of the divine power that could, in a way still utterly beyond my understanding, deliver me from guilt and give me life.

Not that I was thereafter happy. For years I would recurrently go through hours and days when my heart was burdened with the memory of what I had done. Nor did I quickly gain understanding. It took not merely years but decades for me to comprehend, and to live under the authority of, the act of divine forgiveness that took place on the cross. But from the moment I came upon the psalmist's words about the Lord's day, I knew that my life had not ended on those ships out in Manila Bay.

These events reached a climax only when I became a Christian. Only then did I begin to understand that the light of God's day came not only from the act of creation but also from the act of redemption that was accomplished on the cross. For several years, I remained a Christian Scientist and therefore not a Christian. I resorted to the most absurd theological expedients to explain to myself how God was able to shield the day he had made from the destructive impact of deeds like mine. Humbled and lost though I was, I'm afraid God found me a slow and halting follower. Nevertheless, his mercy endured, and I began my long journey toward Christianity.

This was a highly intellectual journey, even though it began with traumatic physical events. Often I told myself that I would put the events in Manila Bay behind me by becoming a good person, but I certainly did not succeed in becoming any better than the average person. I was shackled by pride, sensuality, and callousness. But I did get myself seriously involved in the quest for truth. Soon after being discharged from the navy, I entered into graduate work, which lasted for six years, and then into university teaching. I became a professional intellectual.

It would be roughly accurate to say that for about twenty years I stumbled along in the dark but caught occasional glimpses of light far ahead. Gradually the light grew brighter. Many of these glimpses came through a pagan of great spiritual stature—Plato. I think that the natural setting in which Plato lived and wrote, with the dry air, the lucid sunlight, and the sharply etched mountains one can still experience in present-day Greece, was enough like the desert setting in which I grew up to render his thought particularly evocative for me. In teaching the history of political philosophy, I always devoted many weeks to Plato. Subsequent history, as I taught it, tended to become a record of decline from Plato on (although, in opposition to Plato, I emphatically endorsed the separation of temporal and spiritual authorities that arose from Christianity as well as the ideal of liberty to which this separation eventually led).

Glimpses of light were also provided by more recent thinkers. I became intensely interested in existentialism, which was very fashionable in the postwar years. I was attracted mainly to existentialists who were religious and Christian, not atheists such as Sartre. I read extensively in Kierkegaard, Karl Jaspers, and Gabriel Marcel.

To speak as casually as this about writers who interested me, however, conveys an inadequate impression of the crucial role that books played in my spiritual progress. Although I had many good friends as a graduate student and then as a young instructor,

I always had religious concerns that set me apart from practically all of the young political scientists and historians with whom I associated. That these concerns were inchoate and exceedingly vague, if deeply rooted, increased my isolation, for I was unable to articulate them. The consequence was that books assumed a peculiar importance in my life. I was nourished and kept alive by certain writers, and it was these writers who gradually led me to Christianity.

Standing slightly taller than any of the others in my memory is the great, but now largely forgotten, Christian philosopher Nicolas Berdyaev. I'm not sure why a naïve young man from a small town in the American West should have been so powerfully drawn toward an exiled Russian aristocrat. Some of his key ideas were never acceptable to me—his emphasis on creativity, for example, and his concept of a primal, cosmic freedom that placed limits even on God and introduced into God's life a tragic note. Moreover, Berdyaev paid little attention to the Christian theme that concerned me above all others as a consequence of my war experiences: sin and forgiveness.

Still, his writings enchanted and shaped me. First of all, he set an example of bold, wide-ranging thought—on a Christian basis. Beyond this, he taught me to take the mystery of human freedom very seriously (although I incorporated it into a Western liberalism, which was not at all what Berdyaev had in mind). He swayed me in the direction of a sharply dualistic metaphysic (most authoritatively expressed, perhaps, in Paul, although approaching the extreme of gnosticism in Berdyaev himself). He made eschatology—the idea of the reappearance of Christ and the end of history—a dramatic possibility among the ideas that occupied my mind. And he enabled me to understand the spiritual significance of Kant, and especially of the first Critique. I will always think of Berdyaev as an old, revered teacher. But Berdyaev did not make me a Christian—at least, not he alone.

It is harder to define the impact on my intellect and feelings of Fyodor Dostoevsky. The influences emanating from novels are probably more subtle and various than those emanating from philosophical writings. However, I read all of Dostoevsky's major novels five or six times over a period of several years, and I'm sure those works did much to confirm and shape my Christian faith. Thus Dostoevsky reinforced my awareness, gained first from Berdyaev, of freedom as the incomprehensible and uncontrollable core of a human being. He helped me (as Berdyaev had not) to see freedom as a bottomless reservoir of evil but, at the same time, to see God's mercy as more powerful than human sin. He enabled me to realize that sin cannot be overcome by human devices of the kind that governments wield but only by suffering and by grace. And he implanted deeply in my mind the sense that when Christianity fades, as it has in our time and as Dostoevsky prophetically foresaw that it would, strange and terrible consequences are apt to follow, consequences like those dramatized in Raskolnikov (*Crime and Punishment*), Stavrogin (*The Possessed*), and Ivan Karamazov (*The Brothers Karamazov*).

A third great thinker who always comes to mind when I try to remember those who drew me into a Christian universe was, paradoxically, not a Christian. This is the Jewish philosopher Martin Buber. Buber's thought is perhaps too simple to be quite adequate; the concept of I-Thou relations leaves numerous metaphysical issues untouched. And his political thought is not only too simple but too optimistic as well; it seems that only a wondrous naïveté could have allowed Buber to ignore the questions about his socialism that were tacitly posed by thinkers such as Augustine, Machiavelli, and Hobbes, as well as by various modern writers influenced by the Christian doctrine of original sin. Nonetheless, Buber was a very great intellect, if we mean by that someone possessed of profound and exceptional insights. Buber's concept of dialogue, an activity embracing not only human beings, but also God ("the eternal Thou"), is among the permanent furnishings of my mind. And it has decisively shaped my understanding of Christianity. If Christ is the Word, then he is a dialogic figure, an interlocutor, so to speak, in conversations between God and man.

Berdyaev, Dostoevsky, and Buber did not merely affect the way I looked at things. Partly from a natural affinity that seemed to bind me to them and partly because I read them so fully and frequently, they became, as it were, permanent residents in my intellectual universe. My thinking tended to be a kind of continuing consultation with them. This is true of two other thinkers as well, one of whom was Karl Barth. I still remember the moment I came across one of the huge, black volumes making up the *Church Dogmatics*. The book looked most forbidding. For one thing, it was long (just short of 700 pages), and the print was small. Also, Barth discussed matters like sin and damnation, and I dreaded reading something that would make me feel that, due to my deeds in the Pacific, I was lost.

But I purchased the volume and read it. I found not only that my fears were unfulfilled (far from it, in view of Barth's eloquent emphasis on God's mercy) but also that I received doctrinal instruction of a kind not gained from anything else I had read. In subsequent years I purchased and read the rest of the 12 giant volumes making up Barth's masterwork (and some of them twice). Barth was a rigorous and highly orthodox theologian. He was also a dramatic writer. The *Church Dogmatics*, along with his electrifying *Epistle to the Romans*, provided me with a theological education. Barth was an extremist, a theological Bolshevik, one might say, and I have never in any strict sense been a follower of his. But for years he has been indispensable to my spiritual morale, and he has probably taught me more about Christian doctrine than any other author.

Finally, I must mention the one American among my regular intellectual instructors and companions—Reinhold Niebuhr. By the time I started reading Niebuhr, shortly after finishing graduate work, I had given up Christian Science entirely (which did not happen in a single dramatic moment but through a slow process of erosion). Niebuhr greatly helped me to consolidate this development. He presented a pessimistic (or, more accurately, realistic) view of human nature and history; he did this in an eminently clear and logical fashion; and he brilliantly related his insights to the contemporary political world.

His assistance helped me get on my feet, not only as a Christian but also as an inhabitant of the harsh political world of the twentieth century. If Niebuhr had a single guiding idea, it was that of original sin—sin as not merely one human trait among others but as an orientation of the soul, distorting and misdirecting all human traits. He wielded this idea with powerful effect in examining the political illusions of our time. Much of the tragic folly of our times, not only on the part of extremists such as Lenin but also on the part of middle-of-the-road liberals and conservatives, would never have arisen had we not, in our technological and ideological pride, forgotten original sin.

The twenty years during which I was inching my way toward Christianity was a time of intense study and reflection. I was absorbed daily and hourly by the enigmas and demands of the intellectual universe in which I dwelled, a universe populated not only by the five names I have mentioned but by numerous others—philosophers, theologians, political writers, and novelists. I lived with books, as well as with notepads for jotting down the thoughts that came to me. I was absorbed in trying to understand my life, and life generally, and the short steps forward that I made were recorded in the lectures I inflicted on my students and in the articles and books I began to write.

It may sound as though my days, and my journey toward Christianity, were very cerebral, and indeed they were. Too much so, probably. I had a wife, someone of worth so inestimable that I count her along with my faith as one of the signs that God has not given me up. I also had two sons, little boys whom I delighted in and loved. I fear, however, that I was too deeply involved in intellectual trials and undertakings—and too wearied and exasperated by my failures—to be very satisfactory as a husband and father.

But God does not forgive us just for grave misdeeds, long repented of, such as those I committed in Manila Bay. He forgives us, I believe, minute by minute, in response to the continuing stream of minor and not-so-minor misdeeds that, for most of us, mark the course of our fallen lives. Hence, in spite of my inadequate performance of family duties, I continued to be carried ahead on the raft of divine grace. I finally completed the long voyage that had begun in Christian Science and ended in Christian faith, the journey that led me from Plato to Christ, and from John Stuart Mill (of whom I wrote a systematic, if inept, defense in my doctoral dissertation) to such mentors as Berdyaev and Barth.

I still have not described the actual event of my becoming a Christian. There is good reason for this: no such event occurred. I can say only that I was not a Christian during my time as a graduate student and a young instructor, whereas well before reaching the age of fifty I was. I can see two main reasons behind this development, one "existential," or personal, the other intellectual. The existential reason is that with my scarcely insignificant moral failures, I could only live as one forgiven by God. After Manila Bay I felt I had forfeited the right to live; only grace could restore that right. The intellectual reason is that among all the numerous creeds I studied, Christianity was by far the most interesting and convincing. Whether it would have been so apart from my war experiences, I cannot say.

It is rather unchristian, however, to give reasons for being a Christian. I have learned this, I suppose, from studying Barth's doctrine of election. If you are a Christian, this is not because *you* have made a choice but because *God* has made a choice. Christianity was written into your destiny on the day of your creation. This is not so arrogant a statement as a non-Christian might suppose. As my own case makes so starkly manifest, to be chosen by God presupposes no merit whatever of your own. Nor is it in any other sense an achievement that redounds to your credit. It is only a matter of unending gratitude.

Just as Christianity is not something you choose, nor something you hold on to for certain specific reasons, neither is it something to which you can assign a value. Living as a Christian does, to be sure, bring hints of ultimate peace and joy that impel us to think of Christianity as possessing great value. Thinking that way is risky, however. It may subtly insinuate into our minds the idea that there is a higher standard in terms of which the value of Christianity can be judged. But that demeans Christianity, which is itself the highest standard. We judge all else by the Christian standard and cannot judge Christianity itself. In other words, attributing value to Christianity may cause us to forget that Christianity is not a part of life, not even a part that is immeasurably more valuable than any other part. It is simply life itself.

Christian existence, one must also remember, is a drama of estrangement (for me, Christian Science) and reconciliation, of sin (Manila Bay) and redemption. Living through such a drama is likely sometimes to be trying and difficult. Even grace may be harsh. Suffering may be the fire in which a new soul is forged. In my own experience, only once, far out in the Pacific Ocean—at the ends of the earth—have I been consciously lifted up by grace. But of course I am not saying that grace has had no part in my life. Let me illustrate the part I think it has had by something told me by a friend.

The friend lived in my hometown in the West. He would often hike, alone, into the Sierra foothills prospecting for gold and glorying in the dramatic mountain and desert scene that lay all about him. There were known to be mountain lions where he hiked. Mountain lions are mysterious, even mystical, creatures. They are almost never seen, even in areas they inhabit. They are benign, for rarely do they attack human beings, although they are among the large predatory cats and can kill sizable animals in an instant; they also possess great beauty and grace.

I once asked my friend whether he had ever seen a mountain lion on any of his prospecting ventures. He said that he hadn't. He said also, however, that often when he hiked into a mountain canyon, then late in the afternoon turned back, retracing his steps, he would find the tracks of a mountain lion near his own tracks, made earlier in the day. He would know that a mountain lion had been paying him close attention, even though he never saw the lion.

My friend's experience might serve as a parable of my own life with God. I can't claim ever to have had even a glimpse of God. When I look back on my life, however, I see his tracks all around the places where I have been.

JAMES VAN THOLEN

SURPRISED BY DEATH

(From *Christianity Today*)

While we were still weak, at the right time Christ died for
the ungodly. . . . But God proves his love for us in that
while we still were sinners Christ died for us.

—Romans 5:6, 8, NRSV

*In 1996 James Van Tholen, then 31, and his wife, Rachel, moved to
Rochester, New York, where Jim became pastor of a Christian Reformed
Church. Members of the church found themselves drawn to Jim's ministry, especially to his preaching, which gleamed with biblical intelligence and humane understanding.*

*Then, the unthinkable occurred: in the late winter of 1998, physicians
identified and surgically removed a liposarcoma from behind Jim's right
knee. Within weeks Jim had another tumor behind his chest wall, and then
spots on both femurs and one kidney. Recent tests confirm cancer up and
down Jim's spine, with the result that he now thinks about how he moves,
always conscious of the risk of spinal cord compression (and paralysis).*

*From March until October, Jim struggled to recover from surgery
and to absorb forms of chemotherapy that offered no cure but could
prolong his life somewhat. By October, the chemotherapy had suppressed Jim's cancer enough that he was able to return to his pulpit.*

*What follows is the sermon Jim preached from Romans 5:1–11 on
the morning of his return, October 18, 1998. As the members of the*

*congregation listened to their young preacher's sermon, they understood
something about dying and rising with Christ that they hadn't known
just that way before.*

Cornelius Plantinga, Jr., dean of the chapel at
Calvin College and a former teacher of Van Tholen's
at Calvin Theological Seminary

This is a strange day—for all of us. Most of you know that today
marks my return to this pulpit after seven months of dealing with
an aggressive and deadly form of cancer. Now, with the cancer
vacationing for a little while, I am back. And of course I'm glad to
be back. But I can't help feeling how strange this day is—especially because I want to ignore my absence, and I want to pretend
everybody has forgotten the reason for it.

But we can't do that. We can't ignore what has happened. We
can rise above it; we can live through it; but we can't ignore it. If
we ignore the threat of death as too terrible to talk about, then
the threat wins. Then we are overwhelmed by it, and our faith
doesn't apply to it. And if that happens, we lose hope.

We want to worship God in this church, and for our worship
to be real, it doesn't have to be fun, and it doesn't have to be guilt-
ridden. But it does have to be honest, and it does have to hope in
God. We have to be honest about a world of violence and pain, a
world that scorns faith and smashes hope and rebuts love. We
have to be honest about the world, and honest about the difficulties of faith within it. And then we still have to hope in God.

So let me start with the honesty. The truth is that for seven
months I have been scared. Not of the cancer, not really. Not
even of death. Dying is another matter—how long it will take
and how it will go. Dying scares me. But when I say that I have
been scared, I don't mean that my thoughts have centered on
dying. My real fear has centered somewhere else. Strange as it
may sound, I have been scared of meeting God.

How could this be so? How could I have believed in the God of grace and still have dreaded to meet him? Why did I stand in this pulpit and preach grace to you over and over, and then, when I myself needed the grace so much, discover fear where the grace should have been?

I think I know the answer now. As the wonderful preacher John Timmer has taught me over the years, the answer is that grace is a scandal. Grace is hard to believe. Grace goes against the grain. The gospel of grace says that there is nothing I can *do* to get right with God, but that God has made himself right with me through Jesus' bloody death. And that is a scandalous thing to believe.

God comes to us before we go to him. John Timmer used to say that this is God's habit. God came to Abraham when there was nothing to come to, just an old man at a dead end. But that's God for you. That's the way God likes to work. He comes to old men and to infants, to sinners and to losers. That's grace, and a sermon without it is no sermon at all.

So I've tried to preach grace, to fill my sermons up with grace, to persuade you to believe in grace. And it's wonderful work to have—that is, to stand here and preach grace to people. I got into this pulpit and talked about war and homosexuality and divorce. I talked about death before I knew what death really was. And I tried to bring the gospel of grace to these areas when I preached. I said that God goes to people in trouble, that God receives people in trouble, that God is a God who *gets* into trouble because of his grace. I said what our Heidelberg Catechism says: that our only comfort in life and in death is that we are not our own but belong to our faithful Savior, Jesus Christ.

I said all those things, and I meant them. But that was before I faced death myself. So now I have a silly thing to admit: I don't think I ever realized the shocking and radical nature of God's grace—even as I preached it. And the reason I didn't get it where grace is concerned, I think, is that I assumed I still had about forty years left. Forty years to unlearn my bad habits. Forty years to let my sins thin down and blow away. Forty years to be good to animals and pick up my neighbors' mail for them when they went on vacation.

But that's not how it's going to go. Now I have months, not years. And now I have to meet my creator who is also my judge— I have to meet God not later, but sooner. I haven't enough time to undo my wrongs, not enough time to straighten out what's crooked, not enough time to clean up my life.

And that's what has scared me.

So now, for the first time, I have to preach grace and know what I'm talking about. I have to preach grace and not only believe it, but rest on it, depend on it, stake my life on it. And as I faced the need to do this I remembered one of the simplest, most powerful statements in the entire Bible.

You may have thought that the reason for my choice of Romans 5 lay in the wonderful words about how suffering produces endurance, and endurance produces character, and character produces hope. Those are beautiful words, true words, but I'm not so sure they apply to me. I'm not sure I've suffered so much or so faithfully to claim that my hope has arisen through the medium of good character. No, many of you know far more about good character than I do, and more about suffering, too.

It wasn't that beautiful chain with character as the main link that drew my attention to Romans 5; instead, it was just one little word in verses 6 and 8. It's the Greek word *eti*, and it has brought comfort to my soul. The word means "yet" or "still," and it makes all the difference between sin and grace. Paul writes that "while we were *still* weak Christ died for the ungodly." He wants us to marvel at the Christ of the gospel, who comes to us in our weakness and in our need. Making sure we get the point, Paul uses the word twice in verse 6 in a repetitious and ungrammatical piling up of his meaning: "*Still* while we were *still* weak, at the right time Christ died for the ungodly."

I'm physically weak, but that's not my main weakness, my most debilitating weakness. What the last half year has proved to me is that my weakness is more of the soul than the body. This is what I've come to understand as I have dwelled on one question: How will I explain myself to my God? How can I ever claim to have been what he called me to be?

And, of course, the scary truth is that I can't. That's the kind of weakness Paul is talking about. And that's where *eti* comes in— while we were *still* weak, while we were *still* sinners, while we were *still* enemies of God, we were reconciled with him through the death of his Son. I find it unfathomable that God's love propelled him to reach into our world with such scandalous grace, such a way out, such hope. No doubt God has done it, because there's no hope anywhere else. I know. I've been looking. And I have come to see that the hope of the world lies only inside the cradle of God's grace.

This truth has come home to me as I've been thinking what it will mean to die. The same friends I enjoy now will get together a year, and three years, and twenty years from now, and I will not be there, not even in the conversation. Life will go on. In this church you will call a new minister with new gifts and a new future, and eventually I'll fade from your mind and memory. I understand. The same thing has happened to my own memories of others. When I was saying something like this a few months ago to a friend of mine, he reminded me of those poignant words of Psalm 103:15–16: "As for mortals, their days are like grass; they flourish like a flower of the field; for the wind passes over it, and it is gone, and its place knows it no more." For the first time I felt those words in my gut; I understood that my place would know me no more.

In his poem "Adjusting to the Light," Miller Williams explores the sense of awkwardness among Lazarus's friends and neighbors just after Jesus has resuscitated him. Four days after his death, Lazarus returns to the land of the living and finds that people have moved on from him. Now they have to scramble to fit him back in:

> Lazarus, listen, we have things to tell you. We killed the sheep you meant to take to market. We couldn't keep the old dog, either. He minded you. The rest of us he barked at. Rebecca, who cried two days, has given her hand to the sandalmaker's son. Please understand—we didn't know that Jesus could do this.
>
> We're glad you're back. But give us time to think. Imagine our surprise. . . . We want to say we're sorry for all of that. And one thing more. We threw away the lyre. But listen, we'll pay whatever the sheep was worth. The dog, too. And put your room the way it was before.

Miller Williams has it just right. After only a few days, Lazarus's place knew him no more. Before cancer, I liked Williams's poem, but now I'm living it. Believe me: hope doesn't lie in our legacy; it doesn't lie in our longevity; it doesn't lie in our personality or our career or our politics or our children or, heaven knows, our goodness. Hope lies in *eti*.

So please don't be surprised when in the days ahead I don't talk about my cancer very often. I've told a part of my story today, because it seemed right to do it on the first day back after seven months. But what we must talk about here is not me. I cannot be our focus, because the center of my story—*our* story—is that the grace of Jesus Christ carries us beyond every cancer, every divorce, every sin, every trouble that comes to us. The Christian gospel is the story of Jesus, and that's the story I'm called to tell.

I'm dying. Maybe it will take longer instead of shorter; maybe I'll preach for several months, and maybe for a bit more. But I am dying. I know it, and I hate it, and I'm still frightened by it. But there is hope, unwavering hope. I have hope not in something I've done, some purity I've maintained, or some sermon I've written. I hope in God—the God who reaches out for an enemy, saves a sinner, dies for the weak.

That's the gospel, and I can stake my life on it. I must. And so must you.

PROCLAIMING THE
LORD'S DEATH

(From *Christian Century*)

High view of the ministry of the Word and pronounced free church sensibilities notwithstanding, I finally caved in. I sought refuge from bad preaching in the celebration of the Eucharist.

My gripe was not with the oratorical skills of preachers in the churches I frequented, though many would have done well to add some rhetorical polish. My problem was not even that sermons were "unbiblical" in the sense that ministers failed to seek inspiration in the scriptures, though some seemed to be commenting on the biblical texts in order to drape their own opinions with the mantle of the prophets' and apostles' authority. More than with rhetoric or the use of the scripture, I was disturbed by the failure of many preachers to make the center of the Christian faith the center of their proclamation. Except in superficial ways, they often kept silent on the topic that should have demanded all their eloquence—Jesus Christ crucified for the ungodly.

Writing to the church in Corinth, the apostle Paul noted that "the message of the cross is foolishness to those who are perishing, but to us who are being saved it is the power of God." Today, however, the message of the cross seems just as foolish to those who should be helping the perishing get saved as it does to the perishing themselves! Many preachers are hesitant to follow the great apostle who decided "to know nothing among" his listeners "except Jesus Christ, and him crucified." Instead, to those who seek wisdom, they offer sapiential musings; to those who demand signs, they give advice on how to transform the world.

Forget about "God's foolishness" which is "wiser than human wisdom," they say implicitly, as they concentrate, say, on putting yesterday's news into perspective or on helping people understand this or that psychological hang-up. Forget about "God's weakness" which is "stronger than human strength," they suggest as they zero in on alleviating pressing social needs or curing physical ailments.

My point is not that physical, psychological and social wellbeing is unimportant or that the church should remain uninvolved. To the contrary. But if the church were primarily about these issues, a perfectly good argument could be made that on a Sunday morning, instead of going to church, one should get cozy in one's armchair with the *New York Times* in hand and a large mug of cappuccino close by. A morning spent with a good newspaper or book would certainly better prepare one to engage the problems of the world than sitting at the feet of preachers who talk about "wisdom" and "signs."

Fortunately, the choice is not between going to church to hear a sermon or staying at home with a newspaper or book. In church one can also receive the sacrament of the body and blood of Jesus Christ (and pray for a good sermon in addition). Some time ago, Emil Brunner suggested that the sacraments are the best antidote to a minister "who lives by his own wisdom rather than from the scriptures. Even the most audacious minister has not dared to lay hands on the Sacraments."

Brunner continues, "One may so interpret the words of Scripture that the words speak the opposite of their intent; but the Sacraments, thank God, speak a language independent of the language of the Pastor. They are a part of the message of the Church least affected by theological or other tendencies; and that is their special blessing." Brunner may have underestimated the audaciousness of some ministers who feel as entitled to redesign the sacraments as they feel inclined to avoid the cross of Christ. But where the sacraments are left intact, they point straight back to Christ's self-giving on the cross.

Dissatisfied with ministers who live by their own wisdom, I turned to the Eucharist. Its celebration takes the participants back to the night in which the Lord of Glory was betrayed and to the day on which his crucified body was suspended between the heavens and the earth. Its "special blessing" lies in not letting us forget that Christians' lives rest on Christ's body broken and his blood spilled and that their calling is to "live in love, as Christ loved us and gave himself up for us, a fragrant offering and sacrifice to God." In the Eucharist the church receives itself anew by the power of the Holy Spirit as that which it is and ought to be—the body of Christ given for the salvation of the world. Augustine put it beautifully to his congregation: "So if it's you that are the body of Christ and its members, it's the mystery meaning you that has been placed on the Lord's table; what you receive is the mystery that means you. It is to what you are that you reply *Amen,* and by so replying you express your assent."

The gathering of believers is the place where by the power of the Spirit and through the celebration of the Eucharist we are made into the body of Christ—for our own salvation and for the salvation of the world. And so on any Sunday morning I happily leave my newspaper at home and head for a church whose primary purpose is neither to enlighten nor to empower me, but "to proclaim the Lord's death until he comes."

Will the stress on the Eucharist produce a church withdrawn from public engagement? It could. But it need not. Indeed, as

William T. Cavanaugh argues in his fascinating book *Torture and Eucharist* (1998), a proper celebration of the Eucharist is a liturgically enacted counterpolitics to the polities of this world. By drawing the church back to the cross of Christ, the Eucharist furnishes the church with resources to resist the injustice, deceitfulness and violence that mark the world for which Christ died.

DALLAS WILLARD

JESUS THE LOGICIAN

(From *Christian Scholar's Review*)

Few today will have seen the words "Jesus" and "logician" put together to form a phrase or sentence, unless it would be to *deny* any connection between them at all. The phrase "Jesus the logician" is not ungrammatical, any more than is "Jesus the carpenter." But it "feels" upon first encounter to be something like a category mistake or error in logical type, such as "Purple is asleep," or "More people live in the winter than in cities," or "Do you walk to work or carry your lunch?"

There is in our culture an uneasy relation between Jesus and intelligence, and I have actually heard Christians respond to my statement that Jesus is the most intelligent man who ever lived by saying that it is an oxymoron. Today we automatically position him away from (or even in opposition to) the intellect and intellectual life. Almost no one would consider him to be a *thinker*, addressing the same issues as, say, Aristotle, Kant, Heidegger or Wittgenstein, and with the same logical method.

Now this fact has important implications for how we today view his relationship to our world and our life—especially if our work happens to be that of art, thought, research or scholarship. How could he fit into such a line of work, and lead us in it, if he were logically obtuse? How could we be his disciples at our work, take him seriously as our teacher there, if when we entered our fields of technical or professional competence we had to leave him at the door? Obviously some repositioning is in order, and it may be helped along simply by observing his use of logic and his obvious powers of logical thinking as manifested in the Gospels of the New Testament.

Now when we speak of "Jesus the logician" we do not, of course, mean that he developed *theories* of logic, as did, for example, Aristotle and Frege. No doubt he *could* have, if he is who Christians have taken him to be. He could have provided a *Begriffsschrift*, or a *Principia Mathematica*, or alternative axiomatizations of Modal Logic, or various completeness or incompleteness proofs for various "languages." (He is, presumably, responsible for the order that is represented through such efforts as these.)

He could have. Just as he could have handed Peter or John the formulas of Relativity Physics or the Plate Tectonic theory of the earth's crust. He certainly could, that is, if he is indeed the one Christians have traditionally taken him to be. But he did not do it, and for reasons which are bound to seem pretty obvious to anyone who stops to think about it. But that, in any case, is not my subject here. When I speak of "Jesus the logician" I refer to his *use* of logical insights: to his mastery and employment of logical principles in his work as a teacher and public figure.

Now it is worth noting that those who do creative work or are experts in the field of logical theory are *not* necessarily more logical or more philosophically sound than those who do not. We might hope that they would be, but they may even be illogical in how they work out their own logical theories. For some reason great powers in theory do not seem to guarantee significantly greater accuracy in practice. Perhaps no person well informed about the history of thought will be surprised at this statement, but for most of us it needs to be emphasized. To have understanding of developed logical theory surely *could* help one to think logically, but it is not sufficient to guarantee logical

thinking and except for certain rarified cases it is not even necessary. Logical insight rarely depends upon logical theory, though
it does depend upon logical relations. The two primary logical
relations are implication (logical entailment) and contradiction,
and their role in standard forms of argument such as the Barbara
Syllogism, Disjunctive Syllogism, Modus Ponens and Modus Tol-
lens—and even in strategies such as *reductio ad absurdum*—can be
fully appreciated, for practical purposes, without rising to the
level of theoretical generalization at all.[1]

To *be* logical no doubt does require an understanding of what
implication and contradiction are, as well as the ability to recognize their presence or absence in obvious cases. But it also
requires the *will* to be logical, and then certain personal qualities
that make it possible and actual: qualities such as freedom from
distraction, focused attention on the meanings or ideas involved
in talk and thought, devotion to truth, and willingness to follow
the truth wherever it leads *via* logical relations. All of this in turn
makes significant demands upon moral character. Not just on
points such as resoluteness and courage, though those are
required. A practicing hypocrite, for example, will not find a
friend in logic, nor will liars, thieves, murderers and adulterers.
They will be constantly alert to appearances and inferences that
may logically implicate them in their wrong actions. Thus the literary and cinematic genre of *mysteries* is unthinkable without play
on logical relations.

Those devoted to defending certain pet assumptions or practices come what may will also have to protect themselves from
logic. All of this is, I believe, commonly recognized by thoughtful people. Less well understood is the fact that one can be logical only if one is committed to being logical as a fundamental

---

[1]See my paper, "Degradation of Logical Form," in *Axiomathes*, 1–3 (1997): 1–22,
especially pp. 3–7.

value. One is not logical by chance, any more than one just happens to be moral. And, indeed, logical consistency is a significant factor in moral character. That is part of the reason why in an age that attacks morality, as ours does, the logical will also be demoted or set aside—as it now is.

Not only does Jesus not concentrate on logical *theory*, but he also does not spell out all the details of the logical structures he employs on particular occasions. His use of logic is always enthymemic, as is common to ordinary life and conversation. His points are, with respect to *logical explicitness*, understated and underdeveloped. The significance of the enthymeme is that it enlists the mind of the hearer or hearers *from the inside*, in a way that full and explicit statement of argument cannot do. Its rhetorical force is, accordingly, quite different from that of fully explicated argumentation, which tends to distance the hearer from the force of logic by locating it outside of his own mind.

Jesus' aim in utilizing logic is not to win battles, but to achieve understanding or insight in his hearers. This understanding only comes from the inside, from the understandings one already has. It seems to "well up from within" one. Thus he does not follow the logical method one often sees in Plato's dialogues, or the method that characterizes most teaching and writing today. That is, he does not try to make everything so explicit that the conclusion is forced down the throat of the hearer. Rather, he presents matters in such a way that those who wish to know can find their way to, can come to, the appropriate conclusion as something *they* have discovered—whether or not it is something they particularly care for.

"A man convinced against his will is of the same opinion still." Yes, and no doubt Jesus understood that. And so he typically aims at real inward change of view that would enable his hearers to become significantly different as people through the workings of their own intellect. They will have, unless they are strongly resistant to the point of blindness, the famous "eureka" experience, not the experience of being outdone or beaten down.

With these points in mind, let us look at some typical scenes from the Gospels, scenes that are of course quite familiar, but are now to be examined for the role that distinctively logical thinking plays in them.

(1). Consider Matthew 12:1–8. This contains a teaching about the ritual law: specifically about the regulations of the temple and the sabbath. Jesus and his disciples were walking through fields of grain—perhaps wheat or barley—on the sabbath, and they were stripping the grains from the stalks with their hands and eating them. The Pharisees accused them of breaking the law, of being wrongdoers. Jesus, in response, points out that there are conditions in which the ritual laws in question do not apply.

He brings up cases of this that the Pharisees already concede. One is the case (I Samuel 21:1–6) where David, running for his life, came to the place of worship and sacrifice supervised by Ahimelech the priest. He asked Ahimelech for food for himself and his companions, but the only food available was bread consecrated in the ritual of the offerings. This bread, as Jesus pointed out (Matthew 12:4), was forbidden to David by law, and was to be eaten (after the ritual) by priests alone. But Ahimelech gave it to David and his men to satisfy their hunger. Hunger as a human need, therefore, may justify doing what ritual law forbids.

Also, Jesus continues (second case), the priests every sabbath in their temple service do more work than sabbath regulations allow: "On the sabbath the priests in the temple profane the sabbath, and are innocent" (Matthew 12:5). It logically follows, then, that one is not automatically guilty of wrongdoing or disobedience when they do not keep the ritual observances as dictated, in case there is some greater need that must be met. This is something the Pharisees have, by implication, already admitted by accepting the rightness in the two cases Jesus referred to.

The still deeper issue here is the use of law to harm people, something that is not God's intention. Any time ritual and compassion (e.g., for hunger) come into conflict, God, who gave the law, favors compassion. That is the kind of God he is. To think otherwise is to misunderstand God and to cast him in a bad light. Thus Jesus quotes the prophet Hosea: "But if you had known what this means, 'I desire compassion, and not sacrifice' [Hosea 6:6], you would not have condemned the innocent" (Matthew 12:7; cp. 9:13). Thus the use of logic here is not only to correct the judgment that the disciples (the "innocent" in this case) must be sinning in stripping the grain and eating it. It is used to draw a further implication about God: God is not the kind of person who condemns those who act to meet a significant need at the expense of a relative triviality in the law. Elsewhere he points out that the sabbath appointed by God was made to serve man, not man to serve the sabbath (Mark 2:27).

Now the case of sabbath keeping—or, more precisely, of the ritual laws developed by men for sabbath observance—is one that comes up over and over in the Gospels, and it is always approached by Jesus in terms of the *logical inconsistency* of those who claim to practice it in the manner officially prescribed at the time. (See for example Mark 3:1–3, Luke 13:15–17, John 9:14–16, etc.) They are forced to choose between hypocrisy and open inconsistency, and he does sometimes use the word "hypocrisy" of them (e.g., Luke 13:15), implying that they *knew* they were being inconsistent and accepted it. In fact, the very idea of hypocrisy implies logical inconsistency. "They say, and do not" what their saying implies (Matthew 23:2).

And legalism will always lead to inconsistency in life, if not hypocrisy, for it will eventuate in giving greater importance to *rules* than is compatible with the *principles* one espouses (greater importance to sacrifice, for example, than to compassion, in the case at hand), and also to an inconsistent practice of the rules themselves (e.g., leading one's donkey to water on the sabbath, but refusing to have a human being healed of an 18-year-long affliction, as in Luke 13:15–16).

(2). Another illustrative case is found in Luke 20:27–40. Here it is the Sadducees, not the Pharisees, who are challenging Jesus. They are famous for rejecting the resurrection (vs. 27), and accordingly they propose a situation that, they think, is a *reductio ad absurdum* of resurrection (vss. 28–33). The law of Moses said that if a married man died without children, the next eldest brother should make the widow his wife, and any children they had would inherit in the line of the older brother. In the "thought experiment" of the Sadducees, the elder of seven sons died without children from his wife, the next eldest married her and also died without children from her, and the next eldest did the same, and so on through all seven brothers. Then the wife died (small wonder!). The presumed absurdity in the case was that in the resurrection she would be the wife of *all* of them, which was assumed to be an impossibility in the nature of marriage.

Jesus' reply is to point out that those resurrected will not have mortal bodies suited for sexual relations, marriage and reproduction. They will have bodies like angels do now, bodies of undying stuff. The idea of resurrection must not be taken crudely. Thus he undermines the assumption of the Sadducees that any "resurrection" must involve the body and its life continuing *exactly as it does now*. So the supposed impossibility of the woman being in conjugal relations with all seven brothers is not required by resurrection.

Then he proceeds, once again, to develop a teaching about the nature of God—which was always his main concern. Taking a premise that the Sadducees accepted, he draws the conclusion that they did not want. That the dead are raised, he says, follows from God's self-description to Moses at the burning bush. God described himself in that incident as "the God of Abraham, the

God of Isaac, and the God of Jacob" (Luke 20:35 [Exodus 3:6]).
The Sadducees accepted this. But at the time of the burning
bush incident, Abraham, Isaac and Jacob had been long "dead,"
as Jesus points out. But God is not the God of the dead. That is,
a dead person cannot sustain a relation of devotion and service
to God, nor can God keep covenant faith with one who no
longer exists. In covenant relationship to God one lives (vs. 38).
One cannot very well imagine the living God communing with a
dead body or a non-existent person and keeping covenant faithfulness with them.

(Incidentally, those Christian thinkers who nowadays suggest
that the Godly do not exist or are without conscious life, at least,
from the time their body dies to the time *it* is resurrected, might
want to provide us with an interpretation of this passage.)

(3). Yet another illustration of Jesus' obviously self-conscious
use of logic follows upon the one just cited from Luke 20. He
would occasionally set teaching puzzles that required the use of
logic on the part of his hearers. After the discussion of the resurrection, the Sadducees and the other groups about him no longer
had the courage to challenge his powerful thinking (vs. 40). He
then sets them a puzzle designed to help them understand the
Messiah—for which everyone was looking.

Drawing upon what all understood to be a messianic reference, in Psalm 110, Jesus points out an apparent contradiction:
The Messiah is the son of David (admitted by all), and yet David
calls the Messiah "Lord" (Luke 20:42–43). "How," he asks, "can
the Messiah be David's son if David calls him Lord?" (vs. 44). The
resolution intended by Jesus is that they should recognize that
the Messiah is not *simply* the son of David, but also of One higher
than David, and that he is therefore king in a more inclusive
sense than political head of the Jewish nation (Rev. 1:5). The
promises to David therefore reach far beyond David, incorporating him and much more. This reinterpretation of David and the

Messiah was a lesson learned and used well by the apostles and early disciples (see Acts 2:25–36, Hebrews 5:6, and Phil. 2:9–11).

(4). For a final illustration we turn to the use of logic in one of the more didactic occasions recorded in the Gospels. The parables and stories of Jesus often illustrate his use of logic, but we will look instead at a well-known passage from the Sermon on the Mount. In his teaching about adultery and the cultivation of sexual lust, Jesus makes the statement, "If your right eye makes you to stumble, tear it out, and throw it from you; for it is better for you that one of the parts of your body perish, than for your whole body to be thrown into hell," and similarly for your right hand (Matthew 5:29–30).

What, exactly, is Jesus doing here? One would certainly be mistaken in thinking that he is advising anyone to actually dismember himself as a way of escaping damnation. One must keep the context in mind. Jesus is exhibiting the righteousness that goes beyond "the righteousness of the scribes and Pharisees." This latter was a righteousness that took as its goal to not do anything wrong. If not doing anything wrong is the goal, that could be achieved by dismembering yourself and making actions impossible. What you cannot do you certainly will not do. Remove your eye, your hand, etc., therefore, and you will roll into heaven a mutilated stump. The price of dismemberment would be small compared to the reward of heaven. That is the logical conclusion *for one who held the beliefs of the scribes and the Pharisees.* Jesus is urging them to be consistent with their principles and do in practice what their principles imply. He reduces their principle—that righteousness lies in not doing anything wrong—to the absurd, in the hope that they will forsake their principle and see and enter the righteousness that is "beyond the righteousness of the scribes and Pharisees"—beyond, where compassion or love and not sacrifice is the fundamental thing. Jesus, of course, knew that if you dismembered yourself you could still have a hateful heart, toward God and toward man. It wouldn't really help toward righteousness at all. That is the basic thing he is teaching in this passage. Failure to appreciate the logic makes it impossible to get his point.

These illustrative scenes from the Gospels will already be familiar to any student of scripture. But, as we know, familiarity has its disadvantages. My hope is to enable us to see Jesus in a new light: to see him as doing *intellectual* work with the appropriate tools of logic, to see him as one who is both at home in and the master of such work.

We need to understand that Jesus is a *thinker*, that this is not a dirty word but an essential work, and that his other attributes do not preclude thought, but only insure that he is certainly the greatest thinker of the human race: "the most intelligent person who ever lived on earth." He constantly uses the power of logical insight to enable people to come to the truth about themselves and about God from the inside of their own heart and mind. Quite certainly it also played a role in his own growth in "wisdom" (Luke 2:52).

Often, it seems to me, we see and hear his deeds and words, but we don't think of him as one who *knew how* to do what he did or who really had logical *insight* into the things he said. We don't automatically think of him as a very competent person. He multiplied the loaves and fishes and walked on water, for example— but, perhaps, he didn't *know how* to do it, he just used mindless incantations or prayers. Or he taught on how to be a really good person, but he did not have moral insight and understanding. He just mindlessly rattled off words that were piped into him and through him. Really?

This approach to Jesus may be because we think that knowledge is *human*, while he was divine. Logic means works, while he is grace. Did we forget something there? Possibly that he also is human? Or that grace is not opposed to effort but to *earning*? But human thought is evil, we are told. How could he think human thought, have human knowledge? So we distance him from ourselves, perhaps intending to elevate him, and we elevate him right out of relevance to our actual lives—especially as they involve the use of our minds. That is why the idea of Jesus as logical, of Jesus the logician, is shocking. And of course that extends to Jesus the scientist, researcher, scholar, artist, literary person. He just doesn't "fit" in those areas. Today it is easier to think of Jesus as a "TV evangelist" than as an author, teacher or artist in the contemporary context. But now really!—if he were divine, would he be dumb, logically challenged, uninformed in *any* area? Would he not instead be the *greatest* of artists or speakers? Paul was only being consistent when he told the Colossians that "all the treasures of wisdom and knowledge are concealed in him" (2:3). Except for what?

There is in Christian educational circles today a great deal of talk about "integration of faith and learning." Usually it leads to little solid result. This is in part due to the fact that it is, at this point in time, an extremely difficult intellectual task, which cannot be accomplished by ritual language and the pooh-poohing of difficulties. But an even deeper cause of the difficulty is the way we automatically tend to think of Jesus himself. It is not just in what we *say* about him, but in how he comes before our minds: how we automatically position him in our world, and how in consequence we position ourselves. We automatically think of him as having nothing essentially to do with "profane" knowledge, with learning and logic, and therefore find ourselves "on our own" in such areas.

We should, I believe, understand that Jesus would be perfectly at home in any professional context where good work is being done today. He would, of course, be a constant rebuke to all the proud self-advancement and the contemptuous treatment of others that goes on in professional circles. In this as in other respects, our professions are aching for his presence. If we truly see him as the premier thinker of the human race—and who *else* would be that?—then we are also in position to honor him as the most knowledgeable person in *our* field, whatever that may be, and to ask his cooperation and assistance with everything we have to do.

Catherine Marshall somewhere tells of a time she was trying to create a certain design with some drapes for her windows. She was unable to get the proportions right to form the design she had in mind. She gave up in exasperation and, leaving the scene, began to mull the matter over in prayer. Soon ideas as to how the design could be achieved began to come to her and before long she had the complete solution. She learned that Jesus is maestro of interior decorating.

Such stories are familiar from many areas of human activity, but quite rare in the areas of art and intellect. For lack of an appropriate understanding of Jesus we come to do our work in intellectual, scholarly and artistic fields *on our own.* We do not have confidence (otherwise known as faith) that he can be our leader and teacher in matters we spend most of our time working on. Thus our efforts often fall far short of what they should accomplish, and may even have less effect than the efforts of the Godless, because we undertake them only with "the arm of the flesh." Our faith in Jesus Christ rises no higher than that. We do not see him as he really is, maestro of all good things.

Here I have only been suggestive of a dimension of Jesus that is commonly overlooked. This is no thorough study of that dimension, but it deserves such study. It is one of major impor-tance for a healthy faith in him. Especially today, when the authoritative institutions of our culture, the universities and the professions, omit him as a matter of course. Once one knows what to look for in the Gospels, however, one will easily see the thorough, careful and creative employment of logic throughout his teaching activity. Indeed, this employment *must* be identified and appreciated if what he is saying is to be understood. Only then can his intellectual brilliance be appreciated and he be respected as he deserves.

An excellent way of teaching in Christian schools would therefore be to require all students to do extensive logical analyses of Jesus' discourses. This should go hand in hand with the other ways of studying his words, including devotional practices such as memorization or *lectio divina*, and the like. It would make a substantial contribution to the integration of faith and learning.

While such a concentration on logic may sound strange today, that is only a reflection on our current situation. It is quite at home in many of the liveliest ages of the church.

John Wesley speaks for the broader Christian church across time and space, I think, in his remarkable treatise, "An Address to the Clergy." There he discusses at length the qualifications of an effective minister for Christ. He speaks of the necessity of a good knowledge of scripture, and then adds,

> Some knowledge of the sciences also, is, to say the least, equally expedient. Nay, may we not say, that the knowledge of one (whether art or science), although now quite unfashionable, is even necessary next, and in order to, the knowledge of Scripture itself? I mean logic. For what is this, if rightly understood, but the art of good sense? of apprehending things clearly, judging truly, and reasoning conclusively? What is it, viewed in another light, but the art of learning and teaching; whether by convincing or persuading? What is there, then, in the whole compass of science, to be desired in comparison of it?
>
> Is not some acquaintance with what has been termed the second part of logic (metaphysics), if not so necessary as this,

yet highly expedient (1.) In order to clear our apprehension (without which it is impossible either to judge correctly, or to reason closely or conclusively), by ranging our ideas under general heads? And (2.) In order to understand many useful writers, who can very hardly be understood without it?[2]

Later in this same treatise Wesley deals with whether we are, as ministers, what we ought to be. "Am I," he asks,

a tolerable master of the sciences? Have I gone through the very gate of them, logic? If not, I am not likely to go much farther when I stumble at the threshold. Do I understand it so as to be ever the better for it? To have it always ready for use; so as to apply every rule of it, when occasion is, almost as naturally as I turn my hand? Do I understand it at all? Are not even the moods and figures [of the syllogism] above my comprehension? Do not I poorly endeavour to cover my ignorance, by affecting to laugh at their barbarous names? Can I even reduce an indirect mood to a direct; an hypothetic to a categorical syllogism? Rather, have not my stupid indolence and laziness made me very ready to believe, what the little wits and pretty gentlemen affirm, "that logic is good for nothing"? It is good for this at least (wherever it is understood), to make people talk less; by showing them both what is, and what is not, to the point; and how extremely hard it is to prove any thing. Do I understand metaphysics; if not the depths of the Schoolmen, the subtleties of Scotus or Aquinas, yet the first rudiments, the general principles, of that useful science? Have I conquered so much of it, as to clear my apprehension and range my ideas under proper heads; so much as enables me to read with ease

---

[2]Herbert Welch, ed., *Selections from the Writings of the Rev. John Wesley* (New York: Eaton & Mains, 1901), 186.

and pleasure, as well as profit, Dr. Henry Moore's *Works*,
Malebranche's *Search after Truth*, and Dr. Clarke's *Demonstration
of the Being and Attributes of God?*[3]

I suspect that such statements will be strange, shocking, even
outrageous or ridiculous to leaders of ministerial education today.
But readers of Wesley and other great ministers of the past, such
as Jonathan Edwards or Charles Finney, will easily see, if they
know what it is they are looking at, how much use those ministers made of careful logic. Similarly for the great Puritan writers
of an earlier period, and for later effective Christians such as
C. S. Lewis and Francis Schaeffer. They all make relentless use of
logic, and to great good effect. With none of these great teachers
is it a matter of trusting logic *instead of* relying upon the Holy
Spirit. Rather, they well knew, it is simply a matter of meeting the
conditions along with which the Holy Spirit chooses to work. In
this connection it will be illuminating to carefully examine the
logical structure and force of Peter's discourse on the day of Pentecost (Acts 2).

Today, by contrast, we commonly depend upon the emotional pull of stories and images to "move" people. We fail to
understand that, in the very nature of the human mind, emotion
does not reliably generate belief or faith, if it generates it at all.
Not even "seeing" does, unless you know what you are seeing. It
is understanding, insight, that generates belief. In vain do we try
to change people's heart or character by "moving" them to do
things in ways that bypass their understanding.

Some months ago one who is regarded as a great teacher of
homiletics was emphasizing the importance of stories in preaching. It was on a radio program. He remarked that a leading minister in America had told him recently that he could preach the

---

[3]Ibid., 198.

same series of sermons each year, and change the illustrations, and no one would notice it. This was supposed to point out, with some humor, the importance of stories to preaching. What it really pointed out, however, was that the cognitive content of the sermon was never heard—if there was any to be heard—and does not matter.

Paying careful attention to how Jesus made use of logical thinking can strengthen our confidence in Jesus as master of the centers of intellect and creativity, and can encourage us to accept him as master in all of the areas of intellectual life in which we may participate. In those areas we can, then, be *his* disciples, not disciples of the current movements and glittering personalities who happen to dominate our field in human terms. Proper regard for him can also encourage us to follow his example as teachers in Christian contexts. We can learn from him to use logical reasoning at its best, as he works with us. When we teach what he taught in the manner he taught it, we will see his kind of result in the lives of those to whom we minister.[4]

---

[4]For necessary elaboration of many themes touched upon in this paper, see J. P. Moreland's crucial book, *Love Your God with All Your Mind* (Colorado Springs: Navpress, 1997).

GOOD SHABBESS

Brit Hadasha, a Messianic Jewish synagogue, is just off the interstate in Memphis. If you didn't know that the name meant "New Covenant," you might easily mistake it for a Reform synagogue. David and I sat in his red two-door for a few minutes watching the parking lot fill up with the usual assortment of minivans and SUVs, battered Hondas, and old Volvos. I watched the long-skirted women and children parade into the sanctuary and wondered who they were. Had their fathers, like mine, been devastated when they embraced Jesus? Had they struggled with what it meant to be a Jewish Christian, or had Brit Hadasha presented itself immediately as the obvious answer? And what was I doing here anyway? My hands shook, and I contemplated sitting in the car and reading a novel for the next two hours.

I had devoted more Saturdays than I could count to worshiping in synagogues of one stripe or another. The only time I'd been in Memphis before was as a bridesmaid for my friend Tova. That wedding had been full of Orthodox Jews—kosher-keeping, Orthodox Jews in long sleeves and ankle-length skirts singing Hebrew songs and dancing ecstatic, sex-segregated dances. The wedding was on a Sunday, and I had spent the morning before chanting familiar prayers in the women's section of Memphis's Orthodox shul. But that was before I gave into Jesus, acknowledged that he'd been tugging at my long, modest dresses, prayed the sinner's prayer, and got baptized.

Unlike the most famous Jewish convert to Christianity, I had no datable on-the-road-to-Damascus experience. I can't say that I became a Christian on January 8, 1993, or on my twentieth birthday. But I can tell you about the time I dreamed of Jesus rescuing me from a kidnapping. I can tell about reading *At Home in Mitford*, a charming if saccharine novel about an Episcopal priest in North Carolina that left me thinking that I wished I could pray to a God called Jesus. I can tell about the hours I spent sitting surrounded by the Metropolitan Museum's collection of medieval Christian art. I can tell about my baptism.

A few months after *At Home in Mitford* and a year before the baptism, I sat, drinking cider that scalded my tongue, with a Presbyterian minister I had known for three years. "Scott," I said, "I think I'm beginning to believe in Jesus."

Scott sipped his cider in silence. Finally he said, "You know, Lauren, you can't just divorce Judaism." I felt like I'd been socked in the stomach. He urged me to go see the campus rabbi, and later he said, "I had no idea when you told me you wanted to get together that you wanted to talk about Christianity. I thought maybe you were going to come out to me as a lesbian." Which, on a campus obsessed with identity politics, might have been more congenial than a Jewish student prattling on about Jesus.

That afternoon I walked into the bookstore at Union Theological Seminary and bought a *Book of Common Prayer*, which felt like the boldest, most daring thing I'd ever done. The next day I gave away all my Jewish prayerbooks. I left them anonymously on the steps of a nearby shul, the way an unmarried mother might have left her baby on the steps of an orphanage in some earlier era.

Scott's metaphor, I learned, was useful: trading my ArtScroll siddur for a *Book of Common Prayer* felt exactly like filing for divorce. The more Christian I became, the more I needed to have nothing to do with Judaism. Every new Christian habit, purchase, or prayer was accompanied by the unlearning of a Jewish habit, the forgetting of a Jewish prayer. Compline replaced Ma'ariv. A scary-looking batiked Jesus from India replaced a watercolor of Hasidim dancing in the streets of Mea Sharim. Short skirts replaced long dresses, Amarone replaced Maneshevitz, books on the Eucharist, the Lord's Prayer, the Gospel of John, and the Great Awakening began to crowd my bookshelves, and crates of sixteenth-century Jewish poetry and Hebrew commentaries on the Torah were sold to used bookstores. I got an email from my friend Rachel, then a Jewish studies major at Duke. "I was just at a used bookstore on Franklin Street, and I picked up a Mikraot G'dolot for incredibly cheap. 'Lauren Winner' was scribbled inside the cover—that wouldn't be you, by any chance?" She didn't ask why I was selling off my library.

But Scott was right; I couldn't divorce—or at least not completely. I'm as bound to Judaism as my parents are to one another. They aren't married, but they have daughters, so they still see each other sometimes, at weddings and college graduations, and sometimes they talk on the phone, perhaps about going in together on an expensive birthday present for me or my sister. The more time I spent with other Christians, the more I realized that Judaism had shaped the way I understood basic things like who Jesus was and what he meant when he talked about the yoke of the law. In my church study group—an every-Sunday gathering devoted to discussing the creeds, line by painstaking line—I held forth on how integral Judaism was to Christianity, how it shaped the way I prayed, the way I read Scripture, the way I thought about the church calendar. One week my priest asked me to bring in a Jewish commentary on Genesis, and she was perplexed when I told her that I'd given all my Jewish commentaries on Genesis away.

"But you're always telling us they're the very scrim through which you understand the Bible," she said, reminding me of the uncomfortable tension between my desire to distance myself from everything Jewish and my insistence that Judaism was fundamental to my understanding of Christianity.

Christians I meet, at church or in class or at dinner parties, seem never to tire of hearing about how I came "through Judaism to Jesus," as my friend Frederica put it. I don't know why: perhaps it somehow affirms their sense that they're right, more than the average conversion story. Most seem able to imagine only two possible responses to what they call my "witness." First is sympathy mixed with incredulity: "Aren't you sad that you wasted so many years of your life learning the intricacies of observant Judaism? All the time you spent studying the Talmud? All those hours poured into making sure your kitchen was kosher? All the teeth you broke trying to master biblical Hebrew?" The simple answer is: No, I'm not. But I usually don't give the simple answer; I usually give the speech I so carefully refined in my church study group: Judaism has shaped everything about my Christianity, and I don't regret an hour I spent learning the rabbinic dietary laws or implementing them.

The second response is quite the opposite—not a sympathetic shake of the head at all the hours lost to Judaism, but what my professors would call a fetishized eroticism of the Other. "You're so lucky to have that Jewish heritage! Listen, I know of a great church full of Jews just like you. They've come to fulfillment in Christ, but they retain all their Jewish practices: they sing Hebrew songs, wear yarmulkes, hold their worship services on Saturdays. You should check it out; it's just a few blocks south of the library. I bet you'll feel like you really belong there."

Once a well-meaning Episcopal friend in Virginia urged me to visit the Messianic Jewish group in Richmond, and I snapped at her: "Absolutely not. I hate Messianic Jews." My friend looked shocked.

"Look, I know that this isn't a very Christian way to feel," I said. "It's not a very Jewish way to feel, either. But Messianic Jews make me want to run screaming into the night in the other direction." Whatever impulse made me sell hundreds of Hebrew books, I explained, multiplies itself by twenty when I think about Messianic Jews.

"But you often speak so eloquently," said my friend, "about how you miss Judaism, and how you feel that it's an essential part of your Christian identity."

"Judaism may inform my Christian faith," I replied, "but not *that* way."

"So why do you hate them so much?" she asked.

I thought for a moment. "I just do," I said, with conviction. "I *hate* them."

I moved to England shortly after buying that *Book of Common Prayer*, and that's where I spent my Christian babyhood. That's where I was baptized and confirmed. The theology I learned was Anglican. All those heated debates about creeds took place in a dark, romantic room at Clare College, Cambridge. When I moved back to New York, I was surprised that Manhattan evangelicals weren't fond of choral evensong, and no one in my new church knew who Rowan Williams was.

There were, however, bigger problems than convincing every Episcopalian in New York to read books by the Welsh bishop or sing Anglican hymnody. The more pressing worry was figuring out how to be a Christian in a neighborhood where everyone knew me as an Orthodox Jew. I didn't know how to tell Jewish friends that I had become a Christian, didn't know how to explain to old professors why I suddenly could attend classes on Yom Kippur, didn't even know what to tell my accommodating Catholic acquaintance who, delighted that I was back in New York, had made dinner reservations for us at a kosher dairy restaurant on the East Side.

Just after Labor Day I traveled to New Jersey to meet with a couple, Jews turned Episcopalians. We sat rather awkwardly in the kitchen of their refurbished Victorian, drinking coffee and making small talk. They weren't sure why I had come, and I couldn't explain. Finally I blurted out, "I tuck my cross underneath my blouse every time I see someone in a yarmulke. I slipped into my old shul on Rosh Hashanah and stood in a corner for an hour watching and trying not to pray. The other night, I actually ducked behind a fruit-cart because I saw an old friend from college—it was clear she was coming from Shabbat services, and it was equally clear that I was headed to a trayf Italian joint for dinner."

"Oh," said the wife. "Now I see why you've come. You've come because you're trying to figure out how to put your life back together."

"See this ring?" her husband said. It was a gold ring with a cross, on the third finger of his right hand. "I still take this off sometimes, when I see family."

On the train back to New York, I made up my mind to do several things: buy a book of Jewish folktales and a Hebrew siddur; call up Tova, whom I had avoided since becoming a Christian; and visit a Messianic Jewish synagogue. "Not because I have any interest in joining one," I explained to a friend. "I'm an Anglican, after all! But because—well, I hate them too much." I paused, helpless to do anything but babble in the lingua franca of therapeutic academese. "If I hate them this much, then there's something I need to confront. A demon! Like confronting your father or a food that you hate! I must confront the Other."

So you see, it seemed providential when my friend David—who is no more Jewish than Rowan Williams—said that he planned to spend Saturday morning at Brit Hadasha, home to Memphis's Messianic Jews.

·   ·   ·

Tova, it turned out, was in Memphis that weekend, visiting her family for the end of Sukkot and giving a reading from her new novel, which is set in Memphis. On the drive, I fantasized about running into her. I knew that I wouldn't; I knew that she would be tucked away in her parents' house and her shul, miles from Brit Hadasha, eating a feast her mother had prepared in her family's sukkah and singing my favorite Shabbat songs.

Sukkot is one of the things I gave up because of Jesus. I gave up Purim, which I love, and kashrut, which I love, and dipping challah into honey on New Year's, which I love. All because I was courted by a very determined carpenter from Nazareth. People ask me if I miss Judaism. Yes, of course, I miss it. I especially miss sitting in a sukkah.

God tells us how to celebrate Sukkot in Exodus 23, Leviticus 23, and Deuteronomy 16. First we learn that we are to "hold a festival" for God when we "gather in the results of [our] work from the field." Then we learn that the Feast of Tabernacles—or Sukkot—takes place on the fifteenth day of the seventh month, Tishrei, for seven days. During that time, "every citizen in Israel shall dwell in huts, so that your generations know that I made the children of Israel dwell in huts when I brought them out of the land of Egypt."

And the Bible commands us to be joyful on Sukkot—the only holiday on which we're specifically enjoined to make joy. When the rabbis developed Sukkot ceremonies for the Temple, they added something not discussed in the Torah—a special water-pouring ceremony, where, according to Arthur Waskow, the pouring out of water is a symbol for our outpouring of joy.

On Sukkot, Jewish families each build a hut, a sukkah, to remind ourselves of the sukkot the Jews inhabited while they camped in the desert for forty years. We don't really know what those desert huts were like: Rabbi Akiva says that the desert huts were flimsy, ramshackle, made of twigs and bark and cactus

needles, but Rabbi Eliezar says the sukkot were far grander—
they were "clouds of glory" that accompanied the Jews all through
their desert wanderings, protecting them from night animals and
helping them not lose their way.

Today, the sukkah you would build might be an eight-foot
cube, made from plywood held together with nails and twine.
You would cover the roof with greenery—the cover is called a
schach, and it should be translucent enough to let in starlight—
and invite neighborhood children to hang drawings on the walls.
You would eat all your meals in the sukkah, and drink all your
drinks, and sometimes even sleep there.

I miss Sukkot because it is sitting in the sukkah that you learn
lessons about dependence on God, realize that even the walls of
your three-bedroom house are flimsy. The trick is to grab hold of
the lessons of the sukkah and remember them when you take
apart your shaky hut and resume eating your meals in a shiny,
spacious kitchen well stocked with flavored olive oil and porta-
bello mushrooms.

David interrupted my parking-lot reverie. "I like it here because
these people are pariahs," he said. "They don't fit in anywhere—
not with Jews, not with Christians. Being a Christian means
being a pariah, Lauren; it means not fitting in anywhere in this
world. Your Episcopalians are no pariahs."

When we walked in, a middle-aged woman with short gray
hair and dangly earrings greeted us. "Good Shabbess. Welcome
to Brit Hadasha. Is this your first visit?" David gave a complicated
answer, explaining that he'd been there on Rosh Hashanah but
that it was my first time.

"And where are you from?" Before he could give another complicated explanation, I said "Arkansas," which is where David is
from, took my New Visitor card, and went in to find a seat. A
man clad in a tallis stood at a podium in the front of the room,

and a small choir clustered to his right, leading the congregation through songs that were printed on a transparency and displayed on a large screen. In the corner of the room, a circle of women were dancing, some variation on the hora.

I was prepared for that. I had read a recent ethnography of a Messianic Jewish congregation, and the author had explained that dancing was an important element of Messianic worship services. I felt an unexpected pull to join them. The dances weren't as complicated as those at Tova's wedding, but they were similar. I hadn't yet found a group of Anglicans who loved Jewish folk-dancing. The service consisted mostly of songs, with a little spontaneous prayer thrown in. That it was Sukkot did not seem to factor in to the service at all, which annoyed me. Perhaps the most basic thing I missed about Judaism was the calendar. I was trying to learn to live according to the seasons of Advent and Lent, but so far my body still thought in terms of Jewish holidays.

The absence of Sukkot was just one of many things that irritated me about the service. The pink satin yarmulkes, straight out of a Reform synagogue in the 1980s, irritated me. The gold and magenta banners proclaiming YESHUA irritated me. And the music irritated me. Rather than singing any of the haunting melodies available to anyone who is casually acquainted with the centuries-old Jewish cantorial tradition, the folks at Brit Hadasha were happy singing songs that sounded as though they'd been lifted from the praise-music guide at any nondenominational evangelical church—except that Brit Hadasha's songs had a little Hebrew thrown in. The lyrics made no sense, Yeshua was invariably presented as a buddy and pal, there were no discernible melodies, and everything rhymed.

Throughout the morning, Brit Hadasha's Judaism struck me as just raisins added to a cake—you noticed them, but they didn't really change the cake. The structure of the service bore no relation to the Jewish liturgy, and I didn't get the sense that my fellow worshipers thought that being Jewish led them to understand Jesus any differently than the Baptists down the street. I wanted the service to be organic and seamless. Instead, the seams showed everywhere. Add Hebrew and stir.

I was tense and I showed off, screwing my eyes tightly shut during the few songs that did come from the siddur so that David, and everyone else, would know that I didn't need to read the transliterated overhead projected on the wall. I occasionally offered up a silent prayer that the Holy Spirit would work overtime on my heart and help me stop being judgmental long enough to recognize that these people were worshiping the risen Lord, but I didn't really want this prayer to be answered.

Sukkot comes at the end of the season of repentance; it's the holiday that follows Yom Kippur, the Day of Atonement. Starting the week before Rosh Hashanah, Jews say special penitentiary prayers called *slichot*. We start at midnight the Saturday before Rosh Hashanah, because the rabbis knew that the heavens are most open to prayers at midnight. Among the prayers we say at slichot is one we say again on Rosh Hashanah, and on all the days between Rosh Hashanah and Yom Kippur, and again on Yom Kippur, when God is making his final judgments about who will live and who will die, whom he will forgive and whom he will punish: *Adonai, Adonai, el rachum v'chanun, erech apayim, vrav chesed v'emet, notzer chesed lalafim, nosey avon vafesha v'chatabah v'nakeh:* The Lord, the Lord of compassion, who offers grace and is slow to anger, who is full of loving-kindness and trustworthiness, who assures love for a thousand generations, who forgives iniquity, transgression, and misdeed, and who grants pardon.

It's a list, culled from the thirty-fourth chapter of Exodus, of God's thirteen merciful attributes—attributes that, according to the rabbis, shine most brightly during the season of repentance. The prayer, a reminder to God not of our merit but of his capacity to overlook our sin, is sung to a particularly haunting melody, my favorite from the entire cantorial literature. It's minor, and repetitive, and dirgelike, and some people say that Jews wailed its tune as they walked to the gas chambers in Treblinka and Sobibor. At Brit Hadasha, we sang a mostly-English-but-laced-with-Hebrew song based on the slichot prayer—a zippy tune, full of rhyme and vim and pep.

In the middle of the song I slipped out of the sanctuary, made my way through the circle of dancing women to the ladies' room, and sat on the toilet crying. Whatever part of me had come to Brit Hadasha hoping not only to confront demons but also to find the key to marrying my Judaism with the cross was disappointed. I wasn't going to find any answers in a church that thought clapping and tambourining its way through *Adonai, el rachum v'chanun* was a good idea.

"That must be why I hate them," I said out loud, thinking of my friend from Richmond. "I must hate them because I want them to give me a formula for how to be a Christian Jew, and yet I know that their formula will never be my formula." After I figured that I'd spent more time than was respectable in the bathroom, I returned to my seat next to David, settling in for more praise music, a Torah reading, and the homily. Across the aisle, a redheaded little girl in a white straw hat smiled at me and did a little dance.

The rabbi was in the middle of a sermon series on the Book of Joshua. "Well, that's refreshing," I whispered to David. "A whole sermon series on something from the Old Testament. You would never hear that in a regular church." David shushed me before I climbed onto one of my favorite soapboxes: the Christians-think-the-Bible-starts-with-Matthew soapbox.

This week's sermon was on chapter 7. Achan, from the tribe of Judah, steals some silver and gold and a beautiful robe; Joshua takes Achan to a valley, where he is stoned to death. Ever after, the Book of Joshua tells us, that valley is known as the Valley of Achor, which means trouble.

The rabbi proceeded to read this chapter just like rabbis in the Talmud would. "Where else is the Valley of Achor mentioned in the Bible?" he asked. This was a favorite rabbinic strategy—if a word appears only two or three times in the Bible, then God is telling us that when we come across one mention, we should think on the other passages that use the same word. This, for example, is how the rabbis figured out what activities were forbidden on the sabbath. While there are several words in Hebrew for "work," God uses the same word to describe the activities that are forbidden on Shabbat and the activities that went into building the tabernacle. So, the rabbis reasoned, those tabernacle activities must be forbidden on the sabbath.

Achor shows up in Hosea 2:15, where God promises to turn the Valley of Achor into a door of hope. And what does God mean, the rabbi asked? He tells us in John 10:9, when Jesus declares, "I am the door: whoever enters through me will be saved." The door promised in Hosea, a promise that in turn looked back to Joshua, was Jesus, the only door that could undo the trouble of Achor.

I was dazzled. I hadn't heard a reading of Scripture this clever since I'd become a Christian. The rabbi had done just what I was always saying Jewish Christians could do—read the Bible the way the rabbis of the Talmud did to show how Jesus came from the Torah. Show that when he said he was a fulfillment of the law he meant something more than just those verses in Isaiah that predict the coming of an Anointed One. So struck was I by the rabbi's marriage of the Old Testament with the New that I hardly noticed what came next—an altar call.

During the altar call David wept and the couple behind us hollered out loud, peppering the rabbi's words with amens like a pair of black Baptists. No one answered the altar call, which didn't surprise me but was nonetheless a little sad, an unanswered altar call being kind of like an uneaten piece of pie. I wondered if it had been directed at us—we looked like the only visitors—and I wondered if answering the altar call would have meant accepting Jesus or accepting Yeshua.

The service broke up, and as David went out in search of Kleenex, I sat in my chair feeling awkward. The little redheaded girl came up to me and put her head in my lap. She was, it turned out, one of those wise children who might have come from a Nancy Lemann novel. "Some people," she said, "don't know about Yeshua." Then she began to hum a tune. Maybe I wasn't hearing her right, but I could swear it was "Jesus loves me, this I know."

L A R R Y   W O I W O D E

THE FEEL OF
INTERNAL BLEEDING

I was sleeping on the subway the night the shuttle caught on fire. Forty-second Street sank two feet and had to be cordoned off. My sleep was from too much beer, and I woke at the end of a line, in the Far Rockaways, to find that my guitar, which had been lying on the seat beside me, had been stolen. I was so alarmed that I decided to see William Maxwell.

I had met him a year before, at the University of Illinois, his alma mater, when he had come to deliver a lecture titled "The Autobiographical Novelist." A professor who had directed me in several plays, Dr. Charles Shattuck, a friend from Maxwell's college years, took me for coffee with Maxwell and said, "Here's a writer I want you to meet," and Maxwell said, "When you get to New York, come and see me."

I was in New York because of his statement, leaving behind a young woman I hoped to marry, but for more than a week I had been afraid even to call him.

At the *New Yorker* building, on 20 West 43rd, I should take the elevator up to the twentieth floor, he tells me on the phone, but when the doors part I'm sure I've gone wrong. I'm not at an elegant magazine but in a bare corridor on an abandoned floor, so it looks—institutional green with dark, scuffed linoleum. Then Maxwell comes through a door to a hall, in a suit and tie, and leads me down a dim passage to his office: a table inside the door, a schoolteacher's desk ahead, and beside it, against the wall to the right, a cream-colored couch whose fabric looks like woven silk.

Past the table to the left are windows with low sills. I go to one, partly blinded by the light at this level, and find that I'm facing north: Central Park in a green swoon.

He steps up close, also looking out. "What do you think of the view?" he asks, and his words are fraught with such meaning I can't speak.

He asks if I received the letter he sent to Urbana, and I say no. It must have arrived about the time I left, he says, and was to let me know the poems I sent to him were with Howard Moss, the poetry editor, but Moss has been ill.

He pulls a wooden chair from the table and revolves it toward his desk, and by the time I sit he's in his swivel chair, hands clasped behind his head, elbows out.

"Will you be able to manage alone in the city?"

"Yes." Though the reason I've come to see him is to ask for a job at the magazine.

"In my letter I gave what I called Ciceronian advice. That awful Walt-Disneyish World's Fair may result in a kind of mass irritability, I said, which would not be helpful if you're looking for a job."

I flinch at his reading of my mind.

"So from that point of view I thought it might be worth it for you to think of not coming till fall. But I don't really know that there will be an irritability or that it will affect things for you one way or another. Maybe we had a glimpse of that last night. Did you know the shuttle from Times Square to Grand Central went up in flames?"

"Yes."

"Anyway, you're at the stage of your life where every action, looked back on later, proves to have been destined, so whatever you do don't listen to advice from middle-aged people like me. Here, your story will walk up to you."

Outside—in Times Square, it happens—I run into Jude, from the theater group at the University of Illinois, a young woman with the aged and confused look of a character actress. She says a friend of a friend needs somebody for a play at Hunter College, and as we talk, she says, "Come along," and leads me to the Overseas Press Club, across from Bryant Park. We take an elevator up and walk to a door with ATTENTION, INC. taped across it—a PR mailing firm with rooms so small its offset press sits over the tub in the bathroom and discarded printed pages rise to the faucets like novels gone awash.

The help is mostly unemployed actors—Jude works there; she was on her lunch break—and one of the owners, Van Varner, says, "Come and go as you please, keep your own time," while typewriters clack and the press above the bathtub echoes ka-thock, ka-thock!

The job is enough for food and a room on St. Mark's Place—a Ukrainian and Puerto Rican neighborhood, with older Italian families moving out, not the fashionable place it will be. I promised to give myself a year to write but give in to the woman at Hunter. She needs one more to make up a three-character show, a recent translation of a German expressionist drama, *Three Blind Men*.

The three of us rehearse in a bare front room, eyes shut from day one, groping our way through blocking. I don't care for the play and regret abandoning my plans—I vowed not to step on a stage till the year of writing was up—and on weekends I drink too much, back from rehearsals.

April 1964: Time moves only as counterpoint to the isolated mind, I wrote in the notebook I kept then. *And her inflections in time, her grace notes ad infinitum, were no longer great enough to touch him.*

Which was a way of saying it was not her I missed.

. . . .

The week after I start work at Attention they move to Lex and 34th, a second-floor-through in a squat building. Jude gives me the number of a grad student from Illinois, in the city to finish his doctorate. I get him on the phone and he says with a sigh, in an accent assumed after a year in England, "Come over and I'll help you put together a résumé. That way you can, well, get a real job."

He lives on Pineapple Street in Brooklyn Heights, down from the St. George, an upscale neighborhood, I see, as I walk around before going up. We put together a résumé he feels will work at literary agencies, where I might work as a reader, and suggests I first try Sterling Lord. I carry my résumé up and "have a seat," as I'm told, and page through a file folder of poems and writing samples, in case they ask. After an hour I'm ushered into the office of a kindly looking, older and urbane gentleman.

"I had to look at the guy who put this together," he says, and shakes the résumé at me. "Where did you get it?"

"I typed it up at a friend's and had another friend run it off at the place where I work now."

"Inventive, huh?"

"Inventive?"

"Nobody could do this much by twenty-two. Don't try to give me that. Go on. Get out of here."

It was the only agency that even gave me an interview.

July 1964: It's difficult to change the character under whose identity you first meet someone. If you were grave in their presence the first meeting, you will continue to be grave. If you were clownish, you know they expect that from you, and will be a clown. Of course you'll feel other emotions, but they'll all be under the auspices of the dominant one you exposed that first meeting.

I'm out of money, except for the dozen hours a week I work at Attention, worse off than a student. I send a note asking to see

Maxwell and hear right back, "I'm running off schedule this week, and you might not find me in. If your job permits it, would you like to have a quick lunch with me this coming Thursday? If you could be at the office at 12:30, that would be best for me."

"Going to see Maxwell again?" Van Varner asks. His favorite writers are Hortense Calisher and Muriel Spark, so he says, but he knows Maxwell's novels and stories, and has met him. "I live down the block from Howard Moss," he said once. "Edward Albee is a neighbor." He put on a prim face of fake concern. "I'm a kind of writer, too, you know!"

He's so energetic a jumpiness often overtakes him. "How now!" he'll cry, and spin to the postage meter, rapidly feeding a stack of letters through, baring his teeth in a fixed grin, jerking glances at the unemployed actors sitting around in their depression. His red-sandy hair, like his exuberance going up in flame, is erratically mussed, his tie looks stuffed or crooked in his loosely bulging button-down collar or drags over one side of his suit from his hurry—tapping now one foot then the other as he works the postage meter, his pouter-pigeon chest pulling at the buttons of his shirt.

"Yes, I write!" he adds generally, to any who might be listening. "I do, I do! For *Guideposts!* The truthful little mag of everyday hope!"

Attention handles *Guideposts'* publicity mailing and is in charge of their exhibit at the World's Fair; and Van is indeed on the staff, a contributing editor. The Fair, far out in Queens beside the gaudy stadium of the comic team that is meant to compensate for the loss of the Dodgers, is not so disruptive, as I find one weekend when I take the subway out to deliver brochures. I'm greeted by Norman Vincent Peale, a cherubic version of the photo of Oswald Spengler on *The Decline of the West*, one of her favorite books, often in her arms when we talked at Urbana, along with Theodore Reik's *Of Love and Lust*.

The daughter of Leonard LeSourd, editor of *Guideposts* and the second husband of Catherine Marshall (of *A Man Named Peter*), works at Attention that summer, now and then helping at the *Guideposts* counter in the Billy Graham pavilion at the Fair, a dark beauty with a settled regard on a realm greater than herself, able to look straight at you but not with the look that invites you in, and can swing her body toward you, with plenty to swing, yet not offer it. I'm able to talk to her only in the joking banter of Van, aware she's unapproachable by such as my pig claws, or so I recognize now, God forgive, nor did I ever press an approach, God forbid.

Maxwell and I take an elevator down from his office and he hails a cab and says, "Fifty-ninth at this corner of the Park." He carries a brown paper bag and we sit on a bench up a slope from the lagoon and eat pieces of chicken that come wrapped in wax paper, as if prepared at home. I gulp mine, so desperate to tell him I need a job I finally can't talk. He mentions writers he thinks I should read, and I miss one or two, crammed so full of the question I must ask. Soon we're in a cab and back up the elevator to his office and he's staring at me, hands clasped behind his neck. I tell him I'm trying to write a story, but—

"Good. Whatever you want with your whole heart to do, you will. Chuck Shattuck says you're a writer, and I'm sure you're the kind only you can be. It's written all over your face. It's the half-formed and half-hearted desires and ambitions that go unrealized. But you know what you want, and so that's how it will turn out for you. No force in the world, no person living or dead, can alter that.

"If I seem to be meddling too much, you have to say so. You have to make allowance for my concern for people—that they're not cold, that they're not hungry, that they have a roof over their head, that they don't have to bear alone a terrible weight on their heart, and on and on. I can meddle in that way and you'll have to tell me when to stop because I don't in any way want to come between you and your will to be a writer. Do you have money enough to live on?"

"Yes." It shames me to think I was planning to ask for a job when by his word he has made me a writer.

July. I believe I have found an important part of my subject matter in the use of actors & theater. My concern for the real over the artificial, the symbolic over the formless, the eternal over man, has, with this subject matter, a tremendous opportunity to speak without seeming contrived or didactic. Besides, I am theater.

Aug 22, 1964: Let me, then, for interest and for future reference, put down my expenses . . .

.70—for a "Hamburger Plate," heaped with fries and with a thimble of slaw and a coke,

.25—tip for the waiter,

.35—a pack of cigarettes (Tareytons),

.20—ice-cream cone (black raspberry),

1.00—to a beggar, the same one (and I'm not letting my need for penance sway me) I passed up several days ago. Now he's near death. He can talk only in a breathless rasp, has hardly any coordination (he sat all the time I talked to him), and is nearly blind. He's dirtier now and his sooty face is streaked with tears. His last words, "I'll say a prayer for you, I will. Excuse me, I can't talk"—holding his throat with his hand—"I'll say a prayer for you."

"Please do."

What made him so breakable, broken?

Some weekends I give all my money away to street people and have to walk to Attention, weak-legged and trembling from no food, and often on those days, near noon, the other partner at Attention, Harold, will stick his head into the back room and say, "Who wants to get us burgers from Prexy's?"—a joint down the street. "I'm buying." Harold is the chief typist or typesetter for the press run by Don, who is from Brooklyn and has a gift of mimicry and memory that enables him to reel off dozens of Burns poems in a Scots brogue, although he isn't one of the unemployed actors. He's better.

At the end of a penniless day I have to ask for a cash advance from Austra-at-the-front-desk, a pursekeeper who is scrupulous never to lend as much as I earned the week before. She is executive and receptionist and secretary and gatekeeper, a single and saintly woman who might have been a nun but turned herself over to Van and Harold, or rather to their business, as their servant. Both are bright but don't have a business sense of organization. Van goes off on dancing creative flights and Harold, who can rattle away on a Selectric at eighty words a minute, a graduate of Pace, is a task finisher. His wife, who some days appears wheeling a baby in a stroller, with another child walking beside, gripping its rail, has a severe look but in conversation is gracious, solicitous, and I imagine it's her money that funds Attention and keeps her face in its concentrated grip. She speaks mostly to Austra and Harold.

I finish a story, "Five Letters," about the letters a character reads and responds to over one night, with interspersed passages that tell another story and contradict his letters, Gidean, and take it to Maxwell. I've mentioned Gide to him before—my fascination with the *Journals*. He asks if I've read Colette, then brings me up to date on the difficulties-of-learning-to-play-the-piano-after-fifty, as he's been trying to do and has talked about before, and then says, "I looked at Gide's *Journals*, and the more I hear about his piano playing, the more I'm led to believe he could barely play a lick on it and was making half of it up."

I feel the heat of this and he looks startled, his lips parted, and then we start laughing at the same moment—he with gleeful seizures that it seems will never stop.

"Have you read *Rabbit, Run?*" he asks, wiping at the corner of each eye with a little finger. I say I started it once. He takes me down to a bookstore on the street and puts a copy in my hand.

The next week *My Mother's House & Sido,* pulled from his library, arrives in the mail, with a note saying this is closer to what I do. I'm so taken by Colette I'm reluctant to return the book, and when I do he says, as if he's read me out again, "No, keep it. I intended it for you."

Aug. 11, St. Marks. Absurd as it may sound, I believe that the isolation of my protagonists in a high place (attic, hay mow, five-story room) is an expression of their desire to get nearer a mystic source: God, if you will.

The temptation of large, rococo words. Shun everything that is not precise, honest, and unobtrusive. Allow the thought to carry the words with it; don't limit it with rhetoric or pedantry. I write all this tonight in haste, guilty that I didn't keep at my story.

I ask Van's permission to stay at Attention after hours, to use a Selectric to type it up, and get so tired I lie down on a piece of cardboard in the press room, and wake to screaming. Austra has come in early and seen my legs and is sure a vagrant has broken into the offices and died.

Van asks me to stay after work and I think, This is it. When everybody is gone from the office he grabs some typed pages and comes in a dance to the sorting table where I sit.

"Will you help me with this?"

It's a first-person piece for *Guideposts,* about a young man who returns home and "for the first time" recognizes the worth of his parents; it isn't bad, as far as it goes, the writing is clear, and I'm pleased he has asked me to help. "Is this about you? Are you from Kansas?"

"Oh, no! I'm a Suthen boy. Vahginya."

"This never happened."

"Well, kind of. We don't always get such wonderful stories and have to rewrite or fill in with our own. You know about editors and quality, no? What do you think?"

"It's not bad."

"Not a little forced at the end when I use italics?"

"I was going to say you should drop those and simplify the language right there, so it's more like the character's thoughts at that age. Then it'll be better."

"Thank you. Thank you!" He grasps the sides of my head in his hands and kisses my hair. "If there's ever any favor I can do, ask, even to staying in my extraordinary bachelor's pad, if you like—while I'm on vacation, of course. Usually in July, by the way."

I don't wonder if he's gay, nor is that a criterion of judgment, either way, since I worked with theater people for years when "gay" was recherché and know that gays are usually more circumspect in their approach (partly because of the era, perhaps) than the Don Juans and sybarites.

On a visit to deliver "Five Letters" I learn from Maxwell that he worked with Nabokov on *The Defense*—at the time appearing in episodes in the magazine—and since Nabokov is the hottest thing since fry bread, so I feel, I ask, "What did he say?"

"I hardly remember. It was one of those talks where with not so many words you seem to understand what the other is saying. After the work I walked him back to his hotel and he asked me up and I sat in a chair with my coat on. He was lying on his hotel bedcovers in his suit and shoes with his head on a pillow and his hands clasped under his head, tired. One thing that should amuse you, he said that for too long he labored under the misconception that a writer of his stature had to screw everything in sight. And nearly lost his wife that way."

I take this as a rebuke, as I gradually come to see something he said earlier, "I've come to believe young men in New York tend to employ women for entirely sanitary reasons." When it's clear this has gone past me, he adds, "To keep from dirtying their own bed linen."

．　　　．　　　．

Sept. 21, 1964: No entries now for over a week. Deep in the transition state—the change Maxwell saw in me three weeks ago.

Sept. 24, 2 A.M.: Tuesday, yesterday, Maxwell received my letter and called right away, asking me to come either for lunch or at four o'clock. I don't know why I chose four; I hadn't eaten and didn't have any money. He wanted to see me because of a paragraph in my letter—

"I think I've ruined most of my fiction. Instead of being honest I've been trying to be profound. It's impossible to be profound if you're not. Besides, it seems as soon as you try to be profound about people, since they're what writing is about, you miss all their humanity."

He was overjoyed to hear "the good news."

He wants me to write a factual account of the last week, and I've been cursing myself for not keeping at my notebook. He wants me to write simple exercises—"Just for me," he said, "without any thought of publication."

Maxwell and I call the pages he believes could be my first novel "My Brother's Visit to New York." I look at *New Yorkers* on newsstands or buy issues when I can, and it seems a story I wrote in a rush at Urbana, "Requiem and Fall," is closest to what they do. I prune out the worst literary passages, which I'm learning to identify, retype it, and address it to Mr. William Maxwell, *The New Yorker*, etc.

The next day I sit at Attention under the hypnosis of collating pages when Austra says I have a call: Maxwell. "Can you come up?" he asks. They're going to take it, is my first thought. "We'll look at what I've done to your story and go for lunch. Would sandwiches in Central Park be all right? We'll make it a picnic."

He's gone over the story sentence by sentence, and I'm able to make sense of what he wants after we go through three or four pages, and he senses that. "Can you work on this in addition to 'My Brother's Visit to New York'?"

"Sure, I think."

We sit on a bench in Central Park and he pulls wrapped sandwiches from the paper bag in his lap. I undo mine but can hardly eat. I can't talk; an iron hand lies on my chest and throat. I feel I have to cough, but if I cough I'll weep. All he's done for me presses like the hand of iron, and now the time he takes to sit with me, feed me, well. A pair of swans is circling on the lagoon below as on the cover of an Elizabeth Bowen novel he earlier bought for me to read, and I feel choked worse than on the day I tried to ask for a job. The swans in their orbits are my focus, and I hear his whispery voice and picture his detailed comments on my pages in his rapid hand and see Bowen's title appear over the swans, *The Death of the Heart.* I turn and his forehead is set with its wrinkles of concern, a V at dead center, and he pauses, his lips parted, as sometimes happens when he searches for a word, and I can't take in what he's saying, as if I'm pinned to another time.

It's not the death but a beginning stirring of life so potent I feel I'll gag on it, and then I'm drawn from that by his words falling over me with the force of love. How can I leave? What would I do? Where would I go? We're on a path, then in a cab, and I see how he tips, studying the meter and counting out the exact amount, his concern for the cabby of a part with his concern for me; then I remember seeing my pages on his table, then leaving, breath held.

And by that magic transport that can happen in a car, when you're fifty miles farther down the road with not a shred of memory of how you got there, I'm in my room, staring at the pages on my bedside table. Every suggestion of his, every interleaved word in the typed lines, turns me toward a point I know I have to reach. "Sometimes it feels, I know, like internal bleeding," I hear him say, and look up. It's his voice, though I'm not sure if he said it today or another time.

But I hear it now. I follow his trail of pencil marks, feeling chunks of words and paragraphs break loose and fall from the ceiling in my mind, and when I look up, it's dark outside. My windows show me back in shining black plates. I lie down on the bed in all my clothes. Her.

I wake with the chilly feeling of a child awakened the hour before sunrise for a vacation or a fishing trip, when whatever mechanism it is that keeps heat from leaking from your bones hasn't kicked in yet. I take my closest subway, the Lexington line, to 86th and get out in Yorkville, Germantown, Maxwell's neighborhood—he's home for the rest of the week, I know—and as I walk, oh, that towering feeling, turns in my head, that o-ver-power-ing feeling! Knowing I'm! on the street where you live!

I walk into Gracie Square, a public park, and notice that the fur on the tail of a squirrel is so fine it seems transparent; I see through it to the ground, to the veins of leaves lying in mud, the tail a mirage.

I walk to the river and sit on a green-slatted bench like the one in the park. The sullen, slow river, myself and my senses coming to themselves in the fall air, as they will every year after, in commemoration of this day. My life has begun. I will remember every single hour with him. Mark that down, I think. I will do that and I will not relent. I will return to others, as much as I am able, something of the love he has lavished on me.

NICHOLAS WOLTERSTORFF

TERTULLIAN'S ENDURING QUESTION

(From *The Cresset*)

"What does Jerusalem have to do with Athens," asked Tertullian in memorable, bitingly eloquent words:

> the Church with the Academy, the Christian with the heretic? Our principles come from the Porch of Solomon, who himself taught that the Lord is to be sought in simplicity of heart. I have no use for a Stoic or a Platonic or a dialectic [i.e., Aristotelian] Christianity. After Jesus Christ we have no need of speculation, after the Gospel, no need of research. Once we come to believe, we have no desire to believe anything else; for the first article of our faith is that there is nothing else we have to believe. (*Prescriptions against Heretics* 7)

Tertullian's aim, in his *Prescriptions against Heretics*, was to persuade his readers to stay away from heresies. Just before the passage quoted he had been inquiring into the root of these "doctrines of men and of daemons." Philosophy is the root— that repository of "worldly wisdom, that rash interpreter of the divine nature and order." Heretics are "equipped by philosophy." "From philosophy come those fables, those endless genealogies and fruitless questionings, those words that spread like cancer,"

which we find in the heretics. Heresies are "generated for itching ears by the ingenuity of that worldly wisdom which the
Lord called foolishness. . . ." Lift a heretic and you'll find a
philosopher.

It was to hold us back from the futile and deceiving speculations of the heretics, says Tertullian, that the apostle Paul "testified expressly in his letter to the Colossians that we should
beware of philosophy. 'Take heed lest anyone beguile you
through philosophy or vain deceit, after the tradition of men,'
against the providence of the Holy Spirit. Paul had been at
Athens, and in his argumentative encounters there had become
acquainted with that human wisdom of the philosophers which
attacks and perverts truth, being itself divided up into its own
swarm of heresies by its mutually antagonistic sects."

Having located the root of heresy in philosophy, Tertullian
then poses his rhetorical question: "What does Jerusalem have to
do with Athens, the Church with the Academy, the Christian
with the heretic?" Be done, he says, with Stoicized Christianity,
with Platonized Christianity, with dialectic Christianity. Were
Tertullian living in our own day his list would be much longer: be
done with Kantianized Christianity, with Hegelianized Christianity, with deconstructionist Christianity. Be done with them
all. The stance of the Christian toward all attempts at "worldly
wisdom" must be unrelenting opposition:

> Would to God that no "heresies had ever been necessary in
> order that those who are approved may be made manifest!"
> We would then never be required to try our strength in con-
> tests about the soul with philosophers, those patriarchs of
> heretics, as they may fairly be called. The apostle Paul
> already foresaw the ensuing conflicts between philosophy
> and the truth. He offered his warning about philosophy after
> he had been at Athens, had become acquainted with that

> loquacious city, and had there gotten a taste of its huckster-
> ing wiseacres and talkers. . . . It will be for Christians to clear
> away those noxious vapors, exhaled from philosophy, which
> obscure the clear and wholesome atmosphere of truth. They
> will do so both by shattering to pieces the arguments which
> are drawn from the principles of things—meaning those of
> the philosophers—and by opposing to them the maxims of
> heavenly wisdom—that is, such as are revealed by the Lord;
> in order that both the pitfalls with which philosophy capti-
> vates the heathen may be removed, and the means employed
> by heresy to shake the faith of Christians may be destroyed.
> (*On the Soul* 3)

There is danger confronting those Christians who set out to
shatter the arguments of the philosophers: they may themselves
be seduced by those arguments and become heretics. The danger
cannot be avoided; some in the community must oppose heresy
by uncovering its roots in philosophy and then attacking that.
But to those who suggest that a training in philosophy should
become a more or less standard part of the education of Christians, Tertullian's answer is unequivocal—as indeed are most of
his answers to most of his questions! Addressing the soul, he says:

> I call you not as one formed in the schools, trained in the
> libraries, nourished in the Attic academies and porticoes,
> belching forth wisdom. I address you simple, unskilled,
> uncultured and untaught, as those are who have you and
> nothing else; I address you as a person of the road, the
> square, the workshop, that alone. I want your inexperience,
> since no one of small experience feels any confidence. I
> demand of you that you consult only the things you bring
> with you as a human being, the things you know either from
> yourself or from your author, whoever that may be.

Tertullian's question, "What does Jerusalem have to do with Athens?" remains as much alive today as it was in A.D. 198 when Tertullian posed it. It's not one of those questions which the Christian community has settled and from there gone on to other matters. It remains an enduring question for the Christian academic. It is, in fact, *the* enduring question: What does the Christian gospel have to do with the enterprise of scholarship—in particular, with the scholarship of those who are not Christian?

The question would not have endured if Tertullian's answer, or some alternative, had been universally accepted. It would now be of interest only to antiquarians. In proclaiming that Jerusalem's business with Athens is combating those philosophies spawned by Athens which inspire the heretics who disturb the church, Tertullian was staking out a position within a multifaceted debate which agitated the ancient church. In particular, he was staking out a position in opposition to that articulated by his near-contemporary, Clement of Alexandria. I think that you and I, at the dawn of the third millennium after Christ, can still learn something by reflecting on that debate conducted by our forebears in the faith.

The picture presented by the passages from Tertullian which I have cited is unremittingly that of *disjunction* and *opposition.* Between pagan philosophy and Holy Scripture there is no choice but to choose. "Choose ye this day whom you will serve." To be a Christian is already to have chosen. The Christian lives by Holy Scripture, in opposition to pagan philosophy. To the suggestion that some Christians should advance beyond their acceptance of Holy Scripture to engage in philosophical speculation, Tertullian's answer is crisp: "After Jesus Christ we have no need of speculation, after the Gospel, no need of research. When we come to believe, we have no desire to believe anything else; for the first article of our faith is that there is nothing else we have to believe."

There were those, Clement included, who were citing the New Testament injunction, "Seek, and you shall find," to justify the project of becoming learned Christians. Tertullian's answer is eloquently dismissive:

The reasonable exegesis of this saying turns on three points: matter, time, and limitation. As to matter, you are to consider what is to be sought; as to time, when; and as to limitation, how far. What you must seek is what Christ taught, and precisely as long as you have not found it, precisely until you do find it. And you found it when you came to believe. You would not have believed if you had not found, just as you would not have sought except in order to find. Since finding was the object of your search, and belief the result of your finding, your acceptance of the faith bars any prolonging of seeking and finding. The very success of your seeking has set up this limitation for you. Your boundary has been marked out by him who would not have you believe, and so would not have you seek, outside the limits of his teaching.

If we were bound to go on seeking as long as there is any possibility of finding, simply because so much has been taught by others as well, we would always be seeking and never believing. . . .

I have no patience with the man who is always seeking, for he will never find. He is seeking where there will be no finding. I have no patience with the man who is always knocking, for the door will never be opened. He is knocking at an empty house. I have no patience with the man who is always asking, for he will never be heard. He is asking one who does not hear. . . .

But even supposing that we ought to be seeking now and ever, where should we seek? Among the heretics, where everything is strange and hostile to our truth? . . . Instruction

and destruction never reach us from the same quarter. Light
and darkness never come from the same source. So let us
seek in our own territory, from our own friends and on our
own business, and let us seek only what can come into question without disloyalty to the Rule of Faith. (*Prescriptions
against Heretics* 10–12)

If we are to see the full pattern of Tertullian's thought, we
must understand the import of those final cryptic words. With
rhetoric of hammering force, Tertullian has been arguing that it is
incoherent to suggest that Christians should engage in "seeking
the truth." To be a Christian is to accept the teachings of Scripture; in and by accepting those teachings, one ends one's search
for the truth. And as to the more specific suggestion that, in seeking the truth, Christians should not neglect to look into the
pagan philosophers, Tertullian's response is that this is not only
incoherent, but altogether futile and muddle-headed.

It was not Tertullian's position, however, that Christians are
to refrain from all forms of intellectual endeavor; he was not an
exponent of bare faith alone. His own writing is evidence to the
contrary. It is appropriate for Christians to try both to understand better *what already they believe* and to defend that with intelligence. Provided you honor the Rule of Faith, says Tertullian to
his fellow Christians, you may "seek and discuss as much as you
please, and pour forth your whole desire for curious inquiry if
any point seems to you undetermined through ambiguity, or
obscure from want of clarity. There is surely some brother, a
teacher gifted with the grace of knowledge, someone among
those skilled intimates of yours," who can assist you in this,
while steering you away from inquiries that stray from the Rule
of Faith (*Prescriptions* 14).

§2. The picture drawn by Clement was unmistakably different. For Clement, the fundamental relation of Christianity to

pagan philosophy was not *opposition* but *supersession*. Pagan philosophy is not *anti*-Christian but *sub*-Christian. Or to speak more historically: just as the law and the prophets served for the Hebrews as a preparation for Christ, so philosophy prepared the Greeks. In Clement's own words: "Philosophy was given to the Greeks directly and primarily, until the Lord should call the Greeks. For this was a schoolmaster to bring the Hellenic mind, as was the law, the Hebrews, to Christ. Philosophy, therefore, was a preparation, paving the way for him who is perfected in Christ" (*Stromata* I, 5). Using a different cluster of metaphors to make the same point, Clement says that philosophy "was given to the Greeks as a covenant peculiar to them—being, as it is, a steppingstone to the philosophy which is according to Christ" (*Stromata* VI, 8).

As his words suggest, Clement's reason for embracing this positive picture of Greek philosophy was, at bottom, theological. Sometimes he appeals to the general principle that, according to the teaching of Scripture, all that is good comes from God. Since it seemed obvious to him that there was truth in Greek philosophy, he drew the conclusion that Greek philosophy, insofar as it has a grasp of the truth, comes from God. In other passages, thinking not about the good in general but about truth, Clement appeals to his understanding of what the prologue to the Gospel of John teaches about Logos. Having described Logos, in verse 9, as "the true light that enlightens every man," John goes on in verse 14 to say that Logos "became flesh and dwelt among us." The conclusion Clement drew was that that very same Logos which became incarnate in Jesus Christ is at work in all humanity, leading them toward truth. This is how he puts the point in one passage: "Into all human beings whatsoever, but especially those who are occupied with intellectual pursuits, a certain divine effluence has been instilled; wherefore, even if reluctantly, they confess that God is one, indestructible, unbegotten, and that somewhere above in the tracts of heaven, in His own peculiar appropriate eminence, He has an existence true and eternal from whence He surveys all things" (*Exhortation* VI). There were those in Clement's day who said that it was through *human understanding* that philosophy was discovered by the Greeks. Clement rebukes them: "I find the Scriptures saying that understanding is sent by God" (*Stromata* VI, 8).

One version of the supersessionist view would be that Christianity has so far superseded its two main antecedents, Hebrew revelation and Greek philosophy, that there is no longer any point in paying attention to those superseded antecedents. That was not Clement's version. Beyond a doubt "the teaching which is according to the Savior is complete in itself and without defect," he says, "being 'the power and wisdom of God'; the addition of Greek philosophy does not make the truth more powerful." Or to put it the other way round: the absence of Greek philosophy would not render the perfect Word incomplete, it would not cause the Truth to perish (*Stromata* I, 20). Nonetheless, the study of Greek philosophy remains of great utility for Christians.

For one thing, it is useful for warding off heresy and sophistry. The learned Christian "can distinguish sophistry from philosophy . . . rhetoric from dialectics, and the various sects of barbarian philosophy from the truth itself. How necessary, then, is it for him who desires to be partaker of the power of God to treat of intellectual subjects by philosophizing!" The philosophically learned Christian, "a man of much counsel, is like the Lydian touchstone, which is believed to possess the power of distinguishing spurious from genuine gold" (*Stromata* I, 9). Alluding to the Tertullianists of his day, Clement observes that "some, who think themselves naturally gifted, do not wish to touch either philosophy or logic; nay more, they do not wish to learn natural science. They demand bare faith alone, as if they wished, without bestowing any care on the vine, right away to begin gathering clusters. [Tertullian, as we saw above, does not "demand bare faith alone" of all Christians.] Now the Lord is figuratively described as the vine from which, accordingly to the word, we are to take pains to gather fruit with the art of husbandry." In husbandry "we lop, dig, bind, and perform other operations. . . . So also here, I call him truly learned who brings everything to bear on the truth; so that, from geometry, music, grammar, and philosophy itself, culling what is useful, he guards the faith against assault" (*Stromata* I, 9).

It is clear, however, that Clement did not regard the utility for apologetics of the study of Greek philosophy as exhausting its serviceability for Christians. Indeed, that for him was not its most important use. Though the truth proclaimed by our Savior is the truth necessary and sufficient for salvation, it is not the whole of truth. It is then the calling of Christian intellectuals to go beyond apologetics and incorporate the truth proclaimed by Christ into a larger picture—a more comprehensive "philosophy," if you will. For this purpose, the learned Christian takes fragments of truth from wherever he finds them. Truth as such is the one ever-living Logos. The various sects of barbarian and Hellenic philosophy each vaunts itself as having got hold of that whole truth. In actual fact, however, none has done more than tear off a fragment. Yet "the parts, though differing from each other, preserve their relation to the whole. . . . Be assured, then, that he who brings the separate fragments together and makes them one again will contemplate the perfect Word, the truth" (*Stromata* I, 13). "The way of truth is one. But into it, as into a perennial river, streams flow from all sides" (*Stromata* I, 5).

§3. Disjunction or supersession, opposition or incorporation. Who was right about the relation of Christianity to pagan learning? And who was right about the Christian intellectual? Does the Christian intellectual study the learning of non-Christians solely to discern the error of its ways, confining the scope of his own positive inquiries to the content of the faith itself? Or does the Christian intellectual, convinced that Logos has dispensed portions of truth to all humanity, study such learning not only to discern the error of its ways but also to harvest such fragments of truth as are to be found there, with the goal of combining those, along with the more clear, ample, and fundamental truths of the Gospel, into a larger synthesis?

You will have discerned that the dispute between Clement and Tertullian was a multifaceted dispute: a *cluster* of issues was under discussion, not just one issue. From that cluster I have time, on this occasion, to pick out just one for discussion—one of the most important, however, namely this: How should Christians interpret pagan literature and philosophy? What should be their goal and strategy of interpretation? Or more generally: How should one interpret the textual tradition which one has inherited? Clement espoused one goal and strategy, Tertullian, another. Neither party won the debate in the second century; neither party has won the debate to this day.

Though Clement believed firmly that, as the consequence of the activity of Logos, there is truth to be found in the Greek philosophers, he did not deny that the truth to be found there is mingled with falsehood. Neither did he deny—indeed, he ardently affirmed—that something decisively new had taken place in world history when the Logos which enlightens all who come into the world was enfleshed in Jesus Christ. Unlike every philosophy, be it Greek or barbarian, the teaching of Jesus "is complete in itself and without defect, being the 'power and wisdom of God.'" Accordingly, when confronted with the teaching of some philosopher which contradicts the teaching of our Savior, the Christian does not spend time mulling over which to accept. Everything incompatible with the teaching of our Savior is in error; none of it is a fragment of the truth. Clement was not Hegel born out of season. History is not a vast ongoing series of supersessions, continuing until such time as *Geist* is fully manifested in the abstract thought of some philosopher. Though Christianity supersedes both Hebrew revelation and Greek philosophy, nothing will supersede Christianity. Our Savior did not teach us the *whole* of truth, he did teach us nothing but truth, there was no falsehood mingled in. And the truth he taught us is the most important truth, taught with a clarity never to be superseded in this present existence. The teaching of our Savior is thus a touchstone for the Christian interpreter.

Just as Clement did not deny that the truth to be found in the Greek philosophers is mingled with abundant error, and either of secondary importance or lacking in full clarity, so too he did not deny that the Greek philosophers, unlike our Savior, exhibited a multitude of vices. The most fundamental of their vices was that they were, in Clement's words, "thieves and robbers." Echoing the then-current view that the Greek philosophers had somehow gained direct access to Hebrew prophecy, Clement says that "before the coming of the Lord they received fragments of the truth from the Hebrew prophets, though admittedly not with full knowledge, and they claimed these as their own teachings, disguising some points, and treating others sophistically by their ingenuity" (*Stromata* I, 17). Nonetheless, Clement insists that "sentence of condemnation is not ignorantly to be pronounced against *what is said* on account of *him who says it* (a point also to be kept in view in the case of those who are now alleged to prophesy); rather, *what is said* must be scrutinized to see if it conforms to the truth" (*Stromata* VI, 8).

There is, thus, a definite sobriety about the Christian intellectual of Clementine persuasion as he interprets the Greek philosophers. He does not place them on a pedestal; he recognizes their moral failings. He does not idolize them as the fount of all and only wisdom and clarity; he recognizes that such truth as they grasped is either of secondary importance or but a hazy and hesitant apprehension of what our Savior taught us. Nonetheless, there's truth in the Greek philosophers—truth even about God. And the Christian intellectual interprets principally for that truth, so as to incorporate it within a larger synthesis. The Christian interpreter notes, for example, that because of the "divine effluence" at work in the Greek philosophers, they correctly "teach, even if reluctantly, that God is one, indestructible, unbegotten," and so forth (*Exhortation* VI).

Anybody who takes in hand Aquinas's *Summa theologiae* will at once discern Clementine hermeneutics at work. Having posed a question—for example, "Whether the Existence of God is Self-Evident?"—Aquinas opens his treatment by citing objections to the answer for which he will argue. These objections almost always are, or incorporate, citations from the tradition. Having stated objections from the tradition to his thesis, Aquinas then announces "On the contrary," and as the introduction to his own argumentation he cites a passage from the tradition which is on his side in the dispute. Finally, after he has laid out his own argument for the answer he prefers, he returns to the opening objections. Though on a few occasions he pronounces an objection mistaken, almost always he instead argues that what was cited as an objection need not be, and indeed, *should not* be, so interpreted. When appropriate clarifications, qualifications, and distinctions are made, what appeared to be an objection is seen instead to be getting at an aspect of the full and complex truth.

The strategy, as I say, is clearly Clementine. Though there are indisputably errors in the textual tradition bequeathed to us, nonetheless the bulk of that tradition presents to us a finely articulated apprehension of the truth. And rather than dwelling on the errors, Aquinas regards his interpretative task and challenge to be discerning that particular facet of the truth which is presented by the text at hand, thereby showing how that text properly interpreted fits together with other texts which might have been supposed to contradict it. In thus interpreting the textual tradition, Aquinas typifies the medieval tradition in general; the medieval Western tradition was dominantly Clementine in its interpretative practice.

Hans-Georg Gadamer, in our own day, has argued for recovering the Clementine tradition—though I am not aware of his anywhere calling attention to the Clementine ancestry of the interpretative strategy which he defends. (He does call attention to its medieval ancestry.) Confronted with a text, the initial goal of the interpreter, so Gadamer argues, should be to interpret so that what the text says on the subject (*Sache*) under discussion turns out true. Only if that goal is frustrated, only if there is no reasonable way of interpreting the text so that it comes out true, should we interpret for the opinion of the author on the subject under discussion. The strategy of interpreting for authorial opinion is legitimate only as a fall-back. Here is what Gadamer says in one passage:

> Just as the recipient of a letter understands the news that it contains and first sees things with the eyes of the person who wrote the letter—i.e., considers what he writes as true, and is not trying to understand the writer's peculiar opinions as such—so also do we understand traditionary texts on the basis of expectations of meaning drawn from our own prior relation to the subject matter. And just as we believe the news reported by a correspondent because he was present or is better informed, so too are we fundamentally open to the possibility that the writer of a transmitted text is better informed than we are, with our prior opinion. It is only when the attempt to accept what is said as true fails that we try to 'understand' the text, psychologically or historically, as another's opinion. (*Truth and Method*, second revised edition, p. 294)

§4. My claim that the medievals, for the most part, practiced the Clementine strategy of interpretation, combined with my description of Gadamer as arguing for "recovering" the Clementine strategy, suggests that somewhere along the line the Clementine strategy went into decline. And so it did. But before we get to that, let me return to the second century to characterize Tertullian's alternative strategy of interpretation.

Contrary to what one might have expected, Tertullian did not deny that there is truth to be found in the Greek philosophers. It's definitely a concession on his part rather than an emphasis; and he doesn't do anything with the concession. Yet there it is. In his *Apology* he says, for example:

> We have already said that God fashioned this whole world by His word, His reason, His power. Even your own philosophers agree that *logos*, that is, Word and Reason, seems to be the maker of the universe. This *logos* Zeno defines as the maker who formed everything according to a certain arrangement; the same *logos* (he says) is called Destiny, God, the Mind of Jupiter, and the inevitable Fate of all things. Cleanthes combines all these predicates into Spirit, which, according to him, permeates the universe. Moreover, we, too, ascribe Spirit as its proper substance to that Word, Reason, and Power by which, as we have said, God made everything. (*Apology* 21)

But if this is Tertullian's conviction, why are disjunction and opposition the themes of his interpretative strategy? Why not, as with Clement, supersession and incorporation?

Tertullian is less explicit on the matter than one would like. Nonetheless, I think one can see how he was thinking. Whereas Clement urged his readers to forget about the persons who are philosophers and concentrate on extracting what is true from what they taught, Tertullian had his eye on the very thing that Clement urged his readers to overlook—*the particular philosophers themselves,* and the distinctives of their patterns of thought in which the particularities of their allegiances, convictions, characters, and so forth get expressed.

When we have the full pattern of Plato's thought in view—or Aristotle's, or some Stoic's—and then compare it with the full pattern of the Rule of Faith, what leaps out is *difference.* Plato's thought, in its distinctive totality, is not a hazy and hesitant adumbration of what finally becomes clear in the Christian Rule of Faith—along with fragments of truth which can nicely be synthesized with the Rule. Plato's thought in its totality has a contour of its own; it has its own integrity. It's not a patternless assemblage of fragments. As such, his thought is not *sub*-Christian but *anti*-Christian. Be it granted that the Christian discerns that here and there Plato is hazily and haltingly getting at something which is stated with clarity and affirmed with confidence in the Gospel. Be it granted that the Christian here and there discerns fragments susceptible to being synthesized into a larger Christian philosophy. But to approach Plato thus is to ignore the integrity of his thought. Let Plato be Plato, rather than a failed approach to Christianity. And let Christ be Christ.

Tertullian was clearly suggesting that we cannot account for the fact that the full pattern of Plato's thought is different from that of the Gospel solely by observing that the Logos dispenses its illumination more fully in Christ than in the minds of the Greek philosophers. Perhaps it does. But human beings are not passive recipients of shafts of illumination thrown off by Logos. In the construction of learning there's always a self at work. What goes a long way toward accounting for the difference between Platonic thought in its integrity—or Stoic, or Aristotelian—and Christian, is that pagan selves are different selves from the Christian self: different allegiances, different commitments, different loves, different orientations, different virtues. Further, the ways in which pagan selves are different from the Christian self are not *in addition to* their thought; those differences *shape* their thought. It's with his eye on the differences of pagan selves from the Christian self that Tertullian asks, "Where is there any likeness between the Christian and the philosopher? between the disciple of Greece and the disciple of heaven? between the man whose object is fame and the man whose object is life? between the talker and the doer? between the man who builds up and the man who pulls down? between friends of error and foes of error? between one who corrupts the truth and one who restores and teaches the truth? between truth's thief and truth's custodian?" (*Apology* 46).

Some might reply that the first of each of these disjunctions is scarcely fair and accurate as a description of all Greek philosophers—not of Socrates, for example. Maybe not. Nonetheless, says Tertullian, "Who can know truth without the help of God? Who can know God without Christ? Who has ever discovered Christ without the Holy Spirit? And who has ever received the Holy Spirit without the gift of faith? Socrates, as none can doubt, was guided by a different spirit—his daemon" (*On the Soul* 1).

To most of us, the Clementine strategy of interpretation practiced by the medievals seems very strange. And not only strange. It seems to us that the integrity of author and text are violated when one interprets with the aim of fitting all texts together into some grand synthesis. Aristotle was not just supplementing Plato; Nietzsche was not just complementing Pascal. Each was a unique person working out a unique pattern of thought and expression. You and I relish the inscapes of each of those unique patterns of thought and expression, and the differences among those inscapes. So much is this the case that it has become common practice in this century even to resist trying to interpret the various texts of a

single author so that they constitute a unity—indeed, to resist trying to interpret *single texts* of an author so that they constitute a
unity. Where once upon a time interpreters unquestioningly
accepted the challenge to show how the various Aristotelian texts
fit together, Werner Jaeger taught us instead to acknowledge dis-
sonance within the Aristotelian corpus, the explanation offered
being that Aristotle's texts, written across the span of his career,
represent stages in his struggle to free himself from the intellectual
grip of Plato. And where once upon a time interpreters struggled
mightily to extract a unified teaching from Kant's First Critique,
Norman Kemp-Smith taught us instead to acknowledge disso-
nance within the First Critique, the explanation offered being that
the Critique was written across a twenty-year stretch of time during which Kant was struggling to break free from his earlier metaphysical way of thinking into his new critical way of thinking.

Before the rise of deconstruction, in which Tertullianist interpretation goes berserk, it was, however, in biblical interpretation
that one saw the Tertullianist strategy followed most relentlessly.
Once upon a time the Bible was regarded as one book, containing a unified, inexhaustibly rich body of teaching. Then it came
to be seen not as God's one book but as an anthology of sixty-six
human books—give or take a few depending on one's preferred
canon. Not long thereafter, many of the books came in turn to be
regarded as anthologies: deutero-Isaiah, trito-Isaiah, and so forth.
And then these sub-anthologies came in turn to be regarded as
anthologies of pericopes. An anthology of anthologies of
anthologies, along with the traces of fumbling editorial efforts to
blend these anthologies together.

I judge the Reformation to have been the principal, though certainly not the only, cause of the decline of Clementine, and the rise
of Tertullianist, interpretation. The Reformers no longer regarded
the texts they inherited, excepting a few unalleviatedly heretical
texts, as all together embodying a finely articulated, highly com-

plex body of truth, it being the task and challenge of the interpreter to extract that truth by drawing the right distinctions, making explicit the tacit qualifications, properly disambiguating the ambiguities, honoring the inherent hierarchies of decisiveness, and so forth. To the contrary: the Reformers regarded the bulk of the texts they inherited as riddled with error. Best then to be done with them and return to the church fathers, and behind those, to God's own text, the Bible, in which there was no error at all.

But if the Reformation thus played a fundamental role in the great reversal of interpretative strategy, I judge it was the Romantic movement which secured the victory of the Tertullianist strategy of interpretation in the modern world. For it was the Romantics who taught us the importance of history, the dignity of the particular, and the organic unity of what is truly a text. It's because of our Romantic inheritance that you and I feel in our bones that Clementine interpretation, be it practiced on philosophical texts, biblical texts, or whatever, dishonors the authors and texts of the past, violating their integrity, by riding roughshod over their particularities in the concern to pluck out whatever can be incorporated into a vast synthesis in which everything has its own little place—that synthesis being constructed, of course, by ourselves. Clementine interpretation feels to us like an act of abusive arrogance.

§5. Revulsion is not reasoned objection, however. The question remains open: Which goal and strategy of interpretation is right, the Clementine or the Tertullianist? And in particular: How do you and I, as Christian intellectuals, interpret all those texts which are not Christian? Do we interpret them for what is true in what is said—now and then polemicizing against some of the errors we notice? Or—if we bother with them at all—do we interpret them for the particular contour of thought, allegiance, and sensibility there expressed? And if we do the latter, to what end? Do we follow Clement or Tertullian?

As preface to the answer I wish to propose, let me call your attention to one fundamental point of agreement between Clement and Tertullian. Perhaps you noticed that whereas I spoke of the goal of interpretation for Clement as discerning what is true in what the author said, I described the goal of interpretation which Gadamer espouses as trying to interpret the text as saying what is true. Those are very different goals—though the descriptions are closely similar. Clement first interprets the text, with the aim of discerning what the author said; then, interpretation finished, he sorts out the true from the false with his incorporationist goal in mind. Gadamer, by contrast, conducts interpretation itself in accord with the rule of trying to have the text turn out true on the matter under consideration. In this respect, Gadamer is closer to the medievals than the medievals were to Clement. Both Clement and Gadamer advocate what I called the "Clementine strategy of interpretation." Neither is much interested in what Gadamer calls the particular "opinions" of authors; both interpret for truth. But their way of getting there is very different; they represent different versions of the Clementine strategy. Clement, to say it again, *first* interprets for what is said and *then* looks for truth therein; Gadamer interprets *so as to have it come out true* and judges that to be what's said.

On this point there is full agreement between Clement and Tertullian; and I, in turn, agree with them. One *can* interpret a text with the aim in mind of having it come out true—or, be it noted, with the aim in mind of having it come out false, or boring, or interesting, or shocking, or bland, or disunited, or aesthetically satisfying—or whatever. Instead of construing a sentence literally, on which interpretation it may be bland, one can construe it metaphorically, on which interpretation it may be arresting; instead of construing it ironically, on which interpretation it may express an important truth, one can construe it literally, on which interpretation it may express a silly falsehood. And so forth. One can do this. But to interpret thus is to ignore the fact that texts are engagements among persons, in which one person performs an act of discourse and another tries to discern what act that was and to respond appropriately. If one insists on never doing anything else with texts than use them as occasions for engaging in one's own play of interpretation, on never using them to engage another human being over what she said, then one is—so it seems to me—in a profound way dishonoring that other human being. I insult you if, whenever you say something to me, I subject your words to a play of interpretation rather than attempting to discern what you said and to respond appropriately.

It may be said that one scarcely dishonors the person if one engages in Gadamerian interpretation—that is, engages in a play of interpretation with the goal in mind of having the words come out true. Isn't this, on the contrary, the most respectful of all modes of interpretation—more respectful than if I interpret for what you said, for your "opinion," which, after all, may or may not be true? I think not. You interpret my speech so as to have it come out true, and you succeed in that. But the truth which emerges is not what I said; it's not what I meant, not what I had in mind. Is that to respect *me*? I fail to see that it is. It's to display your own ingenuity as interpreter.

In short, I am a firm advocate of the priority of what I call "authorial-discourse interpretation." I concede the propriety on occasion of what I call "performance interpretation"—that is, interpretation of a text so as to have it come out true, or unified, or rife with aporia, or whatever. But authorial-discourse interpretation ought to have priority, as I describe more fully in my own 1995 work, *Divine Discourse.* To which it's worth adding that those who advocate performance interpretation regularly question interpretations of their own texts by insisting that interpreters have not grasped *what they said.*

So suppose we interpret texts for what the author or editor said, rather than so as to have them come out some way that we prefer. Should we who are Christians, when interpreting the texts of non-Christians, interpret so as to discern, and then appropriate, what's true in what is said, perhaps taking note along the way of errors, or should we interpret so as to grasp the particular contour of that person's thought, then noting its difference from the contour of Christian thought? Should we read Plato for what's true and to be appropriated in Plato, or for the distinct and alien contours of his thought?

My answer is: we should do both. Neither by itself is sufficient.

The first part of my reason is that there is both truth in what Plato thought, and a particular contour to his thought distinct from that of the Christian Gospel. Both are there, awaiting the interpreter's discovery.

The foundation of Clement's practice was his insistence that truth is not the exclusive possession of Christians—not even truth about God. Nobody is entirely blind to reality; most (maybe all) are not even blind to the reality of God. The Christian will no doubt feel that the non-Christian's apprehension of God is for the most part deficient in one way and another, and to one degree or another. She will not—not usually, anyway—find herself *learning* something about God that she didn't already know, or that she couldn't have known by reading biblical exegesis or Christian theology. But when it comes to other matters, she will often find herself genuinely learning things. I am myself hesitant to embrace Clement's explanation for all of this. Perhaps some of it is rightly ascribed to the Logos of which John speaks. But I would say that much of it is the outcome of the workings of the nature with which we human beings are endowed: our perceptual, rational, introspective, memorial nature. Either way, though, we are, of course, ultimately to ascribe truth to God.

On the other hand, Tertullian put his finger on something which Clement consistently overlooked or neglected. Plato's thought has a definite contour distinctively different from that of the Christian Gospel, a contour shaped not just by the way various experiences acted on various parts of his innate generic belief-forming nature, but by the way those experiences acted on the *blend* of Plato's innate generic nature with the contingent particularities of his allegiances, commitments, convictions, and so forth. It's not just our hard-wiring, but our hard-wiring plus our programming, that accounts for what we come to believe.

It was especially Augustine, among the church fathers, who emphasized and developed this point about the ways in which our particular contingent selves shape our learning. It led him to supplement Clement's motto, faith seeking understanding (*fides quaerens intellectum*), with the more complex motto, I believe in order to understand (*credo ut intelligam*). Faith not only seeks understanding; it is a condition of the understanding it seeks. A full exploration of what Augustine meant by this, and how he argued it, would require a lengthy paper by itself. Here it must suffice to say that it was Augustine's conviction that our affections—our loves and hates—have a profound impact on our understanding. If, for example, one loves some part of earthly reality in an idolatrous way, that will skew one's understanding of God and of God's relation to humanity and the world. It may even lead to one's denial of God. Augustine was convinced, accordingly, that the right ordering of the affections which faith secures is a condition of progressing in the understanding of God, and of reality generally.

To look at the full pattern of Plato's thought is to see a pattern of thought different from that of the Christian Gospel; that was Tertullian's point. To focus on what is true in Plato's thought is to see adumbrations of, and supplements to, the Christian Gospel; that was Clement's point. Both were right. What should be added is that often the pieces cannot be cleanly abstracted from the whole; what Plato meant by the piece is often bound up with the whole, and the whole isn't true. That's an implication of the Tertullianist point, that Plato's thought is not a mere assemblage of true and false items. On the Clementine side of the matter it's to be noticed, however, that in some such cases, though what Plato said is strictly false as he meant it, nonetheless, one can see what it was in reality that he *was trying to get at.* He had his eye on something real, though he didn't see it with full clarity nor describe it with full accuracy.

That was the first part of my argument for the conclusion that we need both Clementine and Tertullianist interpretation: what Clement had his eye on, and what Tertullian had his eye on, are both there. To establish that both are there is not yet, however, to establish that both should be of concern to the Christian scholar. Something more has to be said before we can draw that conclusion.

At this point Clement and Tertullian were, in my judgment, each partly right and partly wrong. Let me begin my unraveling by speaking of the *goal* of Christian learning, as distinguished from the *strategy.*

Tertullian believed that the positive goal of Christian learning does not extend beyond the attempt to deepen one's understanding of the Christian Gospel. It's worth noting that just as Augustine agreed with Tertullian that our affections and loyalties pervasively shape our learning, so too he agreed with Tertullian on this point. Augustine's mottoes, *faith seeking understanding* and *I believe in order to understand,* are almost invariably understood by contemporary Christians as affirming the development of sociology in Christian perspective, psychology in Christian perspective, economics in Christian perspective, and so forth. They are almost invariably understood, in short, along Clementine lines. I think it decisively clear, however, that that is not how Augustine understood them. For Augustine, faith seeks to understand *that which already it believes*—a thoroughly Tertullianist point!

Never was this Tertullianist-Augustinian conviction formulated with greater precision and elegance than by that very Augustinian theologian Anselm, in his *Proslogium.* So rather than citing Augustine, let me cite Anselm. Before he sets out his proof for God's existence, Anselm addresses God with the words, "I long to understand in some degree thy truth, which my heart believes and loves. For I do not seek to understand that I may believe, but I believe in order to understand. For this also I believe—that unless I believed, I should not understand. And so, Lord, do thou, who dost give understanding to faith, give me, so far as thou knowest it to be profitable, to understand that thou art as we believe; and that thou art that which we believe." Then, the proof finished, Anselm again addresses God: "I thank thee, gracious Lord, I thank thee; because what I formerly believed by thy bounty, I now so understand by thine illumination, that if I were unwilling to believe that thou dost exist, I should not be able not to understand this to be true."

To my claim that Augustine sided with Tertullian, and against Clement, on the positive goal of Christian learning, it might be replied that Augustine emphasizes, as Tertullian did not and Clement did, the utility of pagan learning for this project of faith seeking understanding. The famous passage from *On Christian Doctrine*, in which Augustine speaks of the Israelites appropriating the gold of the Egyptians, comes to mind. But Tertullian did not deny—as we have already seen—that there is truth in the pagan philosophers. More importantly, it is to be noted that Augustine, after calling attention to the gold and silver to be found among the pagan philosophers, concludes the passage with these words: "These, therefore, the Christian, when he separates himself in spirit from the miserable fellowship of the philosophers, ought to take away from them, and to devote to their proper use in preaching the gospel." No hint here of the broadscoped Christian learning which Clement favored!

I am well aware, then, of disagreeing with the greatest father of the ancient church when I say that, on this issue, I side with Clement and against Augustine—and Tertullian. I do not believe

that positive Christian scholarship is to be confined to understanding better what already we believe. We are allowed, and
sometimes required, to seek to understand what is no part of
faith, what goes beyond faith: butterflies and quarks, plate tec-
tonics and contemporary sculpture, epistemology and leprosy.

Before I leave my defense of Clementine interpretation, let
me emphasize one point which has already become clear: disagree as they did on the goal of positive Christian learning,
Clement, Tertullian, and Augustine agreed on a fundamental
point of strategy: whatever be the segment of reality that one is
engaged in trying to understand, one consults whatever sources
might be of help. And pagan philosophy may well be among
those sources. Clement, Tertullian, and Augustine were all agreed
that there is, to use Augustine's metaphor, gold and silver to be
found in the pagan philosophers. And should one find some relevant truth in some pagan philosopher, one does not then regret
that those who are not Christian are nonetheless in touch with
reality. One gives thanks to God, the author of all good things.

I have been speaking in defense of the goal and strategy of
Clementine interpretation, though with an important qualification. Yes, we do look for truth in the texts of non-Christians; with
this, no one disagreed, though indeed it's much more heavily
emphasized by Clement than by Tertullian, or even by Augustine.
Yes, we do appropriate such truth not just for the end of understanding better what already we believe but for the end of understanding the reality in which we find ourselves—God and God's
creation. And yes, because of the faith and love which shape our
lives, the learning which emerges will have its own distinct
Christian contour. This last is the qualification. It's a Tertullianist-
Augustinian point; not a point Clement makes.

But now to defend Tertullian's favored goal. Tertullian's strategy, so I have argued, was to interpret for the distinctive contour
of Plato's thought, so as to take note of how different that is from

the contour of Christian thought. (You recognize, of course, that I am here using Plato to stand in for the totality of non-Christian thinkers.) The question before us now is this: Why interpret thus? Why not glean from Plato such truth as is to be found there which is useful for one's own incorporationist purposes, and then move on? Why care about the contours of Plato's thought?

A bland answer comes to mind: this too is part of the reality which the Christian intellectual is allowed to study. To this an aesthetic observation might be added: it's interesting. And a moral observation: if the Christian is going to engage in that practice of our common humanity which is scholarship, then he is thereby under obligation to honor his fellow participants by understanding as well as he can how they are thinking and where, to put it colloquially, they are "coming from."

All true, I do not doubt. Especially the last point. It's a point I make to my students once a week, thereabouts. Thou must not bear false witness against other scholars, be they ancient or contemporary. Thou must not take cheap shots. Thou must not sit in judgment until thou hast done thy best to understand. Thou must earn thy right to disagree. Thou must conduct thyself as if Plato or Augustine, Clement or Tertullian, were sitting across the table—the point being that it is much more difficult (I do not say impossible) to dishonor someone to his face.

Tertullian's goal was different from all of these, however. The difference represented *opposition* for Tertullian. It was to bring *opposition* to light that Tertullian thought we should interpret for the distinct contours of pagan thought and take note of how those differ from the contours of Christian thought. Apples are different from oranges; but they're not in *opposition*. Tertullian saw Platonic thought as not just different from Christian thought but in opposition. Human culture, whatever else it may be, is a conflict of religious visions and loyalties, a struggle over God and the good, a contest for allegiance. And Tertullian believed with all his heart that for the health and fidelity of the Christian community, that struggle has to be engaged by its scholars and intellectuals. There are a thousand and one things going on which threaten to distract and lead astray those who follow Christ. It's the responsibility of the scholars and intellectuals of the community to dig beneath the clutter so as to spy the fundamental dynamics at work. Typically those fundamental dynamics prove to be powerful comprehensive systems of thought at work—philosophies. I would myself add that they may instead prove to be patterns of social organization which are only in part the application of the ideas of intellectuals. Be that as it may, however: It is then the responsibility of the scholars and intellectuals of the community to take the measure of those philosophies and join combat.

This, if I understand him at all, is what Tertullian was saying. And I agree. Culture is a struggle for allegiance. Christian learning must accordingly be Tertullianist learning. Tertullianist as well as Clementine—Clementine as well as Tertullianist.

§6. The question which you and I as Christian scholars and intellectuals can never be finished with pondering is how to speak and act with Christian integrity within that practice of our common humanity which is scholarship and learning. We do not, or should not, go off into our own corner to think; we participate in the practice of our common humanity. But we are not under the illusion that it is possible to participate in that practice as generic human beings; accordingly, we struggle to participate there with Christian integrity.

If nothing else, I trust my discussion has made clear that we are not the first generation to have thought about this question. Our forebears in the second century were already discussing it with a profundity both provocative and instructive. To forget or ignore their contribution would not only be to shortchange ourselves, but to dishonor them.

BIOGRAPHICAL NOTES

VINCE BACOTE is a doctoral candidate in theology at Drew University, where he worked on the *Ancient Christian Commentary on Scripture* under the direction of Tom Oden. He is teaching theology at Wheaton College in Wheaton, Illinois.

RANDALL BALMER is Ann Whitney Olin Professor of American Religion at Barnard College. He is the author of a number of books, including *Mine Eyes Have Seen the Glory: A Journey into the Evangelical Subculture in America*, which was made into an Emmy-nominated documentary, and most recently *Blessed Assurance: A History of Evangelicalism in America*.

LIONEL BASNEY, poet and musician, was professor of English at Calvin College in Grand Rapids, Michigan, at the time of his accidental death in the summer of 1999. His essay in this volume was honored as the best essay published in *The American Scholar* in 1999.

SUSAN WISE BAUER is the author of two novels, *The Revolt* and *Though the Darkness Hide Thee*, and co-author, with Jessie Wise, of *The Well-Trained Mind: Classical Schooling at Home*. She lives in rural Virginia, where her husband is a Presbyterian minister.

TOM BEAUDOIN is the author of *Virtual Faith: The Irreverent Spiritual Quest of Generation X*. A doctoral candidate at Boston College, with a dissertation on Michel Foucault, he is at work on a book about Catholic identity.

ROBERT N. BELLAH is professor of sociology emeritus at the University of California, Berkeley. Perhaps his most influential work is *Habits of the Heart*, of which he was a co-author and presiding spirit.

HARVEY COX, the grand old man of the "new theology" of the 1960s, is Victor Thomas Professor of Religion at Harvard University. Among his many books are *The Secular City* and *Fire from Heaven*, a study of Pentecostal spirituality.

JEAN BETHKE ELSHTAIN is Laura Spelman Rockefeller Professor of Social and Political Ethics at the University of Chicago. A prolific reviewer and essayist whose work appears regularly in *The New Republic* and other magazines and journals, she is also the author of many books, including *Augustine and the Limits of Politics*.

VIGEN GUROIAN is professor of theology and ethics at Loyola College in Baltimore. In addition to many books in his academic fields, he has also published *Tending the Heart of Virtue: How Classic Stories Awaken a Child's Moral Imagination* and *Inheriting Paradise*, a book on gardening.

JEDD HAFER is a writer and stand-up comic based in Colorado Springs, Colorado.

TODD HAFER is a writer and editor based in Jenks, Oklahoma. His latest book is *Snickers from the Front Pew*, which he wrote with his brother Jedd.

ALASDAIR MACINTYRE is professor of philosophy at Duke University. Among his books are *After Virtue* and *Three Rival Versions of*

Moral Inquiry. His essay in this volume was given as the Dudleian Lecture at Harvard Divinity School on April 16, 1999.

FREDERICA MATHEWES-GREEN is a columnist for *Christianity Today* magazine and beliefnet.com, a commentator on NPR, a speaker widely in demand, and the author of several books, including most recently *At the Corner of East and Now: A Modern Life in Ancient Christian Orthodoxy.* She lives near Baltimore, where her husband is the priest of an Antiochian Orthodox congregation.

RICHARD JOHN NEUHAUS is editor-in-chief of *First Things* and head of the Institute for Religion and Public Life. His most recent book is *Death on a Friday Afternoon: Meditations on the Last Words of Jesus from the Cross.*

EMILY OREN, an architecture student at Cooper Union in New York City, writes the "City Journal" column for *Books & Culture.*

VIRGINIA STEM OWENS is a novelist, essayist, and poet. She directed the Milton Center at Kansas Newman College, a training ground for writers, before moving to Texas to take care of her aging parents. Her most recent book is *Jesus Stories.*

BETHANY PATCHIN is an art major at the University of Wisconsin.

BEN PATTERSON is dean of the chapel at Hope College in Holland, Michigan. Among his books are *Waiting: Finding Hope When God Seems Silent* and *Deepening Your Conversation with God.*

EUGENE PETERSON is nearing completion of his translation of the Bible, *The Message.* In addition, he is the author of many books, including *A Long Obedience in the Same Direction.*

ROBERT ROYAL, polymath, translator, author of books on Dante and politics and the environmental movement (among other subjects), is president of the Faith and Reason Institute for the Study of Religion and Culture in Washington, D.C.

KRISTER STENDAHL, a New Testament scholar, is Andrew W. Mellon Professor of Divinity Emeritus at Harvard University and bishop emeritus of Stockholm, Sweden. His book *Energy for Life* was recently reissued in a new edition.

GLENN TINDER is professor of political science emeritus at the University of Massachusetts. His most recent book is *The Fabric of Hope: An Essay*. Many readers will recall his cover story for *The Atlantic Monthly* some years back: "Can We Be Good Without God?"

JAMES VAN THOLEN is the pastor of a Christian Reformed Church in Rochester, New York.

MIROSLAV VOLF is Henry B. Wright Professor of Divinity at Yale University. He contributes regularly to the "Faith Matters" column in *Christian Century*. Among his books are *Exclusion and Embrace: A Theological Exploration of Identity, Otherness, and Reconciliation* and *After Our Likeness: The Church as the Image of the Trinity*.

DALLAS WILLARD is professor of philosophy at the University of Southern California. His most recent book is *The Divine Conspiracy: Rediscovering Our Hidden Life in God*.

LAUREN F. WINNER, a doctoral student in the history of American religion at Columbia University, is writer in residence for *Books & Culture*, a staff writer for *Christianity Today*, and an editor at beliefnet.com. She is the co-author, with Randall Balmer, of a

study of American Protestantism that is forthcoming from Columbia University Press.

LARRY WOIWODE is a writer living in North Dakota, author of *Beyond the Bedroom Wall* and many other books—novels, stories, poems. His most recent is a memoir, *What I Think I Did,* the first installment of a projected three-volume autobiography.

NICHOLAS WOLTERSTORFF is Noah Porter Professor of Philosophical Theology at Yale University. Among his many books are *Divine Discourse: Philosophical Reflections on the Claim That God Speaks, Reason Within the Bounds of Religion,* and *Lament for a Son.*

CREDITS